John Zorn

TRADITION AND TRANSGRESSION

John Zorn

John Brackett

Indiana University Press
Bloomington & Indianapolis

This book is a publication of

Indiana University Press
601 North Morton Street
Bloomington, IN 47404-3797 USA

http://iupress.indiana.edu

Telephone orders   800-842-6796
Fax orders   812-855-7931
Orders by e-mail   iuporder@indiana.edu

The paper used in this publication meets the minimum requirements of American National Standard for Information Sciences—Permanence of Paper for Printed Library Materials, ANSI Z39.48-1984.

Manufactured in the United States of America

Library of Congress Cataloging-in-Publication Data

Brackett, John Lowell.
  John Zorn : tradition and transgression / John Brackett.
    p. cm.
  Includes bibliographical references, discography, filmography, and index.
  ISBN 978-0-253-35234-7 (cloth : alk. paper) — ISBN 978-0-253-22025-7 (pbk. : alk. paper) 1. Zorn, John, 1953–—Criticism and interpretation. I. Title.
  ML410.Z75B73 2008
  780.92—dc22
  [B]

                                                                    2008019643

2 3 4 5   13 12 11 10 09

All of the musical examples and transcriptions herein from the music of John Zorn are copyright © Theatre of Musical Optics.

For Krisi, Zach, and Noah

Contents

Acknowledgments

All examples from the music of John Zorn used by permission, © John Zorn.

A number of people have left their trace on this book. I'm not even going to pretend to list all of them here, but here it goes . . .

I would like to begin by thanking the long-forgotten disc jockeys at WRCU (Colgate College) who introduced me to the wonderful world of Zorn by playing *Spillane* (sandwiched between Pink Floyd's *The Dark Side of the Moon* and a burning live version of the Circle Jerks' "Back against the Wall"). Thanks to my parents, John Sr. and Debbie, and my sisters, Katie and Nicole, for putting up with all of the strange noises coming from my bedroom at all hours of the day.

During my doctoral days at UNC–Chapel Hill, discussions, debates, and arguments with a number of teachers, colleagues, and friends helped me in the fine art of listening. Thanks to Allen Anderson, Matthew Brown, John Covach, Andy Flory, Jon Hiam, Aki Kawamoto, Ethan Lechner, Marc Medwin, Severine Neff, Chris Stephenson, and the entire bar staff at Hell. *Lasciate ogne speranza, voi ch'intrate . . .*

While in Utah, John Costa, April Greenan, Jeffrey Price, Bruce Quaglia, and many students offered helpful criticisms and suggestions both in the School of Music and outside on the steps (when I still smoked). Craig Dworkin, Chris Lippard, and Kathryn Bond Stockton were much needed critics outside of the SoM. Thanks also go to Tomomi Nakashima for taking the time to listen to (what must have been perceived as) really odd questions.

Thanks also to Tamar Barzel, George Lewis, and Shuhei Hosokawa for their early (and more recent) encouragement and insights.

At Indiana University Press, Jane Behnken has been the best editor any first-time author could wish for. Her patience is surpassed only by the commitment she has shown in helping to put this book together. Thanks also to Katherine Baber, Dan Pyle for his help with the examples, and Elaine Durham Otto for her editorial assistance. For their comments on earlier drafts of this manuscript (when/where I needed to pull back/push forward), many, many thanks go to Robert Fink and the anonymous reviewer.

I am grateful to the many folks who have helped me realize the image of the book that was in my head. This includes the staff at IUP, the folks at the Downtown Music Gallery, Brian Butler and Kenneth Anger, Wendy Dorsett and Andy Lampert at the Anthology Film Archives, Nick Hopkins for supplying digital copies of many of the musical examples, Kim Tishler at VAGA, Dale Wills at Boosey & Hawkes, Marcus Jungkurth of the OTO, Amanda Guccione at Artists Rights Society, the Francis Bacon Estate, Holly Frisbee at the Philadelphia Museum of Art, Julie McDowell at Hal Leonard Corporation, Heung-Heung "Chippy" Chin for the design, and Scott Irvine for the image. I wish to thank Gray Raulerson and others associated with the online journal *Echo* for allowing me to reprint a version of my essay "From the Fantastic to the Dangerously Real" as chapter 1.

Thanks to my sons, Zach and Noah, for letting me play trucks, garbage man, and baseball with them. Thanks also go to them for reminding me when *SpongeBob SquarePants* was on.

To my wife, Krisi, I can't say enough. She has lived with me and this project for longer than most rational people could stand. Thanks to her for letting me know when it was time to close the books and turn off the computer.

Unlimited thanks go to John Zorn. I couldn't have written a word if not for John's insights, graciousness, suggestions, criticisms, and silences. I know it's just a glimpse. I hope it's at least a start.

Introduction: Paradoxes and Pitfalls; or, How I Learned to Increase My Worries and Write about John Zorn

While writing about the music of the American composer John Zorn, I have had to navigate conceptual and practical paradoxes while trying to avoid potential pitfalls. Perhaps the most pressing challenge I have had to confront involves finding some way—any way—of speaking about Zorn's music. This has not been an easy task given the eclecticism and size of Zorn's compositional output, ranging from the controlled improvisation of his game pieces (*Hockey, Lacrosse, Cobra, Xu Feng*) written in the late 1970s through the mid-1980s, the file-card compositions (*Spillane* and *Godard*), the collage-form concert works (*Cat O' Nine Tails, Carny, Angelus Novus*), and the pieces inspired by his interest in hardcore music (Naked City and Painkiller projects) from the mid-1980s through the early 1990s, the works that reflect his interests in Judaism and Jewish identity (the Masada quartet and its various offshoots, the chamber piece *Kristallnacht*) beginning in the early 1990s, and, finally, to his recent interests in mysticism and occult philosophy (*Goetia, Hermeticum Sacrum, Necronomicon*).

Given this vast body of work, it might seem that any author who wishes to write about Zorn and his music would have more than enough material to discuss. *How* to talk about Zorn's compositions, however, is another story. For example, confronted with a work such as the string quartet *Cat O' Nine Tails*, the various "musical blocks"—cartoon music clichés, quotations from other works, sections of noise, etc.—might be translated in an analytical setting as "this happens then this happens then . . ." *ad nauseum.* Presumably we see enough of this style of writing when grading undergraduate analysis papers that we don't wish to see similar approaches in our own work or in the work of our colleagues. Such a blow-by-blow account/description of Zorn's musical surfaces might imply that the best way to *talk* about Zorn's music is to simply play the music and not say anything at all.

Unfortunately, a strategy such as this will not suffice in the "sophisticated" arena of musical academia. In this setting, analyses present *explanations* and not *descriptions.* Anyone can describe. We want something more: we seek the *whys* that justify the *whats.* But what could these *whys* be, and how are we to locate them in Zorn's music? Faced with these questions, we quickly arrive at two very different conclusions. On the one hand, it is possible that Zorn's music does not measure up to the rigorous standards and analytical expectations typically assumed by card-carrying music theorists or musicologists. For example, we can imagine a position that argues that Zorn's predilections for immediate and direct musical surfaces replaces the "deeper" structures that act on/justify these surfaces (at least as typically conceived in canonic music associated with the western classical tradition). On the other hand, it could be argued that the discursive formations that have developed around the historical and analytical study of music (as practiced in North American universities and colleges) is ill-equipped to deal with Zorn's music, not to mention the music of many other contemporary composers. It's not that Zorn's music "lacks" deep structures but that the notion of deep structure itself is revealed as specious and, as a concept, is devoid of any sort of justification other than tradition and prejudice. Seen from this perspective, Zorn's musical practices proudly display the leaking sewer pipes and termite-infested edifice that used to support the ivory tower.

As is usually the case in such either/or stories, the truth—if I can use the word—lies somewhere between these two positions. Zorn's music exists in a sort of subversive middle ground that utilizes many of the time-honored formalist/analytical assumptions associated with musical academia while highlighting the academy's inability to deal with his seemingly incommensurable compositional strategies and the tensions they present. Ultimately, the original question remains: How can we talk about music such as Zorn's? Or, for my present purposes and interests, is it possible to develop an analytical language or a theoretical framework that even begins to make sense of Zorn's complex, eclectic, and sometimes maddening music? Obviously, we've started playing a new "game of analysis" that Zorn predicted.[1] The problem now is trying to discover the rules.

One way around these and other difficulties might be to situate any comments or analytical insights within the conceptual/theoretical framework of postmodernism. Indeed, in the relatively few academic essays that consider Zorn and his music, some link to postmodernism is generally nearby where the term is invoked to help explain the stark juxtapositions and stylistic incongruities that characterize Zorn's musical surfaces.[2] Combined with these stylistic markers, an attributed disdain for any sort of coherent narrative or concern for unity both function as sonic and conceptual analogues to certain key features associated with postmodernism in general and postmodernist artworks in particular. Renée T. Coulombe, for example, calls Zorn's *Spillane* a "landmark postmodern piece for its sonic juxtapositions of disjunct materials."[3] For Jonathan Kramer, Zorn's *Forbidden Fruit* exemplifies a form of "radical postmodernism" by offering a "considerable dose of postmodern chaos, despite its nostalgia for other musics." Kramer continues: "Listening to *Forbidden Fruit* can be as dizzying as it is electrifying. You never know what is coming next, nor when. The stylistic juxtapositions are amazingly bold. If there were any discernible thread of continuity, the music would surely be more tame, more predictable, more ordinary. But there is not."[4]

Both Coulombe and Kramer attach the label of "postmodern" to Zorn's music based on stylistic features and the way the music sounds. Moving from Zorn's musical surfaces, Kramer goes on to ascribe certain other characteristics typically associated with postmodern practices: a willful avoidance of "unity" (there is no "discernible thread of continuity") and a freewheeling and ironic treatment of disparate musico-historical styles (where the various quotations or stylistic suggestions signal some sort of "nostalgia for other musics").[5]

Certain questions immediately present themselves when moving from aspects of style to larger issues relating to aesthetic intentions and values. For instance, can inferences that attribute an attitude regarding unity, continuity, or narrativity be drawn from how Zorn's music sounds?[6] Does a disjointed and fragmented musical surface automatically signal an alignment with some version of postmodernism? In my opinion, the answer to both of these questions is yes and no. Zorn's interdependent views on unity, continuity, and history reveal the composer's ambiguous and perhaps ambivalent relationship with the descriptive label "postmodern."[7] By considering these complex views, it might be possible to develop a provisional language for talking about Zorn's musical poetics.

Kramer claims that Zorn's music represents a form of "radical postmodernism," a strain of postmodernism that is recognizable by a contempt for and disdain of traditional notions of organic unity. Paradoxically, it is worth pointing out that Zorn—the apparent poster boy of Kramer's portrait of radical postmodernism—consistently uses the terms *organic* and/or *unity* when referring to his own works. Describing the structure of *Spillane* (a work, we recall, Coulombe describes as a "landmark postmodern piece"), Zorn believes:

Spillane has a unity in the sense that each element deals with some aspect of Mickey Spillane's world. But in terms of sound and pitches, what's going on there? I use maybe six recurrent themes that come back and forth in different ways, and one set of chords which is reused again and again. You try to give a composition a coherent sound, the way Varèse used three pitches for *Octandre,* or the way Carter uses intervals.[8]

In addition to the unifying techniques present in *Spillane* (and present, presumably, in other works as well), Zorn also employs a wide array of compositional procedures and strategies that help a piece "hang together." Another way Zorn achieves coherence in his compositions is by adapting, modifying, and incorporating music by other composers into his own works. For example, he describes how his *Elegy* utilizes material from Boulez's *Le Marteau sans Maître,* although

not in the sense that I would actually take phrases out, lift them, and have them like quotes. I used the score the way Schoenberg would use a twelve-tone row or a serial box. I used it as a point of departure. Sometimes I would reverse pitch sequences; sometimes I would use every other pitch from the viola part and give it to the flute; sometimes I would take [a] rhythm from one instrument and pitches from another and put them together. . . . I'll circle certain areas that I like and reuse this material in a myriad of ways. It's never a case where I'll just take the whole bar; it's more like this is just raw material that I'm using—this scale, this set, this multiphonic, etc., etc. It's incredibly organic; it makes so much sense, it blows my mind.[9]

In his narrative and appropriative/manipulative strategies, Zorn seems to be emphasizing a type of *associative* unity where coherence is guaranteed by, among other things, correspondences or similarities. Often these associations play out against familiar formal devices, such as the large-scale canonic structures that run throughout works such as *Le Mômo* and *Contes de Fées* or the thirty-two-bar song form that lies behind Naked City's manic jump-cut tune "Speedfreaks." In other works, some form of coherence is guaranteed by a trace of unity, as in his lipogrammatic *Chimeras,* a work in which each of the twelve movements that utilize pitched instruments (i.e., not the movement scored for percussion) avoid a single pitch class that, over the course of the entire work, reproduces—*in absentia*—the row from Schoenberg's "Sonett von Petrarca" from his Serenade op. 24.[10]

Before I am accused of portraying Zorn's music as functioning much like the music of Beethoven or Brahms, I wish to make it clear that I am not interested in a simple negation of Kramer's claims as to the discontinuous and disunified surfaces of Zorn's music. There are, without a doubt, a number of qualitative differences that exist between the way Zorn understands and conceives of unity and how the concept is typically understood and employed in the academy. For example, development—a key feature typically associated with "traditional notions of organic unity"—is purposefully avoided by Zorn. Indeed, Zorn has described his lack of interest in forms of musical development, preferring musical structures whose continuity, pacing, and flow derive from other means:

> I've never been interested in development. I work on one moment at a time. Cohesion comes eventually, and I don't see it right away. Once in a while I have to go back through the piece in my mind, in time, and catch up to where I am so I don't lose the sense of line and narrative. I'll say, "OK, I've got to calm down a little bit here, or it's time to really pick it up, or change the orchestration." It's a challenge to keep the piece unified.[11]

Returning to the notion of style, "organic artworks" typically strive for a seamless integration between the parts and the whole. Although none of us seriously believes that a writer or composer begins at the beginning and continues uninterrupted to the end, the impression that remains is one of necessity: the parts logically follow one another in an orderly fashion, an order governed by the logic of the whole. "The organic work of art," Peter Bürger writes, "seeks to make unrecognizable the fact that it has been made" and "to the extent [that the organic work's] individual elements have significance only as they relate to the whole, they always point to the work as a whole as they are perceived individually." For Bürger, the "nonorganic" work of art conceived by the various movements that constitute what he calls the "historical avant-garde"—dadaism, futurism, Russian constructivism, and surrealism—"proclaims itself as an artificial construct, an artifact." As a result—and here we return to the impression of Zorn's musical surfaces and an assumed disunity—the parts of the nonorganic work of art "have a much higher degree of autonomy and can therefore also be read and interpreted individually or in groups without its being necessary to grasp the work as a whole."[12]

Given the independent relations between the parts and the whole in the nonorganic artwork, Bürger considers the paradigmatic and constructivist conception of these works. In contrast to the perceived interdependence between the parts and the whole in the syntagmatic organic artwork, self-sufficient parts of the nonorganic work "could be added or some of those present could be omitted and neither additions or omissions would make a significant difference. A change in the order is also conceivable. What is decisive are not the events in their distinctness but the construction principle that underlies the sequence of events."[13] In a frequently cited quotation, Zorn appears to subscribe to such a view, describing how "my concern is not so much [with] how things SOUND, as with how things WORK."[14] Believing that it was possible to manipulate Zorn's discrete musical blocks in any way I chose, I tried my hand at this by digitally rearranging one of Zorn's more manic jump-cut pieces, "Speedfreaks." As pointed out above, this tune from Naked City's *Torture Garden* recording is constructed out of thirty-two distinct blocks of various musical styles, genres, sounds, and noises (more on this in chapter 1). When I presented my rearrangement to Zorn, he made no effort to hide his dissatisfaction: "Compositionally this new version does not work at all for me." He continued by describing how "finding the proper sequence to keep the interest and flow is a delicate operation. And crucial. . . . Energy, keys, tempos, feels, instrumentation . . . all these parameters need to be properly balanced/unbalanced."[15] While aspects of construction certainly play a key role in Zorn's compositions, his comments to me regarding my rearrangement also reveal the careful attention Zorn pays to individual parts and how these parts interact and contribute to the whole.

Bürger's view of the nonorganic artwork—with its interchangeable/exchangeable parts—does not seem to play a part in Zorn's concept of musical unity. This is perhaps not surprising given the fact that Bürger's claims relating to nonorganic works of art derive from the visual arts (a medium where any sense of temporality is confined within a fixed space) and literature (a medium where any possible spatial manipulations are confined and limited by the temporality of reading). Although Zorn is certainly aware of a variety of techniques and styles associated with literature and painting, his poetics of composition is derived primarily from the structural and unifying possibilities associated with film. He has even commented on how his "music is put together in . . . a very 'filmic' way, [like] montage. It's made of separate moments that I compose completely regardless of the next, and then I pull them, cull them together."[16] Zorn's use of the word *montage* here is suggestive, bringing to mind Sergei Eisenstein's views on montage and filmic form. "In my opinion," writes Eisenstein, "montage is an idea that arises from the collision of independent shots: shots even opposite to one another: the 'dramatic' principle."

> [In film], each sequential element is perceived not *next* to the other, but on *top* of the other. For the idea (or sensation) of movement arises from the process of superimposing on the retained impression of the object's first position, a newly visible further position of the object. This is, by the way, the reason for the phenomenon of spatial depth, in the optical superimposition of two planes of stereoscopy. From the superimposition of two elements of the same dimension always arises a new, higher dimension. In the case of stereoscopy the superimposition of two nonidentical two-dimensionalities results in stereoscopic three-dimensionality.[17]

As in music, where ideas can both unfold over time and be superimposed over one another (as when the bass line from Roy Orbison's "Pretty Woman" is used to support Ornette Coleman's "Lonely Woman" as heard on the first Naked City record), film allows for the temporal unfolding of the "dramatic principle" (understood by Eisenstein as "the methodology of form—not to *content* or *plot!*") while, at the same time, giving the impression of space and spatial depth through various editing techniques. An integrated understanding of space and time does not necessarily displace the traditional organic concept of the interdependence between parts and whole but, instead, expands the possibilities of how these interdependencies can be presented.

Sensing the newfound unifying possibilities of filmic montage, Eisenstein has described a filmic form of unity predicated on what he calls a "montage of attractions." Here, the individual parts or events both participate within and contribute to the formation of a unified plane.

> Instead of a static "reflection" of an event with all possibilities for activity within the limits of the event's logical action, we advance a new place—free montage of arbitrarily selected, independent (within the given composition and the subject links that hold the influencing actions together) attractions—all from the [standpoint] of establishing certain final thematic effects—this is montage of attractions.[18]

An interesting correspondence between Zorn's musical poetics (especially his views on unity) and Eisenstein's "montage of attractions" can be understood. In both, the whole constantly guides the placement, sequence, and choice of seemingly independent events. At the same time, however, the individual events, or parts, respond and react to one another forming an attraction that not only relates each part to one another—suggesting an associative interdependence— but is also a form of necessity given their function in relation to the governing whole. Zorn, like Eisenstein before him, seeks to achieve a type of unity that in many ways seeks to extend and develop the part/whole interrelationships commonly associated with modernist artistic and aesthetic sensibilities. The surface presentation of this unity, however, is drastically different from the seamless, quasi-natural surfaces we typically associate with organic works of art.

Zorn's views on musical unity speak against Kramer's portrayal of the composer as a "radical postmodernist" who cares little for narrativity or any sort of continuity. At the same time, Zorn, who has developed a good portion of his musical poetics from theories of film and avant-garde techniques, uncovers the artificial limitations associated with the concepts "organic" and "unified" and, more specifically, how these concepts are typically employed in the analysis of musical works. While it could be argued that the currency of musical unity has been cheapened, I would argue that the "organic" model so near and dear to many music theorists and analysts has, in fact, been bankrupt for some time. While new "strategies of coherence" demand new descriptions or explanations, any perceived presence and/or absence of coherent, unifying structures can no longer function as a distinguishing trait of postmodern practices. Postmodern? Yes/No (Circle ~~One~~ BOTH!)[19]

● It is possible, however, that the image of Zorn could be reassigned so as to correspond to Kramer's (who is adapting a descriptive label forwarded by Hal Foster) other postmodern position: "neoconservative postmodernism," a sort of "postmodernism of reaction." From this vantage point, unity and organicism "have been reduced to a mere possibility in the postmodern age, . . . a rich possibility" that can be perceived in the works of neoconservative postmodernist composers such as Fred Lerdahl, John Harbison, Steve Reich, and others. "Neoconservatives," Kramer writes, "like latter-day modernists, still value textual unity and organicism as totalizing musical structures."[20] While the music of these and other composers proudly displays a certain need for something resembling unity, its place within the neoconservative postmodernist camp also carries with it a certain view of history and tradition. Hal Foster has described how, from this position, postmodernism is understood as a "return to the verities of tradition (in art, family, religion . . .)" and where, crucially, modernism "is reduced to a style . . . and condemned or excised entirely as a cultural mistake; pre- and postmodern elements are then elided, and the humanist tradition is preserved."[21] In certain respects, Zorn's own views regarding history and tradition correspond to Foster's description. However, Zorn does not appear to be interested in "excising" or abandoning many of the key features associated with modernism; in fact, Zorn attempts to extend and develop many of these features by situating himself both within and against certain modernist artistic traditions and their associated ideological underpinnings.

For many listeners, Zorn's musical surfaces might seem to imply a playful, anything goes view of history where historical moments or phenomena are "reified, fragmented, fabricated . . . imploded, and depleted," an attitude Susan McClary has described as "reveling in the rubble."[22] It is also possible to perceive certain associations on these surfaces, as historically familiar quotations and the works in which they appear gradually merge, forming an unexpected totality of buried resonances and peculiar correspondences. Some of these correspondences are easy to recognize, as in Zorn's string quartet *Cat O' Nine Tails,* where a recurring set of musical blocks present single and sometimes superimposed quotations from composers Zorn considers "important to the string quartet tradition" (although not all of the quotes are taken from string quartets).[23] Taking a step back to consider "classical music" as a discrete category, Zorn has also described how he conceives of "classical music . . . in terms of theater, or of thinking of it like a family—[as] sets of relationships."[24] It is also possible to understand Zorn's notion of history from a larger conceptual perspective. Seen from the perspectives of tradition and "relationships," Zorn's fractured musical surfaces, when combined with his idiosyncratic techniques of incorporating and modifying music of earlier composers, reflects a desire for bringing together particular ideas, figures, movements, etc., into a closer conceptual proximity and ultimately situating himself within a particular artistic tradition.

For Andreas Huyssen, this search for tradition is a defining feature of an American form of postmodernism, especially the type of postmodernism that emerged in the 1970s. Huyssen describes how the "postmodern sensibility of our time is different from both modernism and avant-gardism precisely in that it raises the question of cultural tradition and conservation in the most fundamental way as an aesthetic and political issue." Whereas American artists of the 1960s looked to the practices and thought of the European avant-garde from the first three decades of the twentieth century (Bürger's "historical avant-garde"), artists of the 1970s—recognizing the failure of the historical avant-garde's agenda of undermining the institutionalization of art—were left with techniques and modes of thought that had been stripped of their subversive and transformative powers as the avant-garde itself had become institutionalized. Like many American artists working in the 1970s, Zorn (who returned to New York in the mid-1970s after attending college in the Midwest and living on the West Coast) experienced a sense of "rootlessness" brought about by the condition of contemporary postmodernism, a condition that exists within a "field of tension between tradition and innovation, conservation and renewal, mass culture and high art."[25]

Instead of choosing one or more of these binary oppositions, Zorn has chosen to operate within this "field of tensions" while paradoxically situating himself within a particular artistic tradition. This will take a bit of explaining. Zorn's world, it must be remembered, encompasses much more than music, musicians, and composers. It also includes art and art movements, films and directors, actors, authors, philosophers, religion and religious thinkers, and lunatics. In addition to the many canonic figures who have influenced Zorn's musical poetics (Stravinsky, Boulez, Duchamp, Godard), the works of just as many "marginal" individuals have contributed to Zorn's musical sensibilities: the violent *manga* of Suehiro Maruo, the disturbing artistic creations of Hans Bellmer, the transgressive sexuality, violence, and mysticism of Georges Bataille, the dark voyeurism of Weegee, the brute sensuality of Jean Genet, and the magicko-mystical rationality of Aleister Crowley, just to name a few. In fact, it is probably safe to say that the majority of Zorn's influences can be considered "outsiders" or, from the perspective of the academy, marginalized. Zorn has commented that "artists stand on the outside of society. I think that's an important point: I see the artist as someone who stands on the outside; they create their own rules in a lot of ways and shouldn't try to be socially responsible; being irresponsible is the very point of their existence. That's what makes that person able to comment on what's going on around them, because they aren't restricted by the censors or the powers that be."[26]

Zorn's attraction to "outsiders" can be seen in the artistic traditions he draws on. Since the early 1990s, figures associated with surrealism have served as a continual source of inspiration for many of his compositions and his compositional thought. But while a work such as *Amour Fou* borrows its title from a book by André Breton, most of Zorn's surrealist influences are drawn from the work of individuals who operated at the margins of surrealism. For instance, in Zorn's compositional output there are no works dedicated to Dalí, Aragon, Magritte, or other "mainstream" figures typically associated with surrealism. Instead, figures like Bataille and Artaud appear prominently (see Zorn's *The Dead Man* dedicated to Bataille and *Le Mômo* for Artaud), individuals who were both "expelled" from the surrealist circle by Breton. Extending beyond the French sphere of surrealism, the work of Hans Bellmer and Joseph Cornell also figure prominently within Zorn's poetics (see Bellmer's artwork on the covers to Naked City's *Absinthe* and the chamber music recording *Cartoon/S&M* as well as Zorn's piece for cello *Untitled,* dedicated to Cornell, discussed in more detail in chapter 3). Although many art histories would group the work of Bellmer and Cornell with surrealism, Bellmer's dark, perverted visions of the unconscious and Cornell's unabashed sense of history and tradition could never participate in Breton's vision of a transcendental *sur*-realism.

As seen from this brief description of Zorn's relationship to surrealism, it is not surrealism per se that interests Zorn but the "outsider" figures who are sometimes associated with this avant-garde tradition: the marginalia of the avant-garde. Recalling Huyssen's claims regarding contemporary postmodernism's search for tradition after the failure of the historical avant-garde's attempt to bridge art and life, Zorn strategically returns to those outsiders who questioned the motives and aims of these avant-garde movements. By doing so, Zorn seeks to develop the threads left hanging by earlier avant-garde movements while foregrounding the "field of tensions" that have been created by the opposed and totalizing ideological structures of both avant-gardism and modernism. Zorn doesn't seek to topple and replace one set of aesthetic/ideological/discursive structures with another. Instead, he chooses to work within the nearly imperceptible spaces of seemingly opposed structures, an attitude and practice I will describe as *transgressive*.

In the earlier chapters, I situate Zorn's musical poetics within a tradition of transgression that is heavily dependent on the thought and writings of Georges Bataille. For now, Michel Foucault provides a useful preliminary perspective on the forms and aims of Bataillean transgression:

> Transgression is an action which involves the limit, that narrow zone of a line where it displays the flash of its passage, but perhaps also its entire trajectory, even its origin; it is likely that transgression has its entire space in the line that it crosses. The play of limits and transgression seems to be regulated by a simple obstinacy: transgression incessantly crosses and recrosses a line which closes up behind it in a wave of extremely short duration, and thus it is made to return once more right to the horizon of the uncrossable. But this relationship is considerably more complex:

these elements are situated in an uncertain context, in certainties which are immediately upset so that thought is ineffectual as soon as it attempts to seize them.

The limit and transgression depend upon each other for whatever density of
being they possess: a limit could not exist if it were absolutely uncrossable and,
reciprocally, transgression would be pointless if it merely crossed a limit composed
of illusions and shadows.[27]

Zorn's music and musical thought operate according to this play of boundaries, a practice that is performed within the negative space that exists between
perceived categorical distinctions (continuous vs. discontinuous, unified vs.
disunified, modernism vs. postmodernism, radical postmodernism vs. neoconservative postmodernism, etc.). This play of boundaries can be seen most
clearly in Zorn's views on unity and history and his ambiguous place within
postmodernist and modernist traditions. While many "radical postmodernists"
eschew traditional concepts of unity, Zorn openly embraces multiple unities,
various methods for achieving some sort of continuity, and a strong belief in
the unifying functions of narratives (musical, visual, conceptual, etc.). Zorn is
able to achieve these various unities by utilizing postmodernism's fragmented
surfaces. On the other hand, Zorn's attraction to marginalized historical figures
and movements satisfies a postmodern yearning for tradition by conceptually
and practically drawing from tendencies born of modernism. Zorn looks beyond the antitraditionalism voiced by the historical avant-garde to unearth subversive tendencies and subsequently exposes and exploits a variety of aporias in
their intentions and practices. Within this marginalized tradition—a tradition
of transgression, we might say—Zorn seeks to develop ideas that he perceives
as incomplete or that have gone unnoticed by earlier artists, musicians, and
thinkers, ideas on the role of art in contemporary society.

The ease with which Zorn is able to travel between apparent binary oppositions demonstrates the fluidity and permeability of these boundaries while
acknowledging that these barriers are in place. Instead of attempting to form
some sort of synthesis from these oppositions—by collapsing and integrat-
ing this space—Zorn's music explodes that space, like a bomb going off right
next to your ear.[28] As Henri Lefebvre has written of Bataille's conceptual spaces,
Zorn's music "accentuates divisions and widens gulfs rather than filling them,
until that moment when the lightning flash of intuition/intention leaps from
one side to the other, from earth to sun, from night to day, from life to death;
and likewise from the logical to the heterological, from the normal to the het-
eronomic."[29]

To varying degrees, all of the essays presented here describe and detail how
the twin notions of tradition and transgression can be used to understand individual compositions as well as Zorn's overall poetics of music. While the two
concepts are best understood as being interdependent and intertwined, I have

organized the chapters in this book around each concept. Chapters 1 and 2 examine how aspects of transgression, constraints, and the permeable barriers of boundaries inform much of Zorn's musical poetics, while chapters 3 and 4 consider the place of tradition and history within Zorn's poetics of music.

In chapter 1, I attempt to unravel the complex meanings of the graphic and violent images that appear in the liner notes and packaging included with many of Zorn's recordings from the late 1980s and the early 1990s. I focus my attention on the images included on Naked City's *Torture Garden* and *Leng Tch'e* recordings, images drawn from Japanese manga, S/M porn films, and archival photos depicting a form of Chinese torture. More specifically, I consider the various ways in which these images can be read according to how the distinction between reality and fantasy is constructed and used by various groups, societies, and Zorn himself. I first consider an "antipornographic" stance assumed by some feminist writers (and implicitly adopted by Ellie Hisama, who has written on Zorn's artwork) where such images represent a form of reality and where there is little—possibly no—room for fantasy. Next, I examine how the fantasy/reality distinction is used in Japanese society (usages Zorn would have been familiar with given the fact that he lived there for half of the year at this time). Finally, I consider how Zorn might have understood these images by focusing on his interest in the writings of Georges Bataille. In particular, I focus on Bataille's notion of transgression and how Zorn attempted to adopt certain aspects of Bataille's thought in his music and record packaging.

Developing the transgressive possibilities suggested by these and other images, in chapter 2 I consider how Zorn appears to have shifted his attention to forms of "rational transgression" by incorporating aspects of "magick," mysticism, and alchemy in his musical designs. The sources of Zorn's interest in matters such as these derive, in part, from his continued interest in the thought of Bataille (especially Bataille's notion of "base materialism"), his familiarity with a variety of occult philosophies (Kabbalah, Aleister Crowley, etc.), and the influence of the filmmaker Kenneth Anger. Through Kabbalistic and other occult numerical-symbolic associations, Zorn has been able to incorporate mystical features into his more recent compositions, features that emphasize irrational and mystical forms of knowledge. In this chapter, I examine a number of passages and excerpts from works that utilize these and many other forms of "mystical" or "magickal" modes of organization. In particular, I consider Zorn's *Necronomicon* for string quartet from 2003 and his album-length project *IAO: Music in Sacred Light* from 2002.

Chapters 3 and 4 consider Zorn's place within a certain artistic tradition and how Zorn conceives of his compositions as participating in a sort of open-ended dialogue with a variety of influences, a key feature of Zorn's musical poetics. Numerous works by Zorn bear explicit or implicit dedications to a wide array of authors, artists, filmmakers, or philosophers (Jean Genet, Marcel Duchamp, Maya Deren, Walter Benjamin, Antonin Artaud). In chapter 3, I argue that Zorn's dedicated works function in a manner that allows Zorn to enter into a larger historical/aesthetic tradition. Zorn is able to enter into this tradition (loosely understood as a "tradition of transgression") by finding ways to incorporate key aesthetic, theoretical, or structural elements associated with his dedicatees in his own musical compositions. What emerges is a form of influence that is predicated on the notion of the gift and gift giving. Zorn, I argue, conceives of the works of his dedicatees as gifts, and as a responsible recipient of these gifts, he must continue the gift-giving spiral. Zorn accomplishes this by creating new works that both absorb and transform features of the original gift and are then passed along, presumably for future artists or writers. Following a brief outline of some of the main features associated with gift theory, I attempt to apply these ideas in my analyses of Zorn's *In the Very Eye of Night* (dedicated to the filmmaker Maya Deren) and *Untitled* (dedicated to Joseph Cornell).

Chapter 4 offers an analysis of two movements from Zorn's *Aporias*, a work subtitled *Requia for Piano and Orchestra* completed in 1994. Much of the pitch material of *Aporias* is derived from Stravinsky's *Requiem Canticles,* and the analysis describes the many ways Zorn transforms and manipulates Stravinsky's source work. At the same time, the notion of the gift as a model of influence is still very much in effect in this chapter. The intricacies of Zorn's incorporation of influences is evident at many levels: not only does the work depend on Stravinsky's *Requiem Canticles,* but each movement is also dedicated to a single individual whom Zorn considers important to his own growth as a composer and musician. My analytical comments focus on the movements written in the memory of the painter Francis Bacon and Marlene Dietrich. The analyses develop many of the ideas regarding influence and tradition described in chapter 3 by considering (a) how Zorn absorbs musical forms and ideas received from other composers, (b) how these transformations reflect certain aesthetic ideals or traits associated with the intended dedicatee, and (c) how Zorn is able to create a coherent, self-standing composition given the many associative and referential sources that form the basis of the work.

Realizing that there was no easy way to write anything resembling a musical biopic, I have chosen to focus on music written and composed since the late 1980s. I felt it would be impractical (if not impossible) to account for all of Zorn's compositions, recording projects, diverse bands, and performing lineups according to any single, all-encompassing generalization. While this time span includes a great deal of music, there are still some gaps, most notably the absence of any extended discussion relating to Zorn's game pieces and the various ensembles he has led or played with (Sonny Clark Memorial Quartet, the *Spy vs. Spy* project devoted to the music of Ornette Coleman, Slan, Hemophiliac, Emergency). Of these ensembles, Masada—perhaps Zorn's most prominent group—does not receive any extended treatment in the pages that follow. The complexity, variety, and very personal nature of Masada and its variously related performing ensembles within the context of the "Downtown Scene" in general and the "Radical Jewish Culture" movement in particular demand a separate book.[30]

For reasons relating to scope and continuity, a number of aspects of Zorn's music and career are not covered in the chapters that follow. For example, I have not been able to address in any detail the role of improvisation in Zorn's musical works or the complex interactions between Zorn the composer and Zorn the performer. At the same time, Zorn's place in the so-called Downtown Scene demands its own separate treatment. Presumably, such an account would take into consideration not only the eclectic musical practices and artists associated with the scene but also the role that location—specifically New York's Lower East Side—has played in Zorn's evolving poetics of music. For example, it is worth investigating the variety of influences Zorn absorbed when he returned to New York in the mid-1970s: from avant-garde jazz musicians and practices, to the emerging punk and "No Wave" scene, as well as the ideas espoused by filmmakers associated with the so-called Cinema of Transgression, filmmakers such as Beth B, Nick Zedd, Tessa Hughes-Freeland, Richard Kern, and Tommy Turner.[31] In short, the essays that follow should only be understood as a partial glimpse into Zorn's musical poetics.

The diversity of works and ideas that I do cover in the following chapters have presented a related set of challenges involving the very act of writing a book on Zorn and his music from within an academic setting. Certain disciplinary assumptions pertaining to rationality, order, and logic determine not only how certain ideas are formulated but also how these ideas are (re)presented in a traditional book format. The traditional structure of a book proceeds from a single thesis (a "through-line") that is developed in the opening chapter(s) and that is then explicated in later chapters where the "evidence" is "read through" this theory or thesis. If we were to apply this book model to Zorn's music and musical thought, we would fundamentally misrepresent his musical *oeuvre* and the associative forms of unity that his work embodies. A question I asked myself over and over again was this: Given a body of work as complex, varied, and dense as Zorn's, how is it possible to talk about his music in a book? My own idea of the book was that it should try to capture the experience of listening to Zorn's own music.[32] This experiential writing strategy acknowledges the many ambiguities, contradictions, and confusions that Zorn's music presents to us as listeners. Instead of reducing any possible correspondences to their lowest common denominator in the hopes of arriving at a single meaning, I have tried to allow for the emergence of multiple meanings. Given Zorn's diverse interests and my own desire to explain these emergent meanings, it has been necessary to dip into gift theory, mysticism and occult philosophy, a variety of critical theories, feminism, theories of sadomasochistic practices and sexuality, law, film theory, and pornography. Many of these theories/methodologies sit uneasily with one another. Consistent with my wish to highlight the buried correspondences, concealed analogies, resonances, and inscrutable mysteries that form Zorn's poetics, I am not bothered by these theoretical tensions; in fact, this is exactly the point. By pitting one or more theories and perspectives against one another, I have consciously attempted to foreground the types and forms of (anti)correspondences I describe in the following chapters and any light they may shed on Zorn's complex understanding of tradition, transgression, a tradition of transgression, and the transgression of tradition.

Finally, a bit of clarification regarding my use of the term *poetics* is necessary, as it will figure prominently in all of the chapters. Although the term *poetics* has been used and understood in a variety of ways—not just in discussions of music but in relation to many creative acts—I have been guided by Stravinsky's use of the term as it appears in his *Poetics of Music:* that is, the act of "*making* in the field of music."[33] I have interpreted Stravinsky's brief (and ambiguous) description of the term as implying not only making music (whether this is understood as performing or composing or whatever) but also constantly thinking in terms of music. All of the essays that follow attempt in one form or another to make sense of Zorn's various interests (films, directors, actors, writers, philosophers, artists and critics, performers and composers/bands) and how these disparate interests directly impact and impinge upon his musical worldview and how they ultimately come to be encoded in his compositions.

Carl Dahlhaus's discussion of "Schoenberg's Poetics of Music" has also been helpful in formulating and trying to describe Zorn's own "musical poetics." Dahlhaus has described a "concept of musical poetics" that "signifies an idea, permeated by reflection, concerning the making and production of musical compositions." More significantly for Dahlhaus, the outside forces that may have helped to shape a body of musical compositions—forces that might include theoretical pronouncements, compositional systems, and influences— are not to be understood simply as a backdrop on which we can read/interpret individual works but, instead, form an integral part of the works themselves. These "outside forces" are, as Dahlhaus understands them, "the objects of the enquiry, and not its precondition. They belong to the material from which—*in reciprocal interaction with the interpretation of the works themselves*—the musical poetics are to be constructed."[34] It is these "reciprocal interactions" which I have attempted to examine in the essays that follow as I try to come to terms with Zorn's musical poetics.

John Zorn

ONE

From the Fantastic to the Dangerously Real: Reading John Zorn's Artwork

Even for those not familiar with John Zorn's music, the composer's name will probably evoke certain associations. One is the image of Zorn as the quintessential postmodern composer, a theme developed by a number of writers.[1] In such works as *Cat O' Nine Tails* for string quartet, *Carny* for solo piano, and the numerous "hardcore miniatures" associated with Zorn's band Naked City, musical genres and/or styles are juxtaposed in a collage or pastiche style of presentation that is often described as postmodern. The effect of these pieces can be described as a sort of musical "channel surfing" where a minimum amount of information is given—enough to provide the listener with some idea of what musical style is in play—before moving on to the next musical image.[2]

Another image of Zorn is darker and, for some, dangerous. This view derives, in part, from the graphic and disturbing visual images that are included on many of his recordings from the late eighties to the mid-nineties. Most of these images appeared on recordings of his Naked City and Painkiller projects and reflect Zorn's interest in hardcore rock music (bands such as Napalm Death, Carcass, Godflesh, Brutal Truth, and many others), aspects of Japanese underground movements, and his participation in various sadomasochistic (S/M) scenes and practices.[3] Especially with the Naked City project, the violent juxtapositions of musical blocks, an emphasis—at times—on noise, and an attention to volume and "heaviness" are accompanied by violent imagery on the album sleeves and liner notes. Some of these images are reproduced in figures 1.1–1.3.

Figure 1.1. *Manga* by Suehiro Maruo (included on *Torture Garden*).

Figure 1.1 is a *manga* (a form of Japanese cartoon) by Suehiro Maruo; figure 1.2 is a film still (from Zorn's own private collection) from an unidentified "pink film" (a Japanese pornographic film); figure 1.3 is an archival photograph depicting the torture and execution of a Chinese criminal.[4] The recordings can be understood as a loose audio equivalent of these images.[5]

However we wish to conceive of the relation between music and image, the presence of these images on Zorn's recordings drew hostile responses. The loudest came from Asian American women's and anti-bias organizations. In one of the many newspaper articles addressing these images, Elisa Lee, a journalist writing for the San Francisco–based paper *Asian Week* in 1994, asked:

> How is it that in a society where an episode of Roseanne showing a kiss between
> two women causes a flurry of public attention and sparks rumors of censorship, a

Figure 1.2. S/M film still (included on *Torture Garden*).

musician who conducts concerts in front of screens of Japanese pornography, distributes albums with covers of Asian women being hung, mutilated and tortured and dedicates an album to Chinese torture can incite nary a protest in mainstream American media?[6]

Academics have also taken notice of Zorn's music and imagery. Ellie Hisama has addressed Zorn's complex relationship with Japanese imagery and especially his representation of Japanese women.[7] In her essay "John Zorn and the Postmodern Condition," Hisama considers the images reproduced in figures 1.1–1.3 and makes it clear that she finds the "presence of the photographs and film stills extremely disturbing." Claiming to speak "from the position of the object that Zorn represents," Hisama criticizes Zorn from a variety of perspectives: that in terms of what it represents, his music—as musical representations—serves to "aestheticize torture" and that his musical appropriations are insensitive. One of the main aims of her essay is, in her own words, an attempt

Figure 1.3. Archival photo depicting Leng Tch'e (included on *Leng Tch'e*).

to develop a theory of "repulsion," a way to talk about "music that we don't care for [and] of music that we find dull, inept, or downright repulsive [or] of music that we understand to negate, devalue, and disrespect who we are." In an effort to develop this theory of the repulsive, Hisama suggests that we should "embrace interdisciplinarity, drawing upon insights from ethnomusicology, cultural studies, critical theory, ethnic studies, postcolonial theory, queer theory, and feminist theory." If musicologists and music theorists incorporate these (and presumably many other) theoretical perspectives, Hisama believes that we would be in a much better position to "educate the producers and consumers of music such as *Torture Garden* as to how persons of color and women regard their use as currency in a postmodern artistic economy for others' professional and economic gain."[8]

The criticisms directed at Zorn for his use of these images arose during a very specific, racially charged climate. In the United States in the 1980s and early 1990s, Japan was often represented as the "new enemy" who had successfully assimilated the capitalist logic formerly associated with and perfected by the United States. In an ironic twist, Japan and by extension Japanese Americans (not to mention the numerous other ethnic and cultural groups typically included under the label "Asian American") had, in Gary Okihiro's words, succeeded too well as a "model minority" and now represented a new "yellow per-il."[9] The perceived threat posed by Japan (really, an imagined, all-encompassing, and ill-defined notion of "Asia" in general) manifested itself in American culture in many ways during this time, from the murder of Vincent Chin (killed by two unemployed auto workers in Detroit in 1982), the number of books that appeared in the late 1980s and early 1990s that portrayed Japan as "out to get us" (where "us" is understood as "American"), the *Miss Saigon* casting controversy on Broadway in 1991, the mixed readings and interpretations engendered by David Henry Hwang's play (1988)/David Cronenberg's film (1993) *M Butterfly*, to the backlash and violence directed at Korean shop owners during the 1992 L.A. riots.[10]

Like Hisama and many others, I was shocked when I first experienced these images. Of course, for a white, middle-class American male, these images will never *mean* or *represent* to me the same things they do for Hisama. On the one hand, what I always found remarkable about these images was their unreality—the unreality of their scenarios, the unreality of their presentation (i.e., cartoons and film stills), and the vast differences between the sexual interests and view of women expressed in these images and my own. On the other hand, for a viewer like Hisama, what is remarkable about these images is how "real" they actually are or can be. It goes without saying, therefore, that the various types or forms of reality/unreality represented by these images are dependent not only on personal histories and experiences but also on a wide array of discursive formations at work that enable certain types of readings to exist while suppressing others.

In her essays on Zorn, Hisama draws our attention to what she perceives as the nearly irreducible relationship between Zorn the composer and Zorn as the quintessential postmodernist practitioner. On the one hand, the celebration of Zorn as a postmodernist composer typically involves discussions that focus on his use of borrowed materials, his blendings of what have typically been considered "high" and "low" cultural forms, an aggressive (anti-)aesthetic, and a host of other stylistic, signifying traits typically associated with postmodern artistic practices. However, as Hisama points out, what is typically covered up or ignored in discussions that focus on stylistic characteristics of Zorn's music (and postmodernist practices in general) is how, through a sort of cultural flattening of cultural differences, Zorn actually perpetuates and reinforces a variety of ideological and hegemonic practices or views. Hisama notes how "numerous writers have praised Zorn's clever use of musical quotations, his ability to draw disparate sources into a single composition, his nonconformity, and his 'in your face' aesthetic while ignoring the misogyny and racism of his music in its visual, textual, and sonic manifestations."[11] By appealing to and focusing on the free play of images in a postmodern world, so Hisama argues, we miss the many forms of violence (personal, cultural, ideological) that continue to be perpetuated against

Asian Americans, Asian American women, Asian women, and women in general. For Hisama and other Asian American critics, the images that appear on selected album covers and liner notes by Zorn-led projects are decried not only for what they (re)present (extreme violence toward Asians) but also in terms of the appropriative act itself (where the individuals portrayed or represented by the appropriated images are not allowed to speak of and for themselves).

Developing the interpretive differences relating to reality/unreality alluded to earlier, I will examine how these images can be read according to interpretive frameworks that rely on ideas relating to reality and fantasy. How is fantasy understood in relation to the real? How is the "real" partially formed by fantasy? How does fantasy contest the primacy and power of the real? These are all questions that tie together the various ways Zorn's images have been used, understood, and received. I will address these and other questions in three contexts: the (Asian) American reception and interpretation of these images as being an example of a special type of reality (one where fantasy plays no part); a Japanese sociocultural context where these images are understood as complex fantasy (as fantasy that provides an "outlet" and, at the same time, maintains a certain status quo); and Zorn's musical poetics where these images are understood as transgressive acts that highlight the "hidden gaps," or aporias, left open by a reality that relies on notions of rationality, utility, and subjective wholeness (a poetics derived, in large part, from the thought of Georges Bataille). Finally, I will return to the types of reading/interpretive strategies employed by Zorn's Asian American critics to lay bare an underlying tension and inconsistency that also depends on how various discursive realities are constructed and utilized.

The complex ways producers and (willing or unwilling) consumers of these images understand the fantasy/reality distinction(s) will not solve the difficulties they present. If anything, they will make things more difficult. I should make it clear that I am not attempting a defense of Zorn's decisions. That Zorn offended a great many people by including these and other images on his records is undeniable. Instead, I am interested in *how* these images are read within or against interpretive frameworks that—either explicitly or implicitly—rely on distinctions between fantasy and reality. In an effort to adequately describe these various frameworks, I will adopt a multiperspectival mode of presentation.[12] Before addressing the actual images and their contexts from these various perspectives, a brief discussion on some of these fantasy/reality frameworks is necessary.

The Fantastic and the Real

One theory of fantasy is also, by exclusion, a theory of the real. Such a view can be considered a naïve view of fantasy where the real might be defined as "what there is" while fantasy is understood as "what there is not," hence the "unreal." According to this naïve view, what is real is obvious: the real includes everything we all know, perceive, or understand as being true or beyond question. Science, evidence, facts, and intersubjective confirmation all determine, to a large extent those things, beliefs, phenomena, etc., that qualify as real. Anything characterized as fantasy resists the types of verification associated with the real. To be clear, though, it is not that the real is unequipped to deal with fantasy and the fantastic; the real understands that there is no reason to seriously address fantasy.

While a naïve view of fantasy and the real might be adequate when considering unbelievable scenarios or exaggerated representations of people or things, the distinction is not as obvious in everyday, "real-world" situations. A brief mental review of the history of science is enough to convince us that what was at one time considered fantasy—i.e., the not-real—was later admitted to the category of the real. Notice, however, that it is the real that is the arbiter of what is or is not considered fantasy. If something makes the switch from the fantastic to the real, it is only according to the terms of the real; at all times fantasy is silent, having no say in regard to its status. The relative fluidity as to what is considered real or fantasy represents a more common-sense view of the distinction. The common-sense view contains a built-in feature that allows for the "as-yet-to-be-determined" reality of what is, at the present time, fantasy. The common-sense view accommodates change with to-be-developed mechanisms for determining what constitutes the real. Such mechanisms are easy to see in the area of science where more sophisticated theories or testing devices can expand the realm of the real. At the same time, the common-sense view is seen around us in advertising, politics, and other day-to-day interactions. The psychoanalytic notion of wish fulfillment falls under the common-sense view, as the "not-yet-real" is closer than we might think. ("If you want that raise, then you need to do x, y, and z," "Want to date more beautiful women/men, then buy this penis enlarger!" "Wouldn't you look good in a Lexus?") In a related fashion, the possibility that fantasy is an imminent reality and therefore must not become real is common in contemporary politics and relies on the common-sense view. ("If you want to hold on to your personal freedoms, then you must do your part in helping us defeat terrorism.")

With a slight shift in perspective, we can identify the category of the real as being determined by institutions of power. Those "in charge" of the real have at their disposal the ability to identify what is not real. With this shift, what is real is now understood as serving stabilizing forces designed to preserve the status quo (maintaining the hegemony of a particular institution) while, at the same time, assuming some sort of valuative function(s). By ruling over and determining the real, power structures make available—even promote—those things that are useful, productive, and "right." Moreover, what is deemed useful and productive continually serves the powers-that-be. At the same time, institutions of power not only determine the real. They can also construct fantasies, fantasies that serve to perpetuate the real. As an example, Foucault has described how discursive practices established during the "Victorian regime" (and still in effect today) were able to circumscribe ways of talking about, understanding, and practicing sex and sexuality, his so-called repressive hypothesis. Through an increased openness and frankness in discussions relating to sex, religious institutions and other political bodies attempted to rein in and demystify questions relating to human sexuality. "Rather than the uniform concern to hide sex," Foucault writes, "rather than the general prudishness of language, what distinguishes these last three centuries is the variety, the wide dispersion of devices that were invented for speaking about it, for having it be spoken about, for inducing it to speak of itself, for listening, recording, transcribing, and redistributing what is said about it. . . . Rather than massive censorship, beginning with the verbal proprieties of the Age of Reason, what was involved was a regulated and polymorphous incitement to discourse."[13] The result of this openness has not been an "anything-goes," free-love approach to matters relating to sex but, instead, the conservative circumscription of sexuality according to principles of production and utility; that is, heterosexual sex whose aim is procreation. As a result, anything related to sex that could not be understood according to the principles of production or utility is understood as other, deviant, taboo, and, therefore, prohibited fantasy.

Foucault also points out that greater restrictions and prohibitions related to sex and sexuality also had the reverse effect; that is, seemingly more and more "peripheral sexualities" arose, or became more visible, as a result of the centrifugal forces of heterosexual, procreative, and monogamous relationships. Power and its hold on the real was constantly being contested by those forces that it had tried to suppress; it was being challenged from within. Whereas outward and external manifestations of taboo and prohibition-breaking behavior could, to a certain extent, be brought back under control (by legal, educational, medicinal, or other means), it is much more difficult to satisfactorily handle similar external manifestations of transgressive behavior that arise from fantasy and the subject's mental life. Freud's notion of psychic reality seriously undermines the reality/fantasy distinction by positing that external behaviors—neuroses, symptoms, etc.—may actually arise from unconscious memories that have no basis in reality. That is, fantasies (or *phantasies*) constructed by an individual that are believed to be true—i.e., grounded in reality—may actually have been fabricated by the individual. The individual believes some memory to be true (as having actually happened) when, in "reality," no such events ever occurred. The result is the seemingly paradoxical situation that certain external behaviors or acts (associated with the real) can be traced back to (unreal) fantasies of the subject.

If we pursue these implications far enough, we can potentially view the entire project that has constructed, maintained, and sustained the fantasy/reality split as a form of fantasy. Judith Butler has suggested that we can "understand the 'real' as a variable construction which is always and only determined in relation to its constitutive outside: fantasy, the unthinkable, the unreal."

> The positivist version of the real will consign absence to the unreal, even as it relies on that absence to stabilize its own boundaries. In this sense, the phantasmatic, as precisely such a constitutive exclusion, becomes essential to the construction of the real. If this is so, in what sense, then, can we understand the real as an installation and foreclosure of fantasy, a phantasmatic construction which receives a certain legitimation after which it is called the real and disavowed as phantasmatic? In what sense is the phantasmatic most successful precisely in that determination in which its own phantasmatic status is eclipsed and renamed as the real? Here the distinction between the real and unreal contrives a boundary between the legitimate domain of the phantasmatic and the illegitimate.[14]

The fluidity of the reality/fantasy distinction is highly suggestive. However, while I am attracted by the theoretical implications of arguments such as Butler's, I am a bit skeptical (maybe nervous is a better word) about how such theories can be effectively enacted or implemented in practical, "real-world" situations. That is, I perceive the potential for an extreme radical relativism in both thought and practice if ideas such as these are used as legal defenses of criminal conduct, moral or ethical justifications of acts, etc. Perhaps this shows that the notion of the "real"—the useful, the productive, the rational, and the regulated—is just as much a necessity for fantasy as fantasy is for reality.

I recognize that the fantasy/reality distinction requires a much more thorough and rigorous explication than the one I have just presented. However, I do believe that, given the rough outline described above, we can begin to see how distinctions relating to fantasy and reality can be conceived and put to use. At the same time, we can recognize the variety of ways texts or images are "read" by groups or individuals, forms of reading that depend on some understanding of the relation(s) between fantasy and reality.

Reception of Zorn's Images in America: The Revenge of the Real

For Ellie Hisama and other individuals or groups who have expressed disgust or revulsion at Zorn's imagery, the images reproduced in figures 1.1–1.3 are understood as representing a sort of social reality. In particular, the reality depicted is one based on misogyny, racism, and stereotypical constructions of Asian women. The images are understood as dangerous not only in an epistemological, conceptual sense but also in a practical sense where these images can be understood as potentially functioning somewhere along a causal chain that will lead to violent acts toward Asian women. The critics' crusade against these images, and the pressure applied to Zorn to remove them, was understood, therefore, as "a matter of personal survival."[15] Numerous comments by Zorn's detractors speak to the dangerous reality of these images:

> These images are degrading and reinforce all sorts of stereotypes of Asian women being sexual mannequins and victims. (Richard Oyama, San Francisco–based poet)

> It's so obviously dehumanizing . . . one should know when you present an image how it is perceived. When [Zorn] puts out those images, it reinforces things, whether he wants it to or not. (Jason Hwang, New York–based musician)

> The dismemberment of the sonic body [described by Hisama in her analysis of Naked City's tune "Osaka Bondage"] is related to the dismemberment of the actual bodies depicted on the CD covers. (Hisama)[16]

For these and other critics, the images—the *manga*, the film stills, and the archival photos—are understood as unmediated representations of the real. While the images from *Leng Tch'e* are truly "documentary" in nature, the cartoon images and film stills can also be understood as being just as real, for they, too, document a sort of social reality. The "cinematic" nature of the film stills and archival photos do not lie: "These things happen(ed)," they announce to us. The *manga*, although lacking the cinematic reality of the other images, partake in this announcement. While they lack the documentary tone of the other images, the various *manga* images included on Zorn's recordings are drawn from and reinforce the same reality responsible for the photographs and the film images.

A useful framework for understanding the type of social reality constructed and reinforced by these images is provided by Catharine MacKinnon and her views on the use and function of pornography in American society.

> Pornography does not simply express or interpret experience; it substitutes for it. Beyond bringing a message from reality, it stands in for reality; it is existentially being there. This does not mean that there is no spin on the experience—far from it. To make visual pornography, and to live up to its imperatives, the world, namely women, must do what the pornographers "say." . . . Pornography makes the world a pornographic place through its making and use, establishing what women are said to exist as, are seen as, are treated as, constructing the social reality of what a woman is and can be done to her, and what a man is in terms of doing it.[17]

For MacKinnon, the defense that pornographic images (and, in our present context, I believe we can include racist imagery as well) do not "say" anything but are instead inherently meaningless and only acquire meaning through an encoding process by the consumer is untenable and unacceptable. Such a view, MacKinnon argues, would require us to believe that such images are harmless and that any possible harm that can be related to these and other images is the result of people who project their own beliefs, fantasies, and ideologies *into* them. The images, then, are empty containers waiting for semantic content to be added by viewers. In opposition to this viewpoint—which is, incidentally, the viewpoint that provides some sort of protection to these and other images under current state and legal frameworks—MacKinnon argues that such images are much more active and that they do function in a meaningful way: as imperative speech acts:

> Pornography contains ideas, like any other social practice. But the way it works is not as a thought or through its ideas as such, at least not in the way thoughts and ideas are protected as speech. Its place in abuse requires understanding it more in active than in passive terms, as constructing and performative rather than as merely referential or connotative.
>
> The message of these materials, and there is one, as there is to all conscious activity, is "get her," pointing at all women.[18]

In this "image as speech act" view of pornography, the visual is indistinguishable from the linguistic. Furthermore, the linguistic reality of such images function through a process of identification ("Women *are* this . . .") as well as action ("Do *this* to women *because they are nothing but* . . ."). We can see these processes of identification and the potential for enactment at work in the ways critics of Zorn's imagery equate torture with S/M practices. Hisama writes how "the 'Japanesing' of sadomasochism in *Torture Garden* emerge[s] from Zorn's obsessive need to associate the unfathomable and alluring Orient with sex generally, and S/M particularly. . . . Zorn's attempts to aestheticize torture in his use of sonic and visual images trivializes the suffering of millions of people for whom torture [is] neither a postmodern game, nor a choice."[19]

But are S/M practices and torture interchangeable? Taken on their own and devoid of any context, the images on *Torture Garden* and the images accompanying *Leng Tch'e* might appear to present the same idea.[20] Indeed, the practice of Leng Tch'e describes a form of torture used in China during the Manchu dynasty whereby the accused is kept alive with opium as they are slowly cut into 100 pieces ("Leng Tch'e" translates as "100 Pieces"). Figure 1.3 is only one photo of many taken during what was probably the last time this form of torture was employed in China—possibly from April 10, 1905—showing Fu Chou Li, a young man convicted of killing Prince Ao Han Ouan, being cut apart.[21]

Casual viewers of S/M scenes (if there can be such a thing) might easily conflate the performances of sadomasochistic behavior with real-life torture scenes. To do so, however, is to overlook some fundamental differences between the two. First, victims of torture have no say in how they are treated. There is no way that torture victims can exert their will into the process; indeed, the whole point of torture is to destroy the will of the victims, to force them to impart some information needed or wanted by the torturers, those who are in power. In "typical" S/M scenes, by contrast, the power resides in the "dominated" (the submissive, or the "bottom"). It is the bottom who calls the shots (determines what is "wanted") and is able to call off the entire scene if he or she feels that things are getting out of hand. Second, with torture, the infliction of pain is the means by which a torturer will gain something; the torturer gains at the expense of the victim's loss. S/M scenarios, however, more closely resemble religious asceticism where the pain undergone by a victim leads to a pleasurable experience for that victim. There is eventual pleasure in the pain endured. Whereas a sense of self is lost or broken for the victim of torture, the self is affirmed, attained, or sought after by the submissive in S/M practices.[22]

For those critical of Zorn's choice of images, the complex power and identity politics of S/M behavior are disregarded and are, instead, unquestionably equated with practices better described as torture. Furthermore, in the readings that I have been able to consult, it is not even mentioned that there are no men engaged in the S/M depictions included on *Torture Garden;* all of the images show either a single woman or two women.[23] Even if the unbalanced or ambiguous gender depictions were noted, I am not sure that this would fundamentally alter the critics' opinions. Violence against women is depicted in these images and therefore there is only one way to read them: from within the social reality of male domination and male power. Andrea Dworkin has even suggested that all representations of female-female sadism are male dominated and male directed (posed and staged by males, for a male audience, depicting male fantasies of lesbianism while also serving to affirm the idea that women are, at their most fundamental level, dangerous). Furthermore, even in those S/M scenes where the male assumes the role of the submissive, "masochism in the male is transformed into a form of sadism. He suffers to conquer; she suffers to submit."[24] According to this view, within *any* S/M scenes involving women, either the women are the victims of actual violence directed at them because they are women, or they are simply rehearsing and reinforcing deeply entrenched gender stereotypes imposed on them by a patriarchal society. In other words, these women are "acting out" or performing what is expected of them by men, and if this is the case, then these women truly have been robbed of their will, and the analogy between S/M and torture becomes much more tenable.[25]

For Zorn's critics, there is no interpretation necessary in decoding his images: what you see is what you get. An individual's perception is equated to a singular perception of an unequivocal reality ("one should know when you present an image how it will be perceived"). As a result, there is no room for "fantasy," the innocent representation, or the "mere" presentation of ideas. MacKinnon again notes:

> To say that pornography is categorically or functionally representation rather than sex simply creates a distanced world we can say is not the real world, a world that mixes reality with unreality, art and literature with everything else, as if life does not do the same thing. The effect is to license whatever is done there, creating a special aura of privilege and demarcating a sphere of protected freedom, no matter who is hurt. In this approach, there is no way to prohibit rape if pornography is protected. If, by contrast, representation is reality . . . then pornography is no less an act than the rape and torture it represents.[26]

What is depicted in these images "speaks" about us and to us. Furthermore, MacKinnon argues, what it has to say is incredibly dangerous and can be compared to hate speech leading, potentially, to hate crimes.[27] Educating Zorn (and others) about the very real dangers of these images is easily understood as a matter of "personal survival" for his critics as well as those who have been silenced.

The Place and Function of Fantasy in Japanese Culture

A westerner visiting Japan in the late 1980s and early 1990s may well have been shocked by the abundance of nudity and/or sexually suggestive material in everyday Japanese culture (advertisements, television commercials, etc.). Nudity might have been encountered in ads and billboards designed to sell any number of products or viewed on television both in advertising and in specialty shows (such as those ranking or grading some of the best massage parlors in town). Even at the train station, sexually explicit and often violent *manga* would be available for purchase by the businessman (or businesswoman) making his/her way across town. Whereas in the United States sexually explicit material was typically associated with shops on the "wrong side of town" and found on the upper racks of magazine stands, *manga* and other sexually oriented magazines could easily be purchased at book and magazine vendors at the stations. Often no effort was made to hide these items from persons deemed too young or from those who might find such materials offensive. Zorn most certainly encountered and familiarized himself with these and other materials during his extended stays in Japan during this time. In this section, I will consider some ways in which such images might have been read, understood, and used in Japanese culture and society.

Imagine getting on a train in Tokyo and sitting down next to a businessman reading *Rapeman,* a serialized *manga* where the main character is a superhero who avenges jilted lovers (both male and female) by seeking "Vengeance through penetration!" Our first instinct, of course, would be to pick up our belongings and move to another seat.[28] Why someone would read such materials—in a public setting, no less—would be baffling. Perhaps adding to the disbelief, it might come as a shock that most *manga* (and, in this case, "erotic manga" or *ero manga*) made and directed toward an audience of women (*redikomi*) are just as—if not more—explicit in their depictions of rape, violence, and brutality. Writing on women's *ero manga*, Setsu Shigematsu states:

> The pornographic detail of the sex depicted in ladies' comics is on par with pornographic comics for men. The wild and risqué narratives are combined with illustrations of vaginas, clitorises, penises, anuses, breasts, erect nipples, an excess of bodily fluids, and a no-holds-barred array of sexual practices, ranging from autoeroticism, S/M, same-sex encounters, threesomes, foursomes, orgies, sex with transsexuals and transvestites, various rape and pseudo-rape scenarios, gang rape and rape by strangers, fathers, [ex-]boyfriends, girlfriends, and the list goes on.[29]

It's hard to see how the list *could* go on. As someone who has spent a lot of time examining and thinking about the role of ladies' *ero manga*, Shigematsu hypothesizes that instead of being a "reflection" of women's repressed sexual desires, ladies' erotic comics

> function as an alternative site and avenue of eroticism for women, which simultaneously (re)configures and extends the boundaries of publicized sexuality for women by making visible such heterogeneous uses and possibilities of sexual activity. Rather than being a reflection of some pre-existing, hidden desires, ladies' ero manga provides varieties of sex as entertainment for women, marketing a smorgasbord of sexual possibilities, producing sex as a consumable spectacle.[30]

The notion of "naïve fantasy" as a form of entertainment predicated on its unbelievability is a trait present in ladies' and men's *ero manga* and in Japanese pornographic films as well.[31] In such *manga*, the oversized genitalia, breasts, and buttocks are instantly recognized as ridiculous in Japanese society. In other words, the creators of Japanese *manga* appear to be poking fun at themselves when they draw their characters (many of whom lack defining facial features of Asian men and women) with extraordinary genitalia or enormous breasts. At the same time, the acts of violence depicted in explicit *manga* are unbelievable, where the victims endure incredible amounts of pain, pain that a "real" person could never endure. The "unbelievability" of their pain and injuries is underscored by the fact that these same characters may appear again five frames later in the same strip seemingly with no apparent injuries. An example of such an unbelievable scenario is evident even in figure 1.1, where we are (are not?) expected to believe that a young girl who has just had the skin removed from her face can still manage to hug the neck of her attacker in some kind of sick embrace.

Turning our attention to the screen, production in pornographic films is typically shoddy with little concern for creating realistic on-screen representations. The unrealistic nature of these films is compounded by awkward edits or stylized camera angles that foreground the aura of fantasy.[32] Zorn's images of sadomasochistic practices included on *Torture Garden* are stills from a Japanese "pink film" that, like many "erotic productions" (*eroductions*) made and produced in the 1960s and 1970s, is set in the Yoshiwara district (a regulated "pleasure quarter") in the pre-modern Edo period where, after a day of killing and terror, the warriors could enjoy themselves in the comfort and safety of the state-regulated brothels. It is, in other words, a period porno film, much like *Caligula* is to western audiences.

The exaggerated bodily makeup of *ero manga* characters and the poor production techniques and fantastic locations and scenarios of many *eroductions* are instantly recognizable as unreal by Japanese audiences. Relating these production techniques and representations to aspects of storytelling in Japanese society, Anne Allison has written how "Japanese sexual storytelling . . . relies far more on a convention of fantasy that is compelling because it engenders rather than suspends belief. To say this somewhat differently," she continues, "fantasies of sex are often produced along the lines of abnormal, illicit, transgressive, or dirty encounters that leave certain realities off the page and, figuratively, outside representation."[33] What are these "realities" which are absent from *ero manga*, erotic films, and other sexually explicit and/or violent materials? To answer this question, we need to examine a particular aspect of Japanese law.

Article 175 of the Japanese Revised Criminal Code—adapted in 1907 as Japan was entering the "modern" world—reads as follows:

> A person who distributes or sells an obscene writing, picture, or other object or who publicly displays the same, shall be punished with imprisonment at forced labor for not more than two years or a fine of not more than 5,000 yen or a minor fine. The same applies to a person who possesses the same for the purpose of sale.[34]

Of course, any potential legal strength (or weakness) of Article 175 depends on how "obscene" is defined. According to the Misdemeanor Law, Article 1, No. 20, obscene is understood as "a person who brazenly exposes thighs, hips, or other body parts at a place exposed to public view in such a manner as to cause disgust to the public."[35] At around the same time, Article 21 of the Customs Standards Law (1910) describes as obscene any materials entering the country that "are considered of such a nature as to excite sexual desire and give rise in people to feelings of shame or repugnance."[36]

Article 1 of the Misdemeanor Law focuses on the depiction of the body's lower frontal extremities as constituting an "obscene display," and Article 21 emphasizes a social standard regarding sexual desire and the feelings that may result in consumers of obscene materials. Admittedly, both definitions are vague and open to a number of interpretations. In fact, many took advantage of these vagaries and ambiguities. For example, it was possible—within the purview of the law—to show genitalia without pubic hair. While this would seem to contradict Article 1, No. 20, it was permitted because it was understood as not being sexual, where sexual meant productive, procreative sexuality. At the same time, intercourse could be depicted as long as the genitals were concealed.

Article 175 was written and worded in such a way as to conform to Japan's emerging role in a modern (i.e., western) society. According to Allison, Article 175 and the varying definitions of obscenity outlined above were understood as a "corrective to [the] western perception of Japanese 'primitiveness.'"

> [The laws] were a means of covering the national body from charges that it was obscene. To Japanese at the time . . . exposing one's body to bathe or to nurse was considered neither dirty nor sexual. Further, sexuality itself lacked the connotation of dirtiness. Rather, under a Shinto rather than Judeo-Christian religious ideology, these are bodily functions that, along with burping, excretion, and picking one's nose, are viewed as matters more of nature than of shame.[37]

The wish to conform to western ideologies regarding decency, obscenity, and morality was made clear by state and legal officials who informed the general population that public nudity or mixed-sex bathing in bathhouses, "although . . . not so despised among ourselves, . . . is looked upon with great contempt [by foreign countries]. You should therefore consider it a great shame." Fukuzawa Yukichi, the "moralist of the Meiji enlightenment," warned his contemporaries that "sooner or later such conditions in our country will come to the ears of foreigners, exposing us to who knows what attacks and reproaches."[38]

Stepping back for a moment, we come to realize that the prohibition against the depiction of pubic hair and genitalia has, to a large extent, allowed many of the graphic images and subject matter commonly found in Japanese *manga* and erotic films to exist (a possibility suggested by Foucault). The extreme images of sadomasochism, the fetishization of prepubescent girls, anal fixations, etc., are all legal under pre-1991 Japanese law. Because of the restrictions outlined by Article 175, what has emerged in a great deal of Japanese advertising media as well as entertainment is, as Anne Allison points out, a "public culture in which the conjuring of sex that depends on body imagery . . . either decenters the genitals or alludes to them indirectly." Allison mentions alternative (i.e., pubic-free) imagery that includes "peepshots" (upskirt photographs of women and prepubescent girls), an obsessive fetishization of other body parts, and acts of sadomasochism, all of which are considered "something other than 'obscene' and other than 'real' [according to Japanese law]. They are fantasies that can penetrate the public only by covering, effacing, or decentering the pubis."[39]

It seems paradoxical (not to mention disturbingly ironic) that censoring any depiction of the genital region actually gave rise to a variety of images and depictions that might be considered much more "dangerous." As Allison continues, however, the "banning of genitals from public images . . . protects as 'real' one region of the social body from the sexualization of mass culture." This region, she argues, is "family and home and [the] center of this region is the mother":

> Young girls, whose very lack of pubic hair signifies their feminine immaturity, are featured [in "pornographic" materials] instead, as well as sex acts that have no chance of leading to reproduction—voyeurism, sadism, anal penetration, fellatio. What is prohibited as "obscene" by the state, then, is also that which is most sacred and central to the state's national identity—stable families, reproductive mothers, and orderly homes.[40]

The notion of "sexuality" described by the Customs Bureau therefore would not be violated by these seemingly more violent images. In an interesting legal case, importers, distributors, and translators of portions of the Marquis de Sade's *In Praise of Vice* and *The Travels of Juliette* were taken to court on obscenity charges in Japan in the early 1960s. Invoking Article 175, the Tokyo District Court needed to establish three conditions necessary to judge the work obscene: (1) Did the work exhibit a "wanton appeal to sexual passion"? (2) Did the work cause "offense to the average man's sense of shame"? and (3) Did the work exhibit "opposition to proper concepts of sexual morality"? Although conditions 2 and 3 were understood as being present, the defendants were acquitted when it was ruled that the first condition was not met. The court explained that the "brutality and *unreality* of *Juliette* were such as to preclude fulfillment of the first condition."[41] What was not upset was "real" sexuality, the reality that emphasizes the stability of the family, the role of the mother, and the role of the state.

Images of anal sex, rape, sadomasochism, and/or bondage are relegated—almost by law—to the realm of fantasy. At the same time, these images paradoxically uphold traditional Japanese values of family, child-rearing, and stability. As a result, the realms of the real and the fantastic exist in an interesting tension in Japanese culture and society, a fact reflected not only in the forms of pulp entertainment we have been considering but also in city planning. As John Clammer has recognized, "Japan combines conservatism and hedonism in a way that few other societies have managed to do" and where the customs and laws of Japan paradoxically support a conservative sense of public order by legitimating the free play of a very frequently erotic and violent imagination in areas or compartments set aside for this purpose, something which may have to do with the [near] absence of violent crime in Japan. The cheek-by-jowl juxtaposition of a district of love hotels and one of Tokyo's premier high-cultural sites (the Bunka Mura) in the capital's Shibuya district is not an anomaly or the accidental result of bad town planning: it represents a fundamental structure of Japanese society at work.[42]

Such images and juxtapositions can be understood as enabling fantasy and perhaps are used to take people's minds away from the heavily controlled and regimented society in which they live and work. Understood from this perspective, these images are used, consumed, and valued because of their unreality. On the other hand, if sexually explicit *manga,* magazines, or films can be read as reinforcing traditional Japanese society and its values (family and stability), many of the original difficulties presented by these texts and images return. Even though certain images might not be read as saying "perform acts of sado-masochism or rape against women," they still function in maintaining a certain status quo of Japanese society, specifically the limited opportunities available to women through the reinforcement of traditional familial, occupational, and gender roles. Even after arguing against the perceived reality or "truth" of the acts depicted in certain *ero manga* (both men's and ladies'), Allison ultimately concludes that "*ero manga* are misogynistic. That they embed and thereby foster an ideology of gender chauvinism and crude masochism is also irrefutable."[43]

In effect, we have returned to the reading model described in the previous section where the image functions as some sort of imperative speech act. Instead of the direct "do this to women" interpretation put forth by MacKinnon and others, the consumption of sexually explicit and violent Japanese images described above is more indirect, stating "don't *really* do this, do this instead." The aims and outcomes of such indirect imperative statements are just as troubling and disturbing. To make matters even worse, other authors have considered the negative consequences of similar indirect speech acts in *manga* that do not rely on depictions of extreme sex and violence. In her discussion of the popular science fiction *manga* and *anime* (animated film) *Sailor Moon,* Mary Grigsby describes how the superhuman powers possessed by the female main character do not necessarily function as a positive role model for young girls, but serve instead to reinforce traditional gender and societal roles for Japanese women where, in her words, "to be feminine is to consume market goods and be consumed by men."[44] *Manga* and *anime* have also been interpreted according to the direct model. Kanako Shiokawa, for instance, has examined the concept of cuteness (*kawaii*) in girls' comics (*shojo manga*) and its ability to foster passivity, timidity, and weakness in young girls. For Shiokawa:

The notion of "cute" in Japan . . . helps one conform to the age-old aesthetical and social values that favor peace, harmony, and self-discipline, while scorning conflict, disorder, and conceit. Individuality (or, more accurately, being unique and standing out in the crowd) and independence (or pronounced self-reliance and self-sufficiency) traditionally are considered threats, especially in women.[45]

It would seem that Japanese *manga, anime,* and presumably live-action films do not have much to recommend them. Whether or not such images depict sex or violence and whether or not they portray strong female characters, in the final analysis they all end up reinforcing, cultivating, and perpetuating a negative social reality that is dependent on traditional gender and societal roles of women, a possibility suggested by MacKinnon in regard to pornography in general. While this could be understood as a rather strong condemnation of a wide variety of images and forms, as well as Japanese culture, I believe it actually points to some of the limitations of the "image as speech act" model. Given the vast popularity of various forms of *manga, anime,* and even pornography, we would have to believe that millions of Japanese consumers of these and other materials (not to mention other consumers worldwide) are unable to form their own opinions about such materials. At the same time, we are being asked to admit that, in these particular cases, any image contains and therefore presents only *a single* meaning, a meaning that can be read right off its surface. As such, there really is no *act* of reading whatsoever; instead, there is simply an act of presentation that demands that certain actions be taken and certain roles be filled.

Rather than viewing these and other images as reflecting or constructing a sort of social reality—specifically one that subordinates and objectifies women—it is possible to view *manga, anime,* and pornographic films and images as sites of engagement that acknowledge the role of the reader and his or her ability to decode, encode, interpret, use, and misuse texts. At the same time, individual readers and their complex backgrounds—in terms of social, political, economic, gender, and sexual orientation, etc.—not only assist in framing and situating images or texts but also create a set of alternative readings that are foreign or different to the specific "reality" of the mediating reader. As a result, the set of possible interpretations is—if not infinite—exceedingly large. What this means is that, contra the "image as speech act" model described above, these images do not and cannot *mean* any single thing. Understood in relation to the fantasy/reality distinctions I have been describing, Setsu Shigematsu describes how

even reality is typically differentiated by what is called the external/physical/social reality and the internal/mental/psychological and psychic reality. It is in between these realms of reality that manga is consciously read, mediated, and elaborated on through a reader's internal/mental processes, and variously rejected, extrapolated, and/or interwoven into a personal repertoire of memories, pleasures, fears, and fantasies. The making of a reader's personal fantasies, which are individually designed and contrived, might then be understood as constituting a different dimension of fantasy—a singular/internal space of difference that is variously elaborated on and repeatedly transformed.[46]

As an example, Shigematsu considers the rape scenes that frequently occur in ladies' *ero manga* by noting how "it is easy to assume that the reader identifies primarily with the heroine of each story" and who typically endures the rape. However, "the identifications are multiple," and therefore the "subject of desire—the woman who buys and reads the *manga*—may identify with the position of the sexualized object, and/or the transgressing attacker, and/or the voyeur." Often these multiple perspectives are reflected in the graphic layout of the comics themselves as successive frames of the strip offer different angles and viewpoints in the unfolding narrative allowing the reader/viewer multiple modes of access and ways of understanding the action unfolding on the page. Ultimately, Shigematsu believes, the fluid and concomitant acts of both reading and identification "attest to the ways in which women seek to occupy various positions that may traditionally or formerly have been the proscribed social privileges of men." Furthermore, by subtly reconfiguring acts that might typically be conceived as reinforcing certain stereotypical conceptions of women and women's sexuality, such scenes play with and are ultimately "dependent upon the existing cultural-symbolic order, with its prohibitions and taboos." Instead of reinforcing or bolstering these and other deeply entrenched cultural and societal formations, rape scenes and other violent or "deviant" sexual acts in ladies' *ero manga* exploit and highlight the artificially constructed edges and boundaries of these formations.[47]

Zorn never reveals with whom he may or may not identify in these images: the victims, the attacker(s), or a hidden onlooker. For Ellie Hisama and other critics, it has always been assumed that Zorn identifies with the attacker(s) or possibly the voyeur. Presumably it is just as possible that he is not identifying with anyone or, perhaps more likely, everyone.

Fantasy and Reality and Zorn's Poetics of Music

In a response to his critics over the place of these and other images on his CD covers and liner notes, Zorn issued a statement in which he explains that the images "are not meant as a condemnation of one particular group . . . they have been used for their transgressive quality, illustrative of those areas of human experience hidden in the gaps between pain + pleasure, life + death, horror + ecstasy."[48]

Zorn's use of the word *transgressive* in this particular quote is not innocent, carrying with it both a specific meaning and reference. Around the time he began to issue recordings that contained images such as those I have been discussing, Zorn's musical poetics appears to have been greatly influenced by the thought and writings of George Bataille.[49] In fact, Zorn most certainly encountered the images of Leng Tch'e and Fu Chou Li in Bataille's *Tears of Eros*. In the unattributed liner notes included with *Black Box* ("On the Artwork"), the author explains how "further research into the relationship between violence and the sacred led Zorn [in 1990] to the writings of Georges Bataille."[50] A long quote from Bataille on the effects of these photos follows:

> This photograph [of Fu Chou Li] had a decisive role in my life. I have never stopped being obsessed by this image of pain, at once ecstatic and intolerable. I wonder what the Marquis de Sade would have thought of this image, Sade who dreamed of torture, which was inaccessible to him, but who never witnessed an actual torture session. In one way or another, this image was incessantly before his eyes. But Sade would have wished to see it in solitude, at least in relative solitude, without which the ecstatic and voluptuous effect is inconceivable.
> [. . .]
> What I suddenly saw and what imprisoned me in anguish—but which at the same time delivered me from it—was the identity of these perfect contraries, divine ecstasy and its opposite, extreme horror.
> *And this is my inevitable conclusion to a history of eroticism.*[51]

In a passage not included in the notes to *Black Box* (indicated by the ellipsis), Bataille writes:

> Through this violence—even today I cannot imagine a more insane, more shocking form—I was so stunned that I reached the point of ecstasy. My purpose is to illustrate a fundamental connection between religious ecstasy and eroticism—and in particular sadism. From the most unspeakable to the most elevated.[52]

Filtered through a Bataillean lens of eroticism and horror, Zorn intends for these (and other) images and the music they accompany to be read according to Bataille's notion of transgression. Therefore, in an effort to better understand Zorn's own reading of these images (not to mention his music), we must come to terms with certain aspects of Bataille's thought.

Bataille conceives of the realms of the social, the subjective, and the discursive according to two categories, that of the *homogeneous* and that of the *heterogeneous*. Homogeneity—sometimes referred to as the category of *project*—is predicated on utility, production, stability, and rationality. Understood as the "commensurability of elements and the awareness of this commensurability," the homogeneous existence of society, the individual, and discourse is "sustained by a reduction to fixed rules based on the consciousness of the possible identity of delineable persons and situations; in principle, all violence is excluded from this course of existence."[53] *Heterogeneity* describes those "things" or acts that are directly or indirectly forbidden from appearing in the homogeneous realm. The heterogeneous includes aspects of the sacred, religious, and magical (due to a reliance on belief and faith as opposed to scientifically verifiable knowledge), acts of violence, madness, and excess, as well as taboo actions or rituals. Where the realm of homogeneity depends on productive expenditure and utility, the realm of the heterogeneous is predicated on unproductive expenditure and waste. Included within the realm of the heterogeneous, Bataille considers "the waste products of the human body and certain analogous matter (trash, vermin, etc.); the products of the body, persons, words, or acts having a suggestive erotic value; the various unconscious processes such as dreams or neuroses; the numerous elements or social forms that *homogeneous* society is powerless to assimilate. . . . *In summary,* compared to everyday life, *heterogeneous* existence can be represented as something *other,* as *incommensurate* [with homogeneous existence]."[54]

Initially, we might be tempted to equate the domain of the homogeneous with "reality" and that of the heterogeneous with "unreality" or perhaps fantasy. Such a view, however, would oversimplify the complex interactions and interdependencies Bataille perceives between these domains. Bataille does describe the homogeneous as the "sphere of activity" ([or] if you prefer, the real world)" and as a "mirage in which activity encloses us."[55]

At the same time, wars, vermin, eroticism, violence, and other heterogeneous phenomena are certainly very "real" occurrences. However, because we choose to ignore these and other phenomena in an effort to maintain some sense of homogeneous stability, Bataille refers to our tendency to describe the heterogeneous as "aberrations": "*What is the worst aberration? That which we ignore, gravely holding out for wisdom?*"[56] Elsewhere, he refers to the "practical unreality" of heterogeneous elements.[57]

In an attempt to avoid any sort of clear-cut binary divisions between these two realms, Bataille proposes, instead, a continuum where the realms of the heterogeneous and the homogeneous are understood as existing in a complementary, nonoppositional relationship and where the homogeneous necessarily depends on the heterogeneous to justify its existence. The homogeneous is the willful suppression of otherness, taboo, prohibition, and fantasy in the greater interest of progress, stability, and rationality. The elements or objects of the heterogeneous realm are just as "real" as those of the homogeneous; they are only made to seem unreal, undesired, or fantastic through the rationalizing processes of homogeneity.

When the heterogeneous intrudes on the realm of the homogeneous, the subject experiences a "force or shock" that precipitates alternative forms of (non)knowledge, a momentary insight or experience where everything that had been conceived as rational, logical, and beyond any sort of (reasonable) doubt is overturned and thrown into question. Bataille's paradoxical project is therefore aimed at explicating those areas of nonknowledge that are concealed by (homogeneous) knowledge and whose goal is the realization of a subjective moment of "inner experience," of a "luminosity without enlightenment" where the notions of utility and reason are temporarily suspended.[58] Such moments are achieved through acts of transgression.

For Bataille, transgression is not understood as the dismantling of boundaries but rather the pushing or testing of boundaries. With the transgressive act, the rational and the irrational, the beautiful and the horrible, life and death rub up against one another, allowing us to glimpse the proximities, interrelationships, and similarities of phenomena or modes of thought that had always been conceived as being distinct and separate. We recognize the beautiful in the horrible and abject, as well as the hidden horrors of the beautiful.[59] Transgression, therefore, is the play of limits where those heterogeneous materials, acts, or concepts that have been excluded from homogeneous structures and forms are brought back into play.

In addition to actions such as eroticism, sacrifice, and violence, Bataille also considers art—specifically poetry—as being able to enact transgression. Poetry, Bataille writes, possesses "the particular faculty of disordered images [used] to annihilate the ensemble of signs that is the sphere of activity [homogeneity]." For poetry to function in a transgressive manner, however, it is necessary to achieve and maintain a proper—yet tense—balance between the stable structures of homogeneous practices (poetry's traditional forms, designs, practices, and linguistic usages) and those features which are designed to upset and destabilize these structures. Lacking a balance between constraints and freedom, a poem without any rules cannot engage with more traditional forms of poetry and may end up constructing its own set of rules, congealing into a newer, homogeneous mode.[60]

In different ways, the images represented on Zorn's recordings depict, from a Bataillean perspective, heterogeneous acts (the extreme violence of Suehiro Maruo's *manga* to the "unproductive" eroticism represented by the S/M scenes) as well as those instantaneous moments of transgression where eroticism and anguish collide (the expression on Fu Chou Li's face as he is cut into one hundred pieces). However, to stop here would ignore the close connections Zorn perceives between his artwork and the music: "For me, my record covers are *very* important. The cover has got to follow through with what the music is about." Zorn's music does not aim to simply represent heterogeneous or transgressive acts per se. It attempts to wreak violence on homogeneous musical structures, designs, and forms as well as any notion of what may constitute musical "logic." Zorn's music, in other words, attempts to transgress the boundaries that exist between what is typically understood as discursively acceptable, rational, and logical (homogeneous) and that which is considered irrational, unacceptable, and outside of such formations. Such an act requires an acknowledgment of homogeneous musical structures whose logic is ultimately pushed to the breaking point.

To conclude this section, I will consider how the tracks "Speedfreaks" and "Osaka Bondage" (both from Naked City's *Torture Garden*) can be viewed/heard as transgressive musical acts by examining how both enact and embody a "play of limits." I will consider how a specific reaction to Zorn's music—a certain type of laughter—signals the attainment of (musical) limits and accompanies our glimpse into the ruptures—the "hidden gaps"—that open up when determinate and rational meaning is overturned.

"Speedfreaks" is an extreme (perhaps the *most* extreme) example of Zorn's jump-cut style of composition. In this work, numerous stylistic/generic references, noises, and other sonic events fly past at breakneck speed: thirty-two discrete events pass before our ears in less than fifty seconds. Example 1.1 is adapted from the "chart" that the members of the group used when performing and recording this tune.[61] In this example, I have indicated each stylistic reference/noise event (sometimes with instrumentation), the underlying harmony or prevalent pitches employed in each block (where N.C. indicates "No Chord"), and the onset of each block (in seconds).

The most immediate—if not the only—form of continuity present in this tune is a consistent rhythmic pulse that binds and connects each successive event to what has come before and what comes after, a consistency required for the performers. The song was recorded and performed straight through; it is not the result of any sort of "cut-and-paste" editing techniques utilized in the recording studio. This pulse is maintained even in those moments where an extreme sense of rhythmic acceleration/deceleration or even suspension might be perceived (for example, the half-time feel of the "Reggae" block in measure 9 or the vocal, F-modal jazz block in measure 21).

Turning our attention to the unfolding harmonic/pitch design of "Speedfreaks," we are immediately struck by the almost complete absence of anything resembling a functional harmonic progression. It is possible perhaps to hear the progression in measures 9 and 10 as projecting some sort of ii-V^7 progression in B♭; however, such a hearing is quickly thwarted by the noise/thrash block of measure 11. The B♭ does make an appearance a bit later (in measure 15) where it now seems to be part of a V^7-IV-I^7 jazz or pop progression in E♭. Of course, even here, such an interpretation depends on our ability to *hear* and *process* this progression, a difficult task given the extremely fast tempo (where the quarter-note equals approximately two hundred beats per minute).

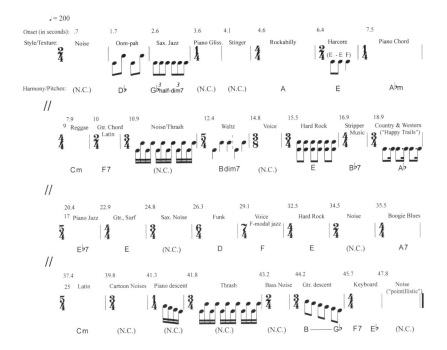

Example 1.1. "Speedfreaks" chart.

The harmonic "illogicality" of "Speedfreaks" might give the impression of complete anarchy where any and all "musical rules" have been abandoned (and where we consider the rhythmic continuity as a conceit necessary for the performance). However, the formal design of this tune provides the necessary balance required by a Bataillean concept of transgression. The 32 discrete musical blocks of "Speedfreaks" is an oblique (and perhaps tongue-in-cheek) evocation of the 32-bar song-form common to many jazz and pop standards. In this form, each eight-measure unit typically unfolds according to the scheme AABA where each A section repeats a melodic line (that may be varied) and a harmonic progression that serves to confirm the tonic. The B section provides the form with its greatest sense of contrast. The contrast of the B section can be the result of an emphasis on a key area other than the tonic and/or, if lyrics are present, by a change in mood, perspective, or content. The B section is harmonically open, ending with a dominant harmony.

In "Speedfreaks," remnants of the formal particulars associated with the standard 32-bar song-form can still be perceived. Notice that the end of the first two A sections (measures 8 and 16, the final measures of the first and second systems) both end with some sort of A♭ harmony—minor at the end of the first system and major at the end of the second system. The harmonic correlation between these two formal junctures might be conceived as insignificant (especially if we focus on the specific melodic/stylistic material heard at these moments) if not for the fact that the opening of the B section (beginning of the third system) starts on E♭, a harmony which could be understood as functioning as the dominant often heard in more traditional AABA formats. The return to the final A is preceded not by its dominant (E♭) but by its tritone substitution (where we could hear the C♯-G tritone pairing as substituting for a more traditional D♭-G pairing that would be included with an E♭7 chord). Finally, Zorn seems to suggest a return to A♭ at the end of "Speedfreaks" with the E♭ sonority played by the keyboard in the penultimate block. The expected A♭ never materializes, however, and is replaced, instead, by a short "chirping" sounds on Zorn's sax and Joey Baron's hi-hat fills. It appears that, with "Speedfreaks," Zorn treats the generic harmonic aspect of the AABA form as a sort of template that can be manipulated and reconfigured. Still, it is this formal constraint (and the harmonies that assist in defining this particular form) which reins in and guides the overall design of "Speedfreaks" and provides the limits or formal prohibitions that the musical surface tries to—but ultimately cannot—break through.

A second tune I would like to consider is "Osaka Bondage," a work that has been described in some detail by Ellie Hisama. Hisama describes "Osaka Bondage" with its noise, thrash/hardcore, and jazz blocks as a mimetic representation of *Torture Garden*'s cover art where the "dismemberment of the sonic body is related to the dismemberment of the actual bodies depicted on the CD covers." Hisama describes "Osaka Bondage" in the following way:

> The sound blocks [of "Osaka Bondage"] proceed from screaming to guitar to sax solo to screaming that evolves into grunting and synthesized lounge music. Some sound blocks are laid out along a common time metric grid, most notably the sections of screaming but also the bass onto which is layered drums and then guitar. Zorn's saxophone solo, played in his characteristic free improvised style, breaks the metric regularity into chaos; the last block of screaming, which is not in the regular $\frac{4}{4}$ meter, is boxed between two blocks of the laid-back, easy-listening style of lounge music that serves as an ironic commentary on the musically transgressive thrash portions of the work. The interspersing of the screaming with smoother styles makes the recurrence of the screams less predictable and subsequently more disturbing.[62]

I have reproduced many of the sections Hisama highlights in Example 1.2.

While there certainly are deviations from a standard $\frac{4}{4}$ metric scheme in "Osaka Bondage" (see the alternating $\frac{3}{4}$ and $\frac{4}{4}$ measures beginning at 0:33 and later between 0:43 and 0:50), it is not true, as Hisama suggests, that any sort of metric regularity is abandoned. Even in the opening noise section (0:00–0:14), drummer Joey Baron can be heard quickly clicking his sticks, establishing/clar-

0:00-0:14: Noise (Vocals, Guitar, Drums, Bass)

0:15-0:22:

0:22-0:27: Slow Hardcore (repeated D-G-A♭ figure in Guitar and Bass)

0:28-0:32: Saxophone solo over implied G minor harmony

0:33-0:36:

0:37-0:42:

0:43-0:50:

Example 1.2. Form and key events in "Osaka Bondage."

ifying a continuous sixteenth-note pulse that underlies the entire track. I do not wish to dwell on this point but, instead, to consider Hisama's portrayal of the thrash and jazz elements that interact within this tune.

The jazz, or "lounge," sections of "Osaka Bondage" are heard beginning slightly after the 0:43 second mark (a little more than halfway through the track) and at the end, commencing at 1:09. These two sections comprise ap-

0:50-1:08 (Variations on this figure begin at 1:00):

1:09-1:14:

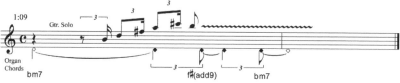

Example 1.2. Form and key events in "Osaka Bondage."

proximately twelve seconds of the tune's overall length of only one minute and fourteen seconds. In contrast to these jazz/lounge sections, musical moments that can be described as "hardcore" or "thrash" rock form the bulk of the musical material of "Osaka Bondage": from 0:15 to 0:42 and again from 0:50 to 1:08. At the same time, these sections project a relatively consistent harmonic center: D. This pitch center is embellished in typical thrash-core fashion with its tritone (A♭) and lowered scale-degree 2 (E♭) (both guitars are tuned down a whole-step from standard guitar tunings so as to accommodate this tonal center).

Hisama describes these thrash sections as "musically transgressive," and while I do not believe she is using the term in as specific a manner as I am (she does not provide any sort of clarification), her description is very suggestive. Presumably, Hisama wishes to convey that—because of the emphasis on noise and screaming—these thrash sections transgress what is typically understood as "musical."[63] At the same time, she describes the lounge sections as providing some sort of "ironic commentary" on the thrash sections as if, because of the presence of clearly recognizable harmonies, clear textures, and easy-to-follow rhythmic and metric structures, the lounge sections are more palatable, more accessible, and more "musical." However, when we consider these competing sections in more detail, we find that the thrash sections are actually more musically stable than the lounge sections. Rather than viewing the thrash sections as functioning in a transgressive manner (where the term is understood in the Bataillean sense I have been describing), it is possible to view the lounge sections as intruding on the boundaries and limitations imposed by the thrash sections.

For instance, the dissonant guitar chord at 0:43 prepares the listener for the first musical block that can be described as evoking a jazz or lounge style.

While it is difficult—if not impossible—to ascribe any sort of tonal significance to this harmony, the A♯ sounding in the upper register (along with the E♮ immediately below) creates a strong expectation for resolution. Such a resolution occurs with the entrance of the keyboard solo as the A♯ resolves up to B, leading us to believe that, because of our deeply engrained knowledge and familiarity with how dissonances should be resolved in tonal contexts, B will also be established as some sort of tonal center (if only for a moment). However, as the keyboard solo continues, the strong-beat arrival on the pitch B is undercut and undermined by the F♯ minor seventh harmony that supports it. Lacking any harmonic support, the lounge section tries to incorporate music originally associated with the thrash sections, notably the rhythms and alternating metric structures heard at 0:33–0:36. Again, this ploy is unsuccessful as the concluding C♯ minor seventh harmony (the final chord of the quarter-note triplets) resolves to the thrash section that immediately follows and its familiar D tonal center. The final jazz section beginning at 1:09 finally provides the B tonal center expected earlier, but because it is the last musical section to occur, it is unable to fully integrate itself within or against the more stable thrash sections that dominate the tune.

These two brief descriptions of "Speedfreaks" and "Osaka Bondage" have attempted to show how Bataillean notions of transgression can be perceived in Zorn's music and not just in the accompanying artwork. Without a doubt, many readers are probably wondering about the value or utility of quasi-formalistic close readings such as those presented above. Given the extremely rapid tempos, do we actually *hear* any of the pitch/harmonic relations described above? While we might not be able to perceive *exactly* what is happening in these or other tunes, it is clear that Zorn is concerned with the details associated with the moment-to-moment interactions as well as the large-scale formations described above. In a conversation I had with the composer about the structure and planning of "Speedfreaks," Zorn described how, in this and other works, "finding the proper sequence to keep the interest and flow is a delicate operation. And crucial. . . . Energy, keys, tempos, feels, instrumentation . . . all these parameters need to be properly balanced and unbalanced."[64]

I do believe that a specific physical reaction to Zorn's music signals, at some level, a recognition of the transgressive qualities and processes enacted by these (and other) musical details. Such a reaction, I believe, is laughter. I am not speaking of a sardonic or derisive form of laughter (a laughter at the expense of others) or the laughter that accompanies a joke whose meaning we "get." Instead, the type of laughter we experience is a type of nervous laughter, a laughter that signals our inability to make sense of situations and when determinate meanings can no longer be grasped. This form of laughter occurs, Bataille writes, when we

pass very abruptly, all of a sudden, from a world in which each thing is well quali-
fied, in which each thing is given in its stability, generally in a stable order, to a
world in which our assurance is suddenly overthrown, in which we perceive that
this assurance is deceptive, and where we believed that everything was strictly anticipated, an unforeseeable and upsetting element appeared unexpectedly from the
unforeseeable, that reveals to us in sum a final truth: that superficial appearances
conceal a perfect lack of response to our anticipation.[65]

This form of laughter accompanies those moments in Zorn's music where
the unexpected and/or the musically irrational or impossible intrudes on and
disrupts our musical expectations: the extreme tempos and the stop-on-a-
dime musical shifts performed by the members of Naked City or the harmonic
"swervings" or deflections that often occur between successive musical moments. The laughter these and other moments evoke in the listener is, according to Bataille, the only response possible. "Laughter," Bataille writes, "leaves
behind the areas that are accessible to speech—and starting with its conditions,
such a laughter is an undefinable leap. Laughter hangs suspended, it leaves you
laughing in suspense . . . [laughter] doesn't affirm anything, doesn't assuage
anything." Bataillean laughter is a response to the "shock or force" that results
from the play of boundaries associated with transgression. Prohibitions must
remain in effect for the transgressive act or acts to have any sort of effect on
the experiencing subject(s). "Laughter is a leap from possible to impossible and
from impossible to possible. But it's only a leap. To maintain this leap would be
to reduce impossible to possible *or the other way around.*"[66]

Zorn's music, the accompanying artwork, and the interaction between the
two create an unstable space where we are confronted with the seemingly impossible, unthinkable, or unimaginable. This transgressive space exists only for
a moment (consider the short lengths of Naked City's tunes), yet the effect of
these transgressive acts remains for much longer as we try to reestablish the
sense of stability that has been displaced by the experience of vertiginous instability that characterizes nonknowledge.

Conclusion

That the images included on Zorn's CD covers and liner notes are complex is beyond any doubt. The complexity derives, in part, from the fact that these images
are stripped from their original contexts—the complete *manga* or entire film as
well as the knowledge of Fu Chou Li's crime and punishment—and are seemingly represented as independent and self-contained depictions of various acts.
At the same time, the recontextualization of these images in relation to Zorn's
music adds new layers of interpretive complexity, where the music and images
can be understood as existing in some sort of mimetic relationship (where the

music is heard as a "sonic analogue" to the graphic images and the "real" violence they depict) or, following the Bataillean perspective outlined above, as representations of transgressive acts that open up, contest, and momentarily merge the separate spaces assumed by the mimetic interpretation.

From a purely theoretical standpoint, the Bataillean perspective offers greater explanatory power in that it enables us to situate and "make sense of" other images included on Zorn's CD covers and liner notes from around this same time (images typically not discussed by Zorn's critics). Focusing on the Naked City recordings, *Heretic, Jeux des Dames Cruelles* (1992) reproduces photos from Serge Nazarieff's collection of historic erotic photography; *Grand Guignol* (1992) uses photos from the Dr. Stanley R. Burns Collection of Historic Medical Photographs and a *manga* by Suehiro Maruo; *Radio* (1993) uses photographs by Man Ray, and *Absinthe,* the band's final studio recording (1993), features hand-colored photographs from Hans Bellmer's *The Doll* (1935).[67] When we consider the artwork from this period as a whole, what emerges is a much larger project whereby Zorn interrogates the boundaries of fantasy and reality, homogeneity and heterogeneity, and the fluid and permeable boundaries that exist between meaning and nonmeaning, knowledge and nonknowledge.

At the same time, the Bataillean perspective allows us to situate Zorn's music and musical poetics within certain practices, principles, and aims common to many of the major avant-garde movements of the twentieth century. For example, the constant interrogation of discursive, cultural, and societal boundaries was a major premise of the dadaists' "anti-art" as well as the varied practices, artists, and thinkers associated with surrealism. Like Zorn, many artists associated with these and other movements aimed to shock viewers with their artworks, often resorting to extreme images of violence and/or sexuality. Thus, as Susan Rubin Suleiman has noted, it was with these avant-garde movements—movements so influential to Zorn's own musical thought—that a "metaphoric equivalence between the violation of *sexual* taboos and the violation of *discursive* norms . . . became fully elaborated."[68]

With this move, sexually explicit or violent visual representations are understood as metaphors for certain forms of linguistic or discursive violence (*écriture*) as described by theorists such as Roland Barthes and Jacques Derrida. Suleiman again writes how *écriture*

> is precisely that element of discursive practice which exceeds the traditional boundaries of meaning, of unity, of representation; and just as for Bataille the experience of transgression was indissociable from a consciousness of the boundaries it violated, so the practice of écriture was indissociable from a consciousness of the discursive and logical rules, the system of prohibitions and exclusions that made meaning, unity, and representation possible but that the play of écriture constantly subverted.[69]

If we allow for an *écriture* of discursive and logical *musical* rules, we recognize the transgressive aims of Zorn's music and musical poetics described in the preceding section.

There are a number of potential "blind spots" in this way of reading. First, if the graphic images such as those that appear with Zorn's CDs are conceived of and treated as signifiers of a deeper, more general metaphor of linguistic and discursive violence, is it even possible to recognize, talk about, or confront those images that depict *actual* scenes of violence, racism, misogyny, or hatred? In other words, does the transgressive interpretive model described above in relation to Zorn and Bataille preclude the possibility that the representation of particular images might actually reflect certain beliefs or wishes of an individual or group? Without any sort of consensus as to standards or restrictions (elements that would seem to undermine the entire transgressive project itself), it would appear that there is not. At the same time, a viewer's ability to distinguish between a range of photographs, artworks, films, or literature that may be considered erotic or that include violent scenes as part of their specific aims or unfolding narratives and those that seem to glorify brutal forms of violence, sexuality, and cruelty would be impossible.[70] If this is the case, then a transgressive perspective ultimately arrives at a similarly extreme (though negated) interpretation of such images as does the "image as speech act" model described in the sections on the reception of Zorn's images in America and Japan. Whereas an extreme version of the "image as speech act" model denies the possibility that these images can mean anything other than what they (re)present (actual violence), the transgressive perspective would seem to deny the possibility that real violence has any meaning outside of any imagined textual or discursive frames. By pursuing each of these ways of reading to their logical conclusions, we arrive at equally untenable and ultimately irreconcilable positions. In short, we have arrived at the extremes of rational, homogeneous thought and stand precariously on the edge of nonmeaning.

Second, it is possible to view Zorn's reliance on aspects of Bataille's thought as a theoretical smoke screen that functions as a disavowal of some sort of underlying fetish for Asian culture in general and Asian women in particular. In support of this possibility, Zorn, in the liner notes accompanying *Spillane*, relates how, during his stays in Japan, he experienced a "strong sense of being outside [Japanese] culture" and that there is a "certain kind of understanding I'll never quite get." At the same time, his sense of being an "outsider" did not deter him from "searching for rare Japanese pop singles, [going] to the movies, old book and poster stores, [eating] incredible food, and [looking] at girls."[71] Zorn's reliance on aspects of Bataille's thought can be viewed perhaps as a strategy by which he can deny any possible pathological fascination with Asian women yet still be able to "use" them in ways that not only satisfy his desires but also allow him to act out against the sense of alienation and rejection he experienced during his stays in Japan. These images and the prominent place they assume on his record covers and liner notes can be read as Zorn's way of "getting back" at a culture that treated him as "Other," a symptom of what Hisama has called Zorn's "Asiophilia."[72]

As a way of returning to the criticisms raised against Zorn by those who speak from an Asian American perspective, it is worth pointing out that appeals to "postmodernism," "pluralism," "multiculturalism," and numerous other buzzwords—while typically used as labels of praise or ideals to be attained—can, for many minority groups, limit access to a wide variety and range of cultural, political, and material opportunities in America. Coco Fusco has pointed out how "what may be 'liberating' and 'transgressive' identification for Europeans and Euro-Americans is already a symbol of entrapment within an imposed stereotype for Others." Fusco writes that "[dominant] cultural and white avant-garde defenses are cast in terms of aesthetic freedom (*But why can't I use what I want as an artist?*) and transgression of bourgeois banality (*But I cross borders and therefore I rebel too*)" and that "what is more fundamentally at stake than freedom . . . is power, the power to choose, the power to determine value, and the right of the more powerful to consume without guilt." "At this historical moment, then," Fusco writes, "the postmodern fascination with the exchange of cultural property and with completely deracinated identity can seem for many people of color less like emancipation and more like intensified alienation." Following Gayatri Chakravorty Spivak, Fusco calls for a position of "strategic essentialism," a "critical position that values identity as politically necessary but not as ahistorical or unchangeable."[73]

Difficulties with such an activist position arise not only from the very real challenges and obstacles faced by any person of color (not to mention gender, sex, class, etc.) who is incessantly confronted by a variety of barriers, limitations, or deeply entrenched modes of representation in contemporary American society, but also, perhaps ironically, by the imagined liberating discursive practices in academia, especially those who trace their genealogy to various strains of poststructuralist thought. As Fusco points out, the ethics and practices of cultural/artistic appropriation when combined with competing views relating to identity and representational politics "involve explicit critiques of liberal humanist claims . . . [and] the relativist postures of certain strains of poststructuralism and their accompanying volunteerist propositions for understanding identity. Scores of feminists and postcolonial theorists have rejected formulations of poststructuralism that declare the death of the subject, the end of meaning, the decline of the social, and the failure of political resistance; these proclamations, they argue, speak only to the realities of those few who once could claim absolute rights, absolute truth, and absolute authority."[74]

I bring in Fusco's work here to serve two purposes: first, to highlight the seedy underside of terms such as *postmodernism, multiculturalism,* and so forth, especially when considering who is doing the appropriating/speaking and who is being ravaged/silenced and, second, to introduce the notion of strategic essentialism as it applies to Asian American positions in relation to Zorn's images and the lingering specter of reality/fantasy that plagues varying interpretive positions. Here I will be on shaky ground because, although Hisama and other critics appeal to a shared notion of Asian Americanness in their collective critiques of Zorn's imagery, it is never clear how the concept or position of Asian American is being used. The "shaky ground" I feel that I am on comes from the fact that Hisama's defensive position relating to her status as Asian American is so underdeveloped and undertheorized in her writings on Zorn that I am forced to reconstruct them in order to make sense of her arguments. While I feel this is something I must do, I can't help but feel that, in the discussion that follows, I am *speaking for* Hisama and other Asian American critics and not *speaking of* their positions.

In Hisama's writings on Zorn, the label "Asian American" is seemingly used as a defensive position that justifies her sense of "repulsion." ("Speaking from the position of the object Zorn represents, I find the presence of the photographs and film stills on these recordings disturbing.") It is this defensive position which has created "the position of the object"—an identity—that Hisama describes. As Susan Koshy and others have pointed out:

> The identity category "Asian American" was a product of the struggles of the 1960s but has been used to organize and interpret the set of immigrant experiences retrospectively and prospectively. . . . The term "Asian American" emerged in the context of civil rights, Third World, and anti-Vietnam war movements and was self-consciously adopted (in preference to "Oriental" or "yellow") primarily on university campuses where the Asian American movement enjoyed the broadest support. . . . From these beginnings, the term "Asian American" has passed into academic, bureaucratic, and thence into popular usage. . . . The Asian American Movement was pivotal in creating a pan-Asian identity politics that represented their "unequal circumstances and histories as being related." Asian American was a political subject position formulated to make visible a history of exclusion and discrimination against immigrants of Asian origin.[75]

Asian American as an identity was born of struggle, lack of opportunity, exploitation, and disenfranchisement. At the same time, it is a fabricated identity category that—in the interest of advancement and equality—conceals as much as (if not more than) it reveals. Recalling Fusco's call for a "strategic essentialism" (from Spivak) described above, the plight and struggles of Asian immigrants in America led—in the formation of the Asian American identity/position—to alliances between a heterogeneous group of peoples, many of whom have very little in common and, in many cases, historically have expressed great animosity toward one another. In the interest of creating a panethnic Asian body that would collectively fight oppression and lack of opportunities in American culture and society, therefore, Korean Americans have been asked to forget their long-standing quarrels and tensions with Japan and China, Chinese Americans with Japanese Americans, and numerous other Asian ethnicities. Ironically, the type of strategic essentializing that gave rise to the notion of Asian American identity is, itself, the result of the same type of essentializing discourse that was formerly known as "Orientalism." As Vincent J. Cheng points out, "What is 'Asian American' if not the flip side of 'Oriental' and or Orientalist bigotry, only now worn with pride?" Further adding to the irony is that, according to the views described above, Asian American identity, to exist at all, necessarily depends on some form(s) of violence. [76]

The erasure of differences in the interest of homogeneity is, for some writers, symptomatic of American (not to mention global) appeals to multiculturalism and/or pluralism. Viet Thanh Nguyen has written how "pluralism is a hallmark of the American nation and culture that Asian American intellectuals often like to assail because it is a form of political organization that represents a vast group of constituencies under a singular identity that is inadequate in terms of fully addressing the cultural, political, and class heterogeneity of American populations." Developing a tension described by Koshy, Nguyen notes how "even as Asian American intellectuals reject American pluralism, they implicitly endorse it for Asian America as a necessary strategy that enables Asian American political agency, unifying a diverse set of ethnicities under a single racial label."[77] In regard to the (ab)use of the concept of "multiculturalism," Lisa Lowe has written how the term "aestheticizes ethnic differences as if they could be separated from history." Within "narratives of multiculturalism," a variety of immigrant, racial, and ethnic cultures are potentially "subject to the leveling operations of both postmodern pastiche and pluralism."[78]

In an effort to get around such a strategically constructed unity of Asian American identity (which as we have seen, requires the willful ignorance of difference that resembles the homogenizing practices and discursive formations associated with multiculturalism/pluralism/postmodernism), some authors have considered the possibility of an emergent, flexible form of Asian American identity that, among other things, does not rely on violence for its existence. Indeed, Hisama draws on the notion of the "interval" as described by filmmaker Trinh T. Minh-Ha. As John Kuo Wei Tchen describes it, the "interval" describes the "space between two contrasting cultural constructs that designates a third, often yet to be realized, place that transcends the attributed polar exclusivity of being Asian and being American."[79] Hisama interprets Minh-Ha's notion of the interval not from the perspective of identity but as an alternative space in which music theory can act. While this is certainly a viable move, I would like to pursue the implications of Minh-Ha's original usage: that of relating to the emergence or becoming of some sort of Asian American identity.

As Stuart Hall has written, cultural identity "is a matter of 'becoming' as well as of 'being.' It belongs to the future as much as to the past. It is not something which already exists, transcending place, time, history, and culture. Cultural identities come from somewhere, have histories. But, like everything which is historical, they undergo constant transformation. Far from being eternally fixed in some essentialized past, they are subject to the continuous 'play' of history, culture, and power." During this emergent formation—this "becomingness"— cultural identities, Hall continues, are "always constructed through memory, fantasy, narrative, and myth. Cultural identities are the points of identification, the unstable points of identification or suture, which are made, within the discourses of history and culture."[80]

Lisa Lowe has written about an emergent Asian American cultural identity that owes much to Hall and, in some respects, fleshes out many of the theoretical implications associated with Trinh T. Minh Ha's notion of the interval. As Lowe points out, the "making of Asian American culture includes practices that are partly inherited, partly modified, as well as partly invented; Asian American culture also includes practices that emerge in relation to the dominant representations that deny or subordinate Asian and Asian American cultures as 'other.'" In the hope of fostering this Asian American cultural identity, Lowe emphasizes how an emphasis on heterogeneity, hybridity, and multiplicity should be stressed and kept in a constant state of tension so as to avoid the essentializing tendencies that may emerge from both *within* the Asian American community and from *without,* specifically the dominant hegemonic institutions that rely on notions of multiculturalism and/or pluralism, terms that, as we have seen, efface more than they provide to minority groups. In Lowe's vision of an emergent Asian American cultural identity, heterogeneity, hybridity, and multiplicity work to contest and disrupt "the discourses that exclude Asian Americans, while simultaneously revealing the internal contradictions and slippages of 'Asian American' so as to insure that such essentialisms will not be reproduced and proliferated by the very apparatuses we seek to disempower."[81]

Lowe's position is a precarious one, as it deftly plays with the rules of the game employed by the dominant institutions that Asian Americans and other minority groups seek to destabilize. It is through a constant play of the boundaries that separate fantasy from reality, truth from fiction, the dominator and the dominated that characterizes Lowe's vision of an Asian American cultural identity.

> The dialectic of Asian American critique begins in the moment of negation that is the refusal to be the "margin" that speaks itself in the dominant forms of political, historical, or literary representation. This transforms the "minority" position from being the only form of inclusion within the universal postulates of the nation to a critique of liberal pluralism and its multicultural terrain. . . . This dialectic not only

addresses the dominant culture and the political state it represents but also reaches back into the reservoir of memory out of which the distinct forms and practices of Asian American culture itself emerge. The "past" that is grasped as memory is, however, not a naturalized, factual past, for the relation to the past is always broken by war, occupation, and displacement. Asian American culture "re-members" the past in and through the fragmentation, loss, and dispersal that constitutes that past.[82]

For Lowe, the formation of alternative Asian American historiographies is selective and nonfactual. A process of reformation, of remembering, involves a selective reconstruction of fragmentary histories and experiences that have been suppressed and denaturalized according to the "universal postulates" expressed and enforced by the "dominant culture and the nation it represents." At the same time, this fictional and selective alternative historiography contains within it the seeds for unmasking similar types of processes associated with "dominant cultures."

In describing alternative historiographical representations—especially those that challenge narratives of development, *telos,* progress, and reconciliation—Lowe draws on arguments set forth in Reynaldo Ileto's "Outlines of a Nonlinear Emplotment of Philippine History." Lowe, excerpting a quotation from Ileto, argues that "in examining historiography, criminality, epidemics, and popular movements, one has only begun to reflect upon those *crucial moments when the state, or the historian, or whoever occupies the site of the dominant centres, performs a cutting operation: remembering/furthering that which it deems meaningful for its concept of development, and forgetting/suppressing the dissonant, disorderly, irrational, archaic, and subversive.*"[83] The selective rememberings/furtherings and forgettings/suppressings ascribed by Ileto to various dominant, hegemonic locations and sites echo the types of organizational and activist tactics suggested by Lowe in her call for an emergent Asian American cultural identity and its concomitant critical strategies/positions of heterogeneity, hybridity, and multiplicity. In both historiographies—the "official" or "sanctioned" histories perpetuated by dominant groups as well as those constructed by marginalized groups—countermemories and/or counterhistories are equally selective in their depiction of the "past," and both depend on fictionalized reconstructions that are at odds with one another. Furthermore, what is "remembered/furthered" by one group in the interest of homogeneity and progress is, for another group, precisely what is "forgotten/suppressed." Furthermore, the justifications for these particular historiographies—an appeal to development, progress, unity, or whatever—are themselves revealed as completely arbitrary and as fantasies on which a fabricated reality is subsequently projected.

In the area of Asian American cultural identity, we have reached a sort of "negative space" that strikingly resembles the spaces in which Zorn's transgressive poetics strives to inhabit. Both, it would appear, depend on and exploit the "blind spots" and inherent contradictions present in officially sanctioned histories and social formations by foregrounding the artificially constructed yet fluid, permeable boundaries separating the real from the fantastic, the true from the false, and the oppressor and the oppressed. Although it must begin with an initial sense of repulsion, a sustained and convincing Asian American critique of Zorn's appropriative acts should expose and undermine any false suppositions or presumptions that might be read into these images. For example, the "de-facement" of the young woman in Suehiro Maruo's manga releases a sort of "negative energy" that despite, or perhaps because of, its extremely violent nature produces the feeling that something (or someone) whole, complete, and unassailable has been violated. Such a feeling is akin to what we perceive when something sacred has been violated, when it has been "defaced." What does this defacement reveal? Where does this sense of sacredness originate? The notion of a whole and complete individual? Or does it highlight (by revealing a "public secret") the wholly incomplete status of Asian American cultural identity?[84] Furthermore, given Lowe's emphasis on the fictionalized "remembering" or the "putting-back-togetherness" of an emergent Asian American cultural identity, how do we make sense of Fu Chou Li's very real "dismemberment" (aside from the obvious analogies with Zorn's musical surfaces)? If bound within and by a variety of intersecting axes of power that suppress and limit the rights and opportunities of the Asian American community, is it possible to focus our attention not *just* on Fu Chou Li's dismemberment but also on the crazed grin on his face as a sort of laugh at those who restrain him and cut him into parts? How effective can the ties that bind Asian Americans to a set of cultural/political/material limitations be when, even as they are being enacted, they are scoffed at? While these are just suggestions, I believe that finding some way to mimic the difficult and conflicting reactions we experience when viewing images such as Zorn's with the conflicting readings that these images engender, it may be possible to move forward in ways where our initial repulsion—as a re-action— is transformed in ways that might, in one form or another, lead to activism.

* * *

At one level, the perceived resonances between Zorn's music and the accompanying artwork reflect his intention of creating a coherent "total package" informed by the thought (not to mention writing style) of Georges Bataille and others who have explored the place(s) and function(s) of violence in society, culture, and art.[85] However, the re-presentation of images depicting torture, violence, and S/M practices have since forced their way beyond the immediate context of Zorn's recordings and have entered a larger debate, a debate on the ways such images can be read or understood. When these de-contextualized images are viewed and debated according to either the "image as speech act" or transgressive models, Zorn's original artistic intention is extended and developed. "Those areas of human experience hidden in the gaps between pain + pleasure, life + death, horror + ecstasy" that Zorn claims are explored in his CDs now becomes an exploration into the hidden gaps and limits associated with certain modes of reading. For instance, whether Suehiro Maruo's *manga* indicates an extreme hatred toward women or is the product of his own artistic fantasy or imagination, or whether the images of S/M practices are viewed as deviant or abnormal sex acts instead of a form of sexual expression preferred by some individuals, or whether the images of Fu Chou Li's execution are understood as a glorification of torture or (as Bataille does) an extreme form of sovereign subjectivity cannot be satisfactorily answered or resolved according to either the "image as speech act" or transgressive forms of reading described above and the diverse social realities and individual fantasies that we bring to these readings.

It is probably clear to most readers that the form of the present chapter reflects the types of theoretical difficulties I have been describing. That is, rather than defending or condemning a particular interpretation of the images that appear on Zorn's CDs, I have chosen to highlight the types of incongruities and limitations associated with a variety of reading strategies. For some readers, my position might be understood as a "cop-out."[86] I believe, however, that to suggest any sort of overarching conclusion regarding the meaning(s) of these images would undermine the very notions of discursive instability and semantic indeterminacy they are designed to elicit—and have elicited—in viewers/listeners. In this regard, I understand the form of this chapter as embodying and enacting the very complexities and uncertainties that Zorn forces us to confront when considering his music, the accompanying artwork, the interactions between the two, and how they can be read.

Magick and Mysticism in Zorn's Recent Works

There are always connections; you have only to want to find them.
—Umberto Eco, *Foucault's Pendulum*

Since the late 1990s, themes of "magick" and mysticism have been pervasive in John Zorn's music.[1] His chamber work *Rituals* (1998), for example, embodies alchemical and/or hermetic designs that are used as a way of organizing and presenting musical as well as extramusical ideas.[2] However, 2002 can be considered the beginning of Zorn's intense interest in "mystical composition." During this year, Zorn published or released a number of compositions and recording projects that are, in some manner and to varying degrees, dependent on aspects of occult philosophy (*IAO*, *Goetia*, and *Sortilège* all appeared in 2002). This trend has continued with the publication of *Necronomicon* and *Hermeticum Sacrum* in 2003 and *Walpurgisnacht* in 2004. At present, it is not known how many other works were also composed during this time (or are currently being written) that are also based on, or inspired by, the occult.

In these and many other works, number symbolisms associated with occult beliefs and practices function as unifying elements and are used to organize many aspects of Zorn's compositional designs, ranging from the form and pacing of a work to specific pitch, rhythmic, and metric choices. At the same time, complex number symbolisms and their fluid meanings create an occult tone to his compositions. Given the aggressive, dark, and provocative images associated with Zorn's earlier musical practices, a continued interest in matters typically described as "evil" or "dangerous" might characterize our immediate reaction to his recent occult-inspired compositions. As I will show, however, the variable and oftentimes contradictory meanings of the number symbolisms Zorn typically employs in these works extend many of the themes developed in the previous chapter, specifically principles associated with Bataillean notions of transgression and the permeability of boundaries. Zorn's occult-inspired compositions, I will argue, operate within the precarious yet necessary balance of conceptual oppositions derived from and associated with a variety of occult traditions.

Before examining the mystical and magical designs of some of Zorn's compositions, a few words on how these more recent interests intersect and develop aspects of Zorn's poetics are in order. In the next section, I will describe how matters relating to various occult traditions can also be understood as being derived from a Bataillean mode of thought, especially Bataille's notion of "base materialism" and its roots in pre-Christian Gnostic beliefs and practices.

Bataille, "Base Materialism," and Gnosticism

For Bataille, we recall, "luxury, mourning, war, cults, the construction of sumptuary monuments, games, spectacles, arts, perverse sexual activity (i.e., deflected from genital finality)" are all activities that "have no end beyond themselves" and are therefore understood as transgressive.[3] These and other forms of active, transgressive phenomena or behaviors correspond to an attitude described by Bataille as "base materialism." For Bataille, base matter "is external and foreign to ideal human aspirations, and it refuses to allow itself to be reduced to the great ontological machines resulting from these aspirations."[4]

Bataille formulates base matter as a foundation for a form of materialism that differs in significant ways from a more traditional understanding of the concept. In his essay "Materialism," Bataille points out that "most materialists, even though they may have wanted to do away with all spiritual entities, ended up positing an order of things whose hierarchical relations mark it as specifically idealist." As a result, Bataille believes, the concept of materialism seems to resemble "a senile idealism to the extent that it is not immediately based on psychological or social facts, instead of on artificially isolated phenomena." In other words, proponents of materialism, opposing any form of materialism *qua* idealism that diminishes the importance and impact of "real-world" phenomena in favor of "ideas," "essences," or "appearances," have argued that "matter matters." These anti-idealist materialists would argue that a more useful way to conceptualize and make sense of existence, the world, etc., must begin with a serious consideration of the function of matter. Bataille, however, believes that these materialists have been more interested in examining "dead matter" and that, as a result, "they have situated dead matter at the summit of a conventional hierarchy of diverse facts." In Bataille's view, what emerges is a form of materialism that differs very little from the idealism it presumably opposes: "Dead matter, the pure idea, and God in fact answer a question in the same way . . . a question that can only be posed by philosophers, the question of the essence of things, precisely the *idea* by which things become intelligible."[5]

Bataille suggests that attention to *active* matter and the ways that matter disrupt or destabilize idealized norms should form the basis of materialism. "When the word *materialism* is used," Bataille writes, "it is time to designate the direct interpretation, *excluding all idealism*, of raw phenomena, and not a system founded on the fragmentary elements of an ideological analysis, elaborated under the sign of religious relations."[6] Bataille's materialist attitude is not one of elevation, enlightenment, or the clarification of ideas through rational thought processes but is instead a position that recognizes the latent instabilities and/or contradictions that emerge when active—and especially base—matter is read against or within attitudes that stress the elevated or the idealized.

As an example, Bataille considers the big toe in an essay of the same name. He points out that it is the big toe that allows humans to separate themselves from animals. By standing up, we distinguish ourselves from primates and proudly announce our "erect" and lofty stature. However, the key to this enlightened, searching, and ideal state is the big toe—still firmly planted in the mud. Bataille describes how "with their feet in mud but their heads more or less in light, men obstinately imagine a tide that will permanently elevate them, never to return, into pure space. Human life entails, in fact, the rage of seeing oneself as a back and forth movement from refuse to the ideal, and from the ideal to refuse—a rage that is easily directed against an organ as *base* as the foot."[7] It is this "back and forth," this wavering, which characterizes the base materialist attitude. It is not simply an overturning of one value system for the other, where the "low" becomes the "high" or the "high" becomes the "low."[8] Instead, base materialism considers the "low" (the base) *within* the "high" and the *interdependency* of the two; base matter, therefore, flattens out oppositions and hierarchies.[9] It *reminds* us, literally, of our "roots" as irrational creatures. At the same time, base matter is typically considered—when it is considered at all—as *remainder:* material that is *left over* and that has consciously or unconsciously been *left out* of the structural and rational organization of homogeneous society.

Bataille's belief that a base materialist attitude can flatten oppositions and dismantle hierarchies leads him to make a connection to beliefs typically described as "Gnostic":

> Base matter is external and foreign to ideal human aspirations, and it refuses to allow itself to be reduced to the great ontological machines resulting from these aspirations. But the psychological process brought to light by Gnosticism had the same impact: it was a question of disconcerting the human spirit and idealism before something base, to the extent that one recognized the helplessness of superior principles.[10]

The objection might be raised that by relating base materialism as an attitude to a set of beliefs that might loosely be described as "religious," Bataille has undermined the transgressive force of base matter; that is, the phenomena of base matter have been elevated and the attitude has been raised to the level of religious idealism. For Bataille, however, Gnostic thought does not represent a religion so much as a position: a position of otherness or difference against Christianity and "Greco-Roman ideology."

> Gnosticism, in fact, before and after the preachings of Christianity, and in an almost bestial way, no matter what were its metaphysical developments, introduced a most impure fermentation into Greco-Roman ideology, borrowed from everywhere, from the Egyptian tradition, from Persian dualism, from Eastern Jewish heterodoxy, elements that conformed the least to the established intellectual order; it added its own dreams, heedlessly expressing a few monstrous obsessions; it was not revolted, in its religious practices, by the basest (and thus most upsetting) forms of Greek or Chaldeo-Assyrian magic and astrology; and at the same time it utilized, but perhaps more exactly it compromised, newborn Christian theology and Hellenistic metaphysics.[11]

For Bataille, then, the similarities between base materialism and Gnosticism are obvious: both have been consciously consigned to the category of "different," or "other," by "rational" homogeneous structures. At the same time, however, the universalizing powers that have sought to suppress such differences are prone to intrusions by the transgressive and active forces upon which they are dependent.

> In practice, it is possible to see as a leitmotiv of Gnosticism the conception of matter as an active principle having its own eternal autonomous existence as darkness (which would not be simply the absence of light, but the monstrous archontes revealed by this absence), and as evil (which would not be the absence of good, but a creative action). This conception was perfectly incompatible with the very principle of the profoundly monistic Hellenistic spirit, whose dominant tendency saw matter and evil as degradations of superior principles.[12]

Finally, Bataille considers the dualist tendencies of traditional Gnostic beliefs, tendencies that recognize the active force of base matter that can still be perceived in contemporary occult practices:

> It is difficult to believe that on the whole Gnosticism does not manifest above all a sinister love of darkness, a monstrous taste for obscene and lawless archontes. . . . The existence of a sect of licentious Gnostics and of certain sexual rites fulfills this obscure demand for a baseness that would not be reducible, which would be owed the most decent respect: black magic has continued this tradition to the present day.[13]

With this last association, we can trace the continued influence of Bataille's thought to Zorn's more recent "mystical" or "magickal" compositions. The concepts and phenomena describable as base matter actively intrude on and disrupt our notions of "right" and "wrong," acceptable and deviant, useful and useless. As *reminder* and *remainder,* certain phenomena and activities considered transgressive reveal the necessity and interdependence of societal, cultural, ethical, and religious limits or boundaries and the activities that lie on either side of these boundaries. Just as there can be no transgression without a limit or a limit without the possibility of transgression, there can be no darkness without light or light apart from darkness. Contemporary occult and mystical practices extend and develop the religio-epistemological traditions of Gnosticism with its emphasis on the necessity of dualist structures. This dualism—evil contained in good, light comprehensible only in relation to darkness—serves to dismantle certain binary oppositions that characterize many of our contemporary discursive structures by revealing latent interdependencies and inherent tensions.[14]

Zorn's recent compositions and their reliance on occult forms of thought and practice emphasize the "stuff" of music: notes, rhythms, dynamics, timbres, etc. Conceived in this manner, music—as "material" capable of conceptual provocation, physical shock, and intellectual confusion—is strikingly similar to Artaud's vision of speech in his "Theater of Cruelty" where "the role of speech in theater is to make use of it in a concrete and spatial sense . . . [and] to manipulate it like a solid object, one which overturns and disrupts things, in the air first of all, then in an infinitely more mysterious and secret domain."[15] For Zorn, like Artaud, this infinitely mysterious domain is one of magick and mystery, a domain beyond the rational and logical structures of everyday (homogeneous) existence. Magick, then, is both the aim and the backdrop. As an aim, Zorn's recent music seeks to open up and explode the spaces where magickal and mystical thought resides. As a backdrop, the specific myths and practices of magick must be employed and utilized so as to attain the desired aim. For Zorn, this means a reliance on certain traditions associated with Kabbalah and the thought of Aleister Crowley.

The rest of this chapter will be devoted to analyses of selected passages and entire movements from two works: *Necronomicon* for string quartet and *IAO: Music in Sacred Light.* In these analyses, I will describe the specific magickal or mystical influences/writings/films/traditions that inform each work. At the same time, I will also show how Zorn incorporated certain organizational or interpretive procedures associated with various strains of mysticism and used them as ways to structure his musical material, specifically the role(s) and meaning(s) associated with various occult number symbolisms. Due to the length and complexity of *Necronomicon,* the analytical points relating to this work are of a more descriptive nature and where I consider aspects of the work's overall formal design as well as significant formal features of the last movement, "Asmodeus." The variable and complex meaning(s) of many of the magickal/mystical symbolisms expressed in *Necronomicon* will then be developed in my analysis of a single movement from Zorn's *IAO*, "Sacred Rites of the Left Hand Path."

Necronomicon

Zorn's *Necronomicon* for string quartet (2003) takes its name from the evil (yet entirely fictional) book created by H. P. Lovecraft, one of the most prolific writers of science fiction and horror in twentieth-century American literature.[16] Lovecraft incorporated the Necronomicon into a number of his short stories and novellas, beginning with "The Hound" in 1923 and continuing with *The Case of Charles Dexter Ward* (1927), "The Dunwich Horror" (1928), "At the Mountains of Madness" (1931), and many others. Lovecraft's book developed over the course of its fictional existence, beginning life as a vaguely ancient, mystical text (in "The Hound"), becoming a book closely resembling a Medieval/Renaissance grimoire (as it appears in *The Case of Charles Dexter Ward*), and, finally, a book about an ancient alien race that had inhabited the Earth at one time ("At the Mountains of Madness"). Lovecraft's desire to provide some sort of coherence to his thoughts while, at the same time, attempting to create an aura of "authenticity" to the book led him to write a "History of the *Necronomicon*" in 1927.[17]

Zorn's *Necronomicon* attempts to evoke the dark aura surrounding Lovecraft's fictitious tome. To this end, a handful of recurring numbers are used to structure and organize various aspects of the work. More specifically, the numbers 13, 666, and 15 (along, presumably, with others) can be found throughout the score and are used because of their symbolic meanings within certain occult traditions. It should be pointed out, however, that Zorn does not appear to be interested in forging any sort of "authentic" relationship with Lovecraft as none of these numbers—to my knowledge—play a significant role in any of Lovecraft's writings devoted to the Necronomicon. Instead, Zorn appears to be transplanting certain occult number symbolisms from other traditions, most notably Kabbalah and the thought of Aleister Crowley, traditions examined in more detail in the section on Zorn's *IAO*.

Zorn has alluded to the "formal beauty" of *Necronomicon*'s five movements: I. Conjurations, II. The Magus, III. Thought Forms, IV. Incunabula, and V. Asmodeus.[18] For Zorn, much of the work's perceived "formal beauty" derives from the use of recycled or reworked musical material both in and between movements. Table 2.1 details many of the most significant intra- and intermovement musical relationships that appear in his work, relationships that include material as small as specific chords or as large as entire blocks or phrases of musical material. For example, the viola and cello chords heard in measure 84 of movement I reappear in a slightly modified form in measure 26 of movement V (example

Table 2.1. Intra- and intermovement relations in *Necronomicon*

Movement	Intramovement relations	Intermovement relations
I. Conjurations	m. 1 (1st violin); mm. 71 and 73 (1st violin)	m. 1 (1st violin); mvt. V, m. 25 (1st violin) (in retrograde)
	mm. 1–4 (all parts, cont. 16th-note passagework); mm. 71–74	mm. 11–12 (1st violin) mvt V, m. 13 (1st violin)
	m. 1 (viola and cello chords); m. 84 (viola and cello chords)	m. 38 (1st violin); mvt. V, m. 66 (2d violin)
	m. 19 (2d violin); m. 84 (2d violin)	mm. 62–63 (all parts); mvt. V, mm. 58–60 (all parts)
	m. 58 (violins); m. 68 (violins)	m. 68 (2d violin); mvt. V, m. 63 (2d violin)
	m. 69 (1st violin); m. 84 (1st violin)	mm. 68–69 (1st violin); mvt. V, mm. 64–66 (first violin)
		m. 84 (viola and cello chords); mvt. V, m. 26 (viola and cello) (see ex. 2.1a)
II. The Magus	m. 54–55 (violins); mm. 68–69 (violins)	m. 25 (all parts); mvt. IV, mm. 54–55 (all parts); m. 54 retrogrades all pitches and rhythms (see ex. 2.1b)
		mm. 54–55 (68–69) (violins); mvt. IV, mm. 72–73 (violins)
III. Thought Forms	mm. 1–43 (all parts, cont. 16th-note passagework); mm. 67–71 (see exs. 2.2a and 2.2b)	m. 61 (2d violin); mvt. V, mm. 64–65 (2d violin) (see ex. 2.3)
	mm. 44–45 (1st violin, viola, cello); mm. 57–64	
IV. Incunabula	m. 28 (2d violin, viola, cello); m. 76 (2d violin, viola, cello) pitches/rhythms retrograded	See mvt. II above
V. Asmodeus	m. 1 (all parts); mm. 12 and 53 (all parts)—m. 12 pizz., m. 53 pitches/rhythms retrograded (see ex. 2.6)	See mvt. I above
	m. 5 (all parts); mm. 19–20 (all parts)	mm. 64–65 (2d violin); mvt. III, m. 61 (2d violin)

Movement I, m. 84 (viola and cello)

Movement V, m. 26

Example 2.1a. Viola and cello chords in movement I, m. 84 (2:36) and their reappearance in movement V, m. 26 (0:58) (*Necronomicon*).

2.1a). Example 2.1b is an example of a block of recycled material as measure 25 of movement II reappears (where the pitches and rhythms retrograded) in measure 54 of movement IV.

Considering the intermovement relationships shown in table 2.1, a symmetrical formal design of the work as a whole emerges as represented by figure 2.1. According to this formal plan, intermovement relations exist between move-

Movement II, m. 25

Movement IV, m. 54

Example 2.1b. All parts of movement II, m. 25 (2:07–2:14) reappear (with the pitches and rhythms retrograded) in movement IV, m. 54 (4:29–4:34) (*Necronomicon*).

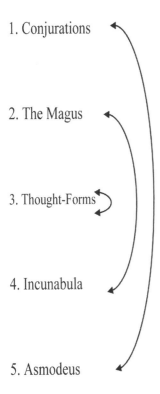

1. Conjurations

2. The Magus

3. Thought-Forms

4. Incunabula

5. Asmodeus

Figure 2.1. Possible formal design based on movement pairs (*Necronomicon*).

ment pairs I/V and II/IV, while movement III—the one movement that exhibits the most pervasive use of intramovement relations—forms the centerpiece of the overall design. Much of the musical material employed in "Thought Forms" is derived from the nearly continuous use of two streams of musical ideas: the interlocking streams of sixteenth-note and triplet gestures passed back and forth among the players as seen in example 2.2a, the opening 10 measures of "Thought Forms." In measures 67 through 71, Zorn condenses and reconfigures a number of ordered (as well as instrumentally and registrally fixed) pitch segments associated with the sixteenth-note stream heard at the opening of the movement. Example 2.2b identifies the sources of these pitch segments in measures 67–71.

The symmetrical formal design represented in figure 2.1 is skewed slightly by the appearance in movement III of a single block of music, an intermovement reference that reappears during the chaotic and frantic close of movement V. The passage in question appears in the second violin in measures 64–65, music first encountered at measure 61 of movement III. (See the solid box connected by an arrow in example 2.3. Other intermovement relations are indicated by

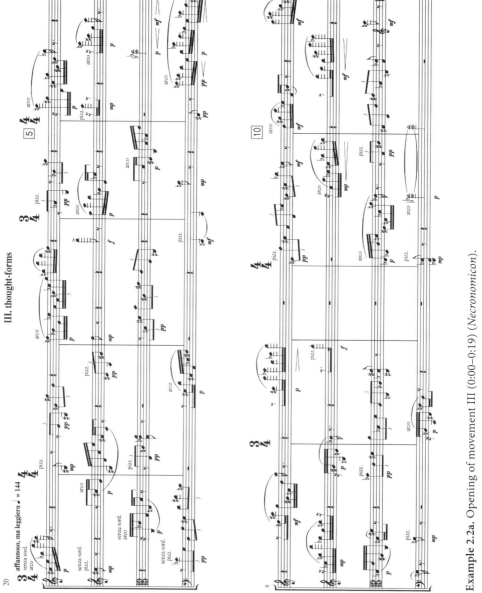

Example 2.2a. Opening of movement III (0:00–0:19) (*Necronomicon*).

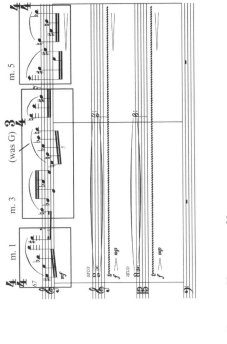

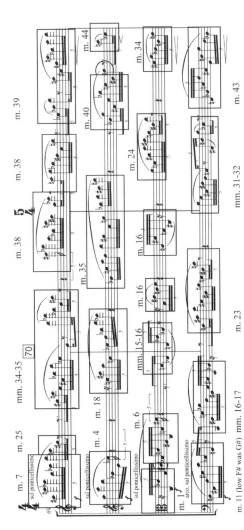

Example 2.2b. Sources of melodic gestures in movement III, mm. 67–71 (2:15–2:25) (*Necronomicon*).

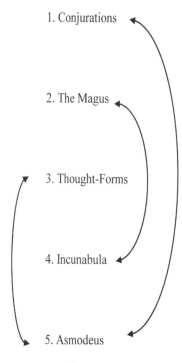

1. Conjurations

2. The Magus

3. Thought-Forms

4. Incunabula

5. Asmodeus

Figure 2.2. Revised formal plan given intermovement relations present in movements III and V (*Necronomicon*).

dashed boxes.) Because of this particular intermovement relation, the "true" formal design of *Necronomicon* is better understood according to the plan shown in figure 2.2. While the movement pairs I/V and II/IV remain intact, V is now also grouped with movement III.

Although we give up the elegant symmetrical design of figure 2.1, another intermovement connection is created through this relation between movements III and V. As described above, two musical streams are present through most of movement III, a sixteenth-note stream and a triplet stream. Both of these streams are rudely interrupted in measures 53–55 by a dense, fortissimo chord repeated fifteen times in the violins and viola (see example 2.4). The number fifteen is significant in Kabbalistic thought where it is sometimes used to signify the "mystic number" of the fifth *sefirah* located on the Tree of Life, *Gevurah* or *Geburah* (see ahead to figure 2.9).[19] This magic number (formed by adding the numbers of the first through fifth *sefirah*) is often associated with the high demon of Kabbalistic demonology, Asmodeus.[20] We can now understood why Zorn inserted the short passage from movement III at the end of movement V (entitled "Asmodeus") once we recognize that movement V is already anticipated in movement III by measures 53–55.[21]

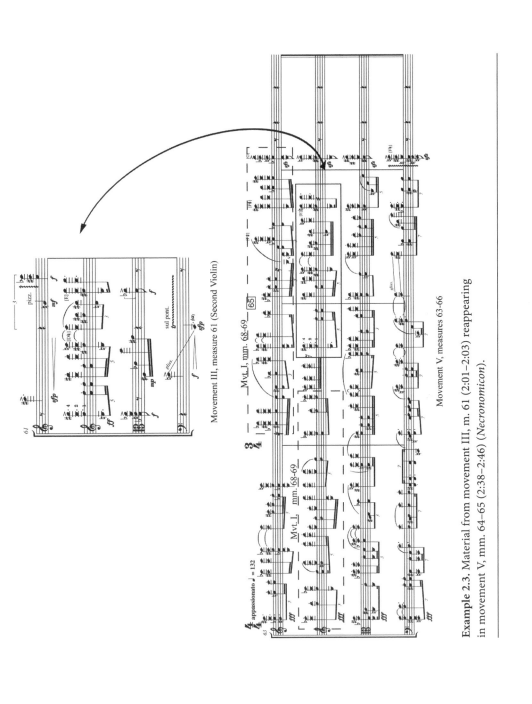

Movement III, measure 61 (Second Violin)

Movement V, measures 63-66

Example 2.3. Material from movement III, m. 61 (2:01–2:03) reappearing in movement V, mm. 64–65 (2:38–2:46) (*Necronomicon*).

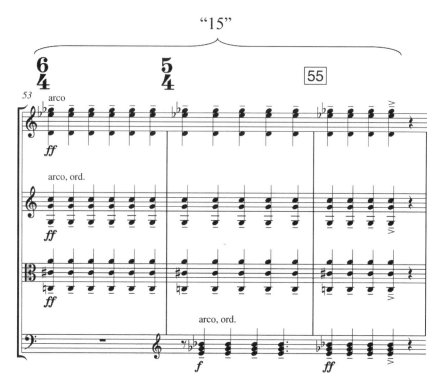

Example 2.4. Chordal passage projecting "15" (signifying "Asmodeus") in movement III, mm. 53–55 (1:35–1:44) (*Necronomicon*).

In movement III, the number 15 and its specific occult reference prepare us for the appearance of "Asmodeus" in the last movement. In addition to the number 15, "Asmodeus" utilizes a number of other numerical symbols and/or references, most notably the numbers 13 (and the dual associations of this number as both "unlucky" and, in Kabbalistic thought, symbolizing "Unity" or "Love") and 666 (the number of the beast in Revelation 13:18 and Aleister Crowley's chosen number). The most obvious structural and formal use of numbers—at least for someone who has the score—is the method by which Zorn groups measures in "Asmodeus." As shown in figure 2.3, the number of beats indicated by each time signature group together into larger blocks equaling 13 (shown by the braces below the signatures) and groups equaling 15 (shown by the braces above). Some measure groupings that add to 13 are easily recognizable, such as measures 2 through 5 (3+5+3+2). Others groupings, however, are not as clear. A group of measures adding to 13 is embedded within measures 1–4 as the ⅜ and ⅝ time signatures of measures 2 and 3, when collapsed into a single measure of ⁴⁄₄, also form 13 (6+4+3). A few overlaps of 13 groupings can be seen at measures 38 and

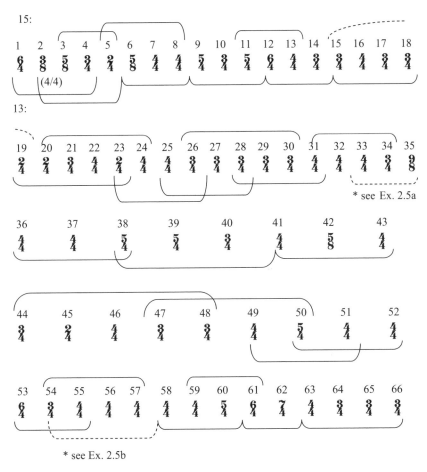

Figure 2.3. Symbolic metric groupings in movement V (*Necronomicon*): braces above=15; braces below=13.

49–51. When measure groupings do not sum to 13, the number is often audible on the musical surface. In measures 33–35 and measures 54–57, for example, the musical surface clearly projects another layer of 13 and the string of attacks played by the entire ensemble (except for the glissando in the cello in measures 34–35) (see examples 2.5a and 2.5b).

Six also plays a prominent role in this movement, especially as it relates to 666. Referring back to figure 2.3, we see that this final movement contains only four measures of 6: measures 1, 12, 53, and 61. Three of these measures—measures 1, 12, and 53—reuse and recycle the same musical material (shown in example 2.6). Measure 12 texturally modifies measure 1 with the pizzicato performance indications while measure 53 transposes the pitch material up an

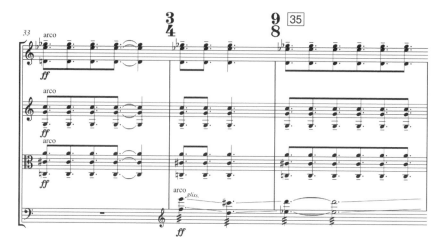

Example 2.5a. Thirteen attack points, movement V, mm. 33–35 (1:13–1:20) (*Necronomicon*).

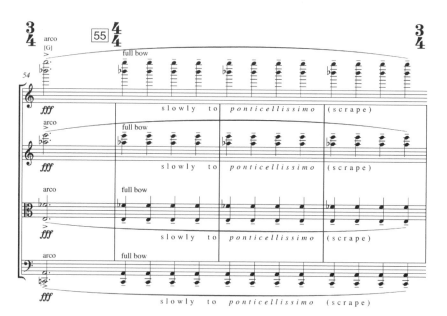

Example 2.5b. Thirteen attack points, movement V, mm. 54–57 (2:10–2:18) (*Necronomicon*).

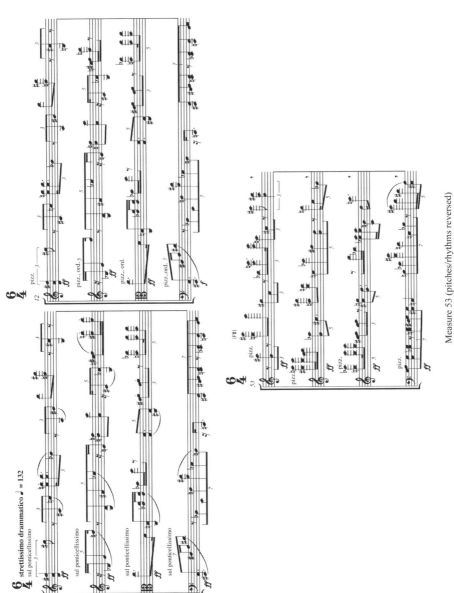

Example 2.6. Prevalence of "6," movement V, mm. 1 (0:00–0:04), 12 (0:26–0:29), and 53 (2:03–2:09) (*Necronomicon*).

octave and retrogrades the pitches and rhythms heard in measures 1 and 12. Taken together, of course, the relations between these measures form a sporadic 6-6-6 grouping that unfolds over the course of the movement. At another level, these measures of 6 occur at measures 1, 12, and 53: 1 and 12 add up to 13 while 1+12+53 equal 66, the total number of measures in "Asmodeus." The final measure of 6 (measure 61)—while it does not group together with the earlier measures—provides the final 6 necessary to complete another 6-6-6 group: measure 61 (in 6) combined with the total number of measures (66).[22]

This brief discussion of *Necronomicon* has focused on how specific occult number symbolisms are employed in this work, especially in regard to the overall form. Specific musical features appearing on the musical surface—chords repeated 13 or 15 times, for example—hint at some of the symbolic meanings associated with these numbers. Without any sort of context for these numbers, however, it is easy to think that Zorn is simply playing on the "evil" associations of specific numbers common in popular thought and belief: 13 as "unlucky" (ask any of the victims in the many *Friday the 13th* movies) or "666" as being the Devil's number (as seen in *The Omen*). While this might be true, I would suggest that the meaning(s) of these and other numerical associations are more complex. In the next section, therefore, I develop these symbolic meanings by discussing the movement "Sacred Rites of the Left Hand Path" from Zorn's *IAO: Music in Sacred Light*. A better understanding of these (and other) number correspondences and their relations to Crowleyian and Kabbalistic mysticism is possible by considering this individual movement and by situating the work in relation to Zorn's dedicatee, the mystical/magickal underground filmmaker Kenneth Anger.

IAO, Kenneth Anger, and Aleister Crowley

Released in May 2002, *IAO* (pronounced *Ee-AH-Oh*) is Zorn's first large-scale project that unequivocally reflects his interest in the occult, esoteric knowledge, and mystical philosophy. According to the description of the record provided on the Tzadik website, *IAO* is a "hypnotic seven-movement suite of Alchemy, Mysticism, Metaphysics, and Magic both black and white" and is inspired, in part, by the writings and thought of Aleister Crowley and "his Magickal disciple, filmmaker Kenneth Anger."[23] The seven tracks that form *IAO* are "Invocation," "Sex Magick," "Sacred Rites of the Left Hand Path," "The Clavicle of Solomon," "Lucifer Rising," "Leviathan," and "Mysteries." According to the notes, the title itself is "Kabbalistically identical to the Beast [Aleister Crowley] and his number 666." While this last point is highly complex, the formula of IAO was, for Crowley, an extremely important concept, in both theory and practice.[24] As a theoretical concept or formula, IAO represents the transformation into a new aeon, that of Horus, whereby "*I* is Isis, Nature, ruined by *A,* Apophis the destroyer, and restored to life by the Redeemer Osiris." In practice, Crowley writes, "the Magician who employs [the ritual of IAO] . . . is conscious of himself as a man liable to suffering, and anxious to transcend that state by becoming one with God."[25]

In addition to the thought of Crowley, Zorn's *IAO* is also inspired by (and dedicated to) Anger. Bringing all of these influences and dedications together, many of Anger's films—films such as *Inauguration of the Pleasure Dome, Lucifer Rising,* and *Invocation of My Demon Brother*—all utilize complex color correlations, symbolisms, and imagery drawn from Crowley's teachings and writings. Often these images, symbols, and references are overlaid with one another creating a type of visual depth that is perfectly suited to Anger's chosen artistic medium. Through editing and other postproduction techniques, Anger overlays individual images and their associated meanings to create an emergent, higher-level semantic resonance where the images and meanings of one layer are transformed by their proximity and location to images at another level. Interpreting Anger's films, therefore, requires an understanding of not only the meanings of individual layers but also how these meanings are transformed when placed onto one another. This technique is best understood not as collage where individual signs or images are placed next to one another and where temporality and spatial relations are discrete and separate but as montage, the technique of superimposition Anger learned from the writings and films of Sergei Eisenstein.[26] Given Anger's interests in the Crowleyian tradition of occult philosophy, where meanings are hidden, complex, and interrelated, the technique of montage is an ideal method of presentation in his films.

The full title of Zorn's work is *IAO: Music in Sacred Light.* The subtitle is a clear reference to Anger's understanding of the role of light in his films. Anger has described how he is "an artist working in Light, and that's my whole interest, really." Anger relates the concept of light to occult beliefs, and his films emphasize the connection between light and Lucifer, where Lucifer's name is understood as being etymologically derived from *lux.* For Anger, "Lucifer is the Light God, and not the devil," a representation he describes as "Christian slander." Lucifer—as the Light God or Venus, the morning star—is Anger's "Holy Guardian Angel" with whom he wishes to communicate through his films. Conceived as rituals or ceremonies, Anger's films function as invocations or sacrificial offerings to Lucifer. On the one hand, the transgressive role played by Lucifer in Anger's films portrays Lucifer as a "Rebel Angel" whose "message is that the Key of Joy is Disobedience." On the other hand, Anger's view of Lucifer carries with it certain redemptive connotations. His biblical character of Lucifer is understood as the Fallen Angel who seeks reunification with the Divine Realm, thereby reinstating the original dualist nature of spiritual existence. Anger's film *Lucifer Rising,* then, is about the "Fallen Angel, the fall from grace, and the hope of redemption, of climbing back up the ladder. It's almost the story in a parable form of the Prodigal Son who goes away and falls from grace and then is accepted in the family again."[27] A few brief examples from Anger's film *Inauguration of the Pleasure Dome* will illustrate the importance of montage and the symbolic meaning of light within Anger's Crowleyian inspired poetics.

According to Anger, *Inauguration of the Pleasure Dome* is based on "Crowley's dramatic rituals where people in the cult assume the identity of a god or goddess."[28] The centerpiece of the film is the consumption of a magickal elixir, a form of occult Eucharist. In his own notes to the film, Anger quotes a passage from Crowley describing the importance of this act:

> A Eucharist of some sort should most assuredly be consumed daily by every magician, and he should regard it as the main sustenance of his magical life. . . . [In this act] The magician becomes filled with God, fed upon God, intoxicated with God. Little by little his body will become purified by the internal lustration of God. Day by day his mortal frame, shedding its earthly elements, will become the very truth of the Temple of the Holy Ghost. Day by day matter is replaced by Spirit, the human by the divine; ultimately the change will be complete; God manifest in the flesh will be his name.[29]

In what P. Adams Sitney calls the most "impressive scene in the film," the character of Cesare—the somnambulist from *The Cabinet of Dr. Caligari*—fetches the magickal elixir that is to be consumed.[30] Sleepwalking through the dark backdrop that has dominated much of the film, Cesare approaches a wall where a hidden door slowly opens, letting out a flood of bright light. As the door opens and the light begins to fill the room, a drawing of Crowley with an inverted pentagram (a five-pointed star) on his forehead is superimposed directly above the doorway (see figure 2.4). The superimposition of these images symbolizes a number of key features of Anger's poetics of film including, obviously, the ever-present figure of Crowley. At the same time, Anger connects Crowley—the Great Beast—with Lucifer, first with the pentagram (a symbol typically associated with Lucifer) and, more specifically, the image of Lucifer as the Light God. Furthermore, Anger connects the image of light with "knowledge" by strategically placing the top of the door with the lower portion of the pentagram between Crowley's eyes, an oblique reference to the location of the pineal eye, or the "third eye" that allows for the communication of esoteric knowledge.

Shortly after this shot in Anger's film, more superimposed images appear as Cesare enters the lit room. First, the so-called Sigil of Baphomet appears, reinforcing the meanings and associations of the inverted pentagram from before.[31] This image, too, begins to dissolve away just as another image begins to dissolve up (figure 2.5). This last image, from S. Michelspacher's *Cabala* (published in 1616), depicts a variety of symbols associated with alchemy and Satan (figure 2.6). In this image, Satan is represented as a fire-breathing beast residing in Chaos. Chaos, according to traditional alchemical and Gnostic beliefs, was the result

Figure 2.4. Superimposition of images in Kenneth Anger, *Inauguration of the Pleasure Dome.* Copyright Kenneth Anger.

of the Fall of Satan, which was causally linked to the Fall of Adam. The Fall, or the lower state of Chaos, is represented by the inverted triangle at the center of the image. Within this triangle is a crucible, the fundamental laboratory instrument for all alchemists. In the corners of the triangle are the symbols for the three basic elements of alchemy (clockwise beginning with the upper left-hand corner): Sulphur ("the expansive force of the universe"), Mercury ("the contractive force in Nature"), and Salt ("the connective or binding force in Nature"). Developing Aristotle's description of the four elements of the material world and their derivation from an original "prime" matter, alchemists attempted to reunite these elements in the hopes of discovering the "primal matter" that would restore existence to its original state, the state of perfection prior to the Fall. The alchemist's work is represented by the crucible and the operations that take place inside of it. The ascending bird flying up the tube of the crucible represents the re-formation of the primal matter, ascending back to M (Mercury, "which is both beginning and end").[32]

Returning to the function of this image within *Inauguration of the Pleasure Dome,* Anger, with this sequence of briefly superimposed images, is referencing "Of the Eucharist; and the Art of Alchemy," a chapter from Crowley's *Magick.*

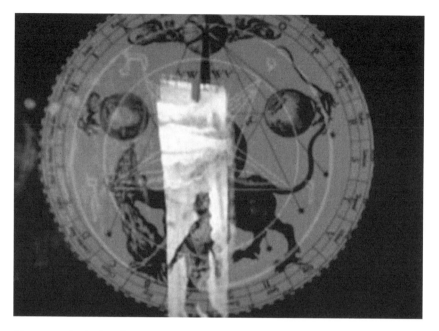

Figure 2.5. Sigil of Baphomet dissolves into alchemical image (Anger, *Inauguration of the Pleasure Dome*). Copyright Kenneth Anger.

Crowley connects the magician's Eucharist—its symbolic meaning, material structure, and the meaning and importance of its consumption—with what he considers to be the primary aim of alchemy:

> the Alchemist is to take a dead thing, impure, valueless, and powerless, and transform it into a live thing, active, invaluable, and thaumaturgic.
>
> The reader of this book will surely find in this a most striking analogy with what we have already said of the processes of Magick. . . . The First Matter is a man, that is to say, a perishable parasite, bred of the Earth's crust, crawling irritably upon it for a span, and at last returning to the dirt whence he sprang. The process of initiation consists in removing his impurities, and finding in his true self an immortal intelligence to whom matter is no more than the means of manifestation. . . . The Magician takes an idea, purifies it, intensifies it by invoking into it the inspiration of his soul. It is no longer a scrawl scratched on a sheep-skin, but a word of Truth, imperishable, mighty to prevail throughout the sphere of its purport. The evocation of a spirit is precisely similar in essence.[33]

In these few frames of film, Anger is able to synthesize an enormous range of meanings and symbols pertaining to Lucifer and light, the transformation of base materials into spiritual food, and the processes and techniques necessary

Figure 2.6. Plate from S. Michelspacher's *Cabala* (1616); source of alchemical image in Anger's *Inauguration of the Pleasure Dome.*

for the practicing magician to attain an enlightened state (a state different from the "sleepwalking" condition of everyday consciousness).

Like Anger, Zorn considers many of his recent works as rituals or ceremonies. Indeed, *IAO*'s opening—"Invocation"—makes no attempt to disguise this fact as we hear chains rattling, knives being sharpened, and water (or oil) being swirled in a cup. All of these sounds and associations are clearly related to the "magical instruments" required by a magician when performing rituals as described by Crowley.[34] Furthermore, in the liner notes to *IAO*, Zorn describes the functional importance of the composer, the musicians, the producers, etc., in realizing this musico-magickal ritual:

> I take "magical weapons" (pen, ink and paper), I write "incantations" (compositions) in the "magical language" (music) . . . I initiate "rituals" (recordings, performances . . . I call forth "spirits" (musicians, engineers, printers, CD sellers and so forth . . .)[.] The composition and distribution of this CD is thus an act of Magick.[35]

In realizing this ritual, Zorn employs montage techniques in both the artwork as well as the music itself. In both of these areas, montage is employed to evoke and symbolize occult ideas or relations pertaining to spirits or demons, Lucifer, and Light.

The liner notes included with *IAO* are written on four separate sheets resembling playing cards or perhaps tarot cards. One side of each card contains information relating to the recording (personnel, track listings, production credits, and explanatory notes) while the other side presents mysterious symbols (in black) superimposed against four circles (in white) against a gold background. Each of the black symbols is a sigil identifying a specific demon or devil as described in the *Grimoirium Verum* (subtitled "The True Grimoire, or The Most Approved Keys of Solomon the Hebrew Rabbi Wherein the Most Hidden Secrets Both Natural or Supernatural Are Immediately Exhibited").[36] Dating from 1517, the *Grimoirium Verum* is composed of three parts: the first part identifies by name and by symbol a variety of demons and the manner(s) by which each demon is invoked. The second part describes the individual powers of each demon (their "natural and supernatural secrets") while the third part ("The Key to the Work") includes specific conjurations, invocations, and methods for dismissing demons.[37] On the cards, the disc, and the accompanying white slip-case of *IAO,* Zorn reproduces seven sigils, five of which are drawn directly from the *Grimoirium Verum.* These include the sigils of Mersilde ("who has the power to transport anyone in an instant, anywhere," on the white slipcase), Bucon (the "demon of hatred," on the reverse side of the card that includes the track listings), Segal (who "will cause all sorts of prodigies to appear," on the reverse side of the card detailing the production/engineering credits), Clistheret (who "allows you to have day or night, whichever you wish, when you desire either," on the reverse side of card listing the performers), and Sirchade ("makes you see all sorts of natural and supernatural animals," on the reverse side of the card that includes quotes from Zorn and Crowley). On the back of the CD is the sigil of Baphomet (described above) and a sigil created by Zorn's longtime designer, Heung-Heung "Chippy" Chin.

The *Grimoirium Verum* is related to another work, *The Key of Solomon (Clavicula Salomonis),* one of the most important texts of Western occult philosophy and ritual magic (and is also the title of one of the tracks on *IAO*).[38]

The Key of Solomon is a complex mixture of white and black magic designed to instruct as well as explain to students of the occult a variety of matters relating to demons or spirits (invocation rituals, demonic powers, etc., as described in Book I of the work) and ritualistic and ceremonial preparations (in Book II). Book I also includes instructions for creating the holy pentacles, seals designed to protect the magician from the particular spirit or spirits being invoked. If constructed according to the complex methods and techniques described in the text, these pentacles will strike "terror into the Spirits," forcing them to obey the wishes of the magician: "If thou invokest the Spirits by virtue of these Pentacles, they will obey thee without repugnance, and having considered them they will be struck with astonishment, and will fear them, and thou shalt see them so surprised by fear and terror, that none of them will be sufficiently bold to wish to oppose thy will."[39] The holy pentacles therefore protect the magician from the particular power(s) of the demons and therefore must be displayed during any ceremony where a spirit is conjured. A number of pentacles included in *The Key of Solomon* are reproduced on *IAO*.

In addition to the complex geometrical designs that distinguish individual pentacles, each one typically contains Hebrew letters, words, and sometimes entire phrases. Figure 2.7 reproduces the fifth pentacle of Saturn, which, according to the description in *The Key of Solomon,* "defendeth those who invoke the Spirits of Saturn during the night; and chaseth away the spirits which guard treasures." In his editorial note, MacGregor Mathers points out the appearance of the Tetragrammaton (IHVH) around the cross in the center, Eloah (ALVH) in the angles of the square, the names of the Angels of Saturn appearing on each side of the square, and—written between the two circles—a versicle from Deuteronomy 10:17: "A Great God, a Mighty, and a Terrible [God]."[40]

The fifth through eighth pentacles of Saturn appear on the personnel card of Zorn's *IAO*. Superimposed on this image is the sigil of Clistheret, who like the spirits represented on the other cards, is an inferior spirit under the rule of the demon Asmodeus (Duke Syrach). Figure 2.8 reproduces the production/recording credits card, a card where the sigil of Segal is superimposed on the third through sixth pentacles of the sun from *The Key of Solomon.* The importance of light in *IAO* is apparent by the inclusion of these particular pentacles. First, the pentacles of the sun are designed to "repress the pride and arrogance of the Solar Spirits, which are altogether proud and arrogant by their nature." Second, the Hebrew texts included on these pentacles describe the importance of light and vision on the path to understanding and Gnostic knowledge. Included with the fourth pentacle (the upper right-hand corner) is a versicle from Psalm 13:3–4: "Lighten mine eyes that I sleep not in death, lest mine enemy say, I have prevailed against him."[41]

The sixth pentacle (lower right-hand corner) contains a fragment from Psalm 69:23 ("Let their eyes be darkened that they see not, and make their loins

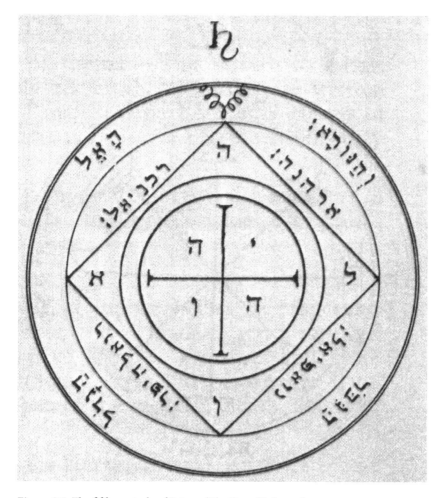

Figure 2.7. The fifth pentacle of Saturn (*The Key of Solomon*).

continually to shake") and Psalm 135:16 ("They have eyes but see not").[42] The superimposition of the demon's sigil (printed in black) against the protecting pentacle of the sun (in white) on this card is clearly Zorn's attempt to evoke the type of visual superimposition(s) present in so many of Kenneth Anger's films. At the same time, the importance of light—discernible by peeling apart the superimposed layers and recognizing the semantic resonances and/or concordances—is also a key component of Zorn's work and is also traceable to Anger's poetics of filmmaking.

Many of these same ideas relating to superimposition and light are represented in Zorn's music. The third track of *IAO*—"Sacred Rites of the Left-Hand Path"—presents these ideas in its opening minute in a complex and dense man-

Figure 2.8. Personnel card from Zorn's *IAO* (the sigil of Segal superimposed over the third through sixth pentacles of the sun from *The Key of Solomon*).

ner that is heavily dependent on principles associated with Kabbalah. The "Left Hand Path" refers to the practice as well as practitioners of black magic. According to Crowley, the Brothers of the Left Hand Path use "spiritual force" in achieving "material ends": "They exchange gold for dross. They sell their higher powers for gross and temporary benefit."[43] Whereas for Crowley the true goal of Magick is the attainment of spiritual enlightenment according to the true or Divine will, followers of the Left Hand Path use Magick for personal use, for material gain, or to change the course of events so as to realize their own desires or wishes.

The association between black magic and the Left Hand Path has a much more complex history, a history that is assumed in Crowley's thought and writings. The notion of the Left Hand Path is traceable to pre-Zoharic Kabbalistic writings where it is offered as an explanation accounting for the presence of evil in the material world. Reflecting the influence of certain Gnostic traditions that consider evil to be intimately connected to both existence and God, many early Kabbalists viewed evil in relation to the Ten Holy Emanations (*Sefirot*) traditionally arranged according to the configuration known as the Tree of Life (see figure 2.9). The *Sefirot* can be understood as the active powers that emanate from the Divine (*Ein-sof,* or *Ain Soph*) that are operative in the material world. Although many different interpretations have been put forward regarding the relations between the Divine and the infinite realm as well as the *Sefirot* and the created world, Gershom Scholem's description suits our present purpose:

> Generally speaking, stress is laid on the fact that the God who expresses Himself in the emanation of the Sefirot is greater than the totality of the Sefirot through which He works and by means of which He passes from unity to plurality. The personality of God finds expression precisely through His manifestations of the Sefirot.[44]

How then are we to account for the presence of evil if all of the active forces of the material world are understood as emanations from the Divine, an entity who is essentially good?

Beginning around the thirteenth century, Kabbalistic texts evincing Gnostic influences began to appear that posited the presence of evil within the divine.[45] As Elliot Wolfson points out, "One of the salient features of this school [of thought] was the positing of a demonic realm morphologically paralleling the realm of the divine: as there are ten holy emanations (*sefirot*), so there are 'ten emanations of the left.'" These "left emanations" were understood as emerging from the left side of the Divine realm, emanating from either the third *sefirah* (*Binah*—"understanding") or the fifth *sefirah* (*Gevurah*—"strength"). This idea regarding the source of evil exerted a powerful influence over later Kabbalists, particularly in the *Zohar* where the left side is described as *Sitra Ahra*—the "Other Side." Subscribing to the idea that the demonic is contained within the divine, the author of the *Zohar* posits two possible explanations as to the origins of this demonic side. Wolfson identifies these two origins as corresponding to (a) the "cathartic view" where the left emanations of the demonic realm are understood as "by-product[s] of the process of the elimination of waste from Divine thought," and (b) the "emanative view" where the "demonic realm" is conceived as a "separate force [that] is viewed as a link in the continuous chain of being."[46]

In "Sacred Rites of the Left Hand Path," Zorn evokes the demonic realm and its relation to the Divine through a variety of symbolic means. The entire track is built over an ostinato (played on a Fender Rhodes) in $\frac{13}{8}$, shown in example 2.7. Immediately, the prominence of 13 as a key component of this track could be construed as an obvious reference to the demonic realm, particularly if we consider 13 as an "unlucky number." According to traditional Kabbalistic interpretations (Gematria), however, the number 13 is numerically equivalent to Love (א ה ב ה) and Unity (א ח ד).[47] Crowley notes that the number is "helpful,

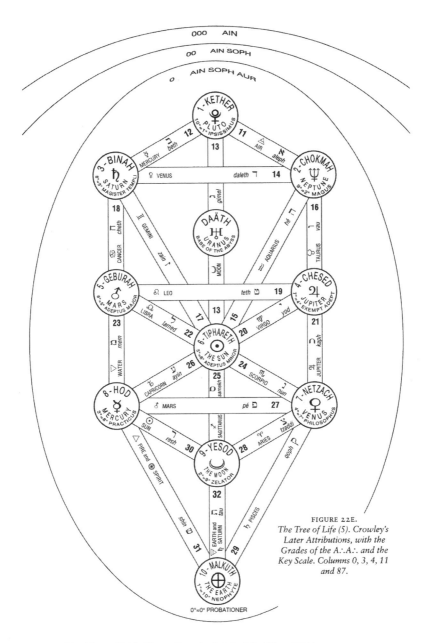

FIGURE 22E.
*The Tree of Life (5). Crowley's
Later Attributions, with the
Grades of the A∴A∴ and the
Key Scale. Columns 0, 3, 4, 11
and 87.*

Figure 2.9. The Tree of Life (from Crowley's *Magick: Liber ABA*).

Example 2.7. Organ ostinato ("Sacred Rites of the Left Hand Path").

since if we can reduce our formula to 13 it becomes 1 without further trouble." Reducing 13 to 1 symbolizes "The Unity—the Finite—the Line, derived from 0 by extension. The Divine Being."[48]

At 0:15, a second musical idea enters—an idea doubled by a piano and synthesizer—and is superimposed over the ostinato (see example 2.8). Initially, this new figure appears to maintain the eighth-note subdivision of the opening idea, but by the second repetition, the piano/synthesizer idea begins to drift away from the regularity established by the ostinato, and we are no longer able to maintain any sort of metric/rhythmic congruity. With the third repetition of the piano/synthesizer idea, the basic four-note gesture is extended as the final G♭ descends to an F♮ and once again aligns with the low F of the ostinato figure. Considering the number of attack points, we recognize that this second idea comprises 13 distinct articulations, recalling the same Kabbalistic associations described above in relation to the ostinato. At the same time, because it takes three measures of the ostinato to correspond with one presentation of the piano/synthesizer figure, a new relation emerges. Three measures of $\frac{13}{8}$ results in 39 eighth-note articulations and, as Crowley points out in *Gematria,* 39 corresponds to the numerical value of the Tetragrammaton (26) and unity (13): "Adonai is Unity" or "Adonai is One" (י ה ו ה א ה ד).[49]

Thus far, "Sacred Rites of the Left Hand Path" has been concerned with presenting numerical values that can best be described as corresponding to the Divine Realm (Jehovah, Unity, Love). Beginning at 0:45, however, the music begins to turn toward the Demonic Realm via the "Left Emanations." Here, a new layer of music is added to the overall texture with the appearance of high- and low-pitched percussion sounds, possibly castanets or sticks played against an unknown surface. In example 2.9, I have transcribed the first five seconds of this percussion layer. Like the piano/synthesizer idea beginning at 0:15, this idea disrupts the sense of meter established by the ostinato. It does this in two ways: first, it begins following the strong downbeat F of the ostinato pattern and, second, it extends beyond the downbeat of the next measure. Following the passage transcribed in example 2.9, the percussion parts oscillate back and forth (albeit irregularly) according to the two patterns shown in example 2.10. Clearly these ideas are drawn from the tail end of the music shown in example 2.9, indicated

Example 2.8. Entrance of organ/synthesizer figure ("Sacred Rites of the Left Hand Path" beginning at 0:15).

by the brace below the staff. The music in example 2.9 can be considered a self-contained idea, preceding the fragmentation and transformation of ideas that follow, shown in example 2.10.

The percussion parts in example 2.9 unfold over 15 eighth-notes, a number that is significant in relation to the "Left Side." As I briefly mentioned in my discussion of the "Asmodeus" movement from *Necronomicon,* 15 is the "mystical number" of the *sefirah Gevurah*—one of the possible sources of the Left Side Emanations within the Divine Realm. The notion of a mystical number refers to the fact that *Gevurah* is the fifth *sefirah* and contains within it all of the previous *sefirah* and their numerical equivalents: *Kether* (1) + *Chokmah* (2) + *Binah* (3) + *Gedullah* or *Hesed* (4) + *Gevurah* (5). This same number also corresponds to the number of "inferior spirits" under the rule of Asmodeus (or Duke Syrach),

Example 2.9. Percussion layer beginning at 0:45 ("Sacred Rites of the Left Hand Path").

Example 2.10. Prevalent rhythmic ideas (following example 2.9) ("Sacred Rites of the Left Hand Path").

of which five are represented on the artwork and liner notes included with *IAO* (see above).[50] As the percussion parts begin to fragment (as shown in example 2.10), notice also that the variable durations oscillate between rhythmic ideas that extend over seven eighth-notes and those that extend over eight eighth-notes (7 + 8 = 15).

Considering aspects of the music heard before the entrance of this percussion part, it is also possible to discern the "immanence" of this number and its associations with the Left Side. Following the four repetitions of the ostinato figure heard at the opening, the piano/synthesizer idea begins at 0:15. Furthermore, the entrance of the percussion idea begins at 0:45, a multiple of 15 that is analogous to the 3 × 13 symbolism of the ostinato heard against the piano/synthesizer figure ("Jehovah is Unity"). At a certain level, then, 15—and its associations with the Left Side—is present in the music that clearly symbolizes aspects of the Divine Realm; in short, the Left is contained within the Right. At the same time, while evil is contained in the good, good is also contained in evil.

Recalling the themes of light and evil described above in relation to Kenneth Anger, it is interesting to note an analogy that is drawn between good/evil and light/darkness that appears in the *Sefer Yetzirah:*

> The Zohar explains that light can only be recognized because of darkness. . . . In a similar manner, good can only be recognized because of the existence of evil. If evil did not exist, then we would not have any free choice whatsoever. We would be like mere puppets. . . . It is only because of the existence between good and evil that free will can exist, where we can choose between them. Conversely, it is only of free will that good and evil can be recognized and defined.[51]

While the number 15 has been associated with elements of the Left Side, it does hold a symbolic place in the Divine realm as well. The fifth path on the Tree of Life—connecting *Tiphareth* and *Chokmah*—corresponds, in an indirect way, to the number fifteen. The Tree of Life contains the ten *sefiroth* and twenty-two pathways connecting the individual *sefirah* (each corresponding to the letters of the Hebrew alphabet). The fifth pathway, therefore, corresponds with fifteen as the fifth pathway following the ten *sefiroth*. This is significant perhaps given that, as Crowley explains in his "Table of Correspondences" included with *777*, each *sefirah* expresses certain "moral ideas" and, in the case of the twenty-two pathways, the "names of the letters indicate . . . the pictorial glyph suggested by the shape of the letter." In Crowley's version of the Tree of Life (as shown in figure 2.9), the fifth pathway (connecting Chokmah with Tiphareth) is identified with the fifth letter of the Hebrew alphabet: hé (ה, the letter H). Crowley describes the shape of this letter as "a *Window* [that serves to] remind us that Understanding . . . is the means by which the Light reaches us. The gap between the two strokes is the window."[52] With this last association, we recognize the interdependencies between good/evil and light/darkness. Like Anger with his films, Zorn is able to represent how each individual element of these two oppositions necessarily depends on the other for its meaning. As a result, these binary oppositions are destroyed and a sort of balance or unity is achieved.[53]

The number 15 figures prominently at other structurally significant points within "Sacred Rites of the Left Hand Path." One of the most obvious points is at 4:05 (divisible by 15) where a series of piano chords—repeated 13 times—unfolds over four repetitions of the ostinato figure and a repeated bass guitar pattern (example 2.11). Furthermore, a more obscure symbolic relation between

Example 2.11. Repeated piano chords beginning at 4:05 ("Sacred Rites of the Left Hand Path").

the numbers 13 and 15 contributes to the overall design of the movement. The 13-note ostinato figure is repeated 100 times over the course of "Sacred Rites of the Left Hand Path," stopping at 6:12. The total length of this track is 6:25 where 13 is the result of the overall length of the track minus the point where the ostinato stops (6:25–6:12). At the same time, the total number of ostinato repetitions (100) divided by 15 equals 6.66 . . . , the only reference that I have encountered in this particular track to the mark of the Beast and Crowley's number.

Zorn spent a great deal of time on postproduction for this recording. In fact, many of the numerical symbolisms described in relation to "Sacred Rites of the Left Hand Path" are built into the way the record is heard by the listener. For example, the track lengths for each of *IAO*'s seven movements reflect the importance of the number 13 (see table 2.2). The lengths of tracks 1–6 either add up to 13 or prominently feature 13 in their total length. "Invocation" actually combines two symbolic numbers in its total length: 13 (the result of 7+0+6) as well as Crowley's personal number, 666 (the result of *six* minutes plus *sixty-six seconds*). The symbolic significance of the final two tracks is somewhat unclear. "Leviathan" lasts 3:13, which can be understood as exhibiting 13 in both forward and backward versions or 39, the result of 3 × 13. It is also possible that the sum—7—is the intended symbolic meaning.[54] We can also derive 39 from the total length of Mysteries: 7 × 5 + 4.[55] In addition to the music that is heard, the music that is "not heard"—the "spaces in-between"—are also strictly organized according to the numbers 13 and 666. The amount of silence occurring between tracks is also given in table 2.2 (the middle column) where 13 seconds of silence appears between tracks 1 and 2, 2 and 3, and 6 and 7. Six seconds of silence appear between tracks 3 and 4, 4 and 5, and 5 and 6, forming 6-6-6.[56]

Table 2.2. Timings on *IAO*

Track	Silence between tracks	Length of track
1. Invocation	13 seconds	7:06 (=13; 666=six minutes and 66 seconds)
2. Sex Magick	13 seconds	13:13
3. Sacred Rites of the Left Hand Path	6 seconds	6:25 (=13)
4. The Clavicle of Solomon	6 seconds	9:22 (=13)
5. Lucifer Rising	6 seconds	5:17 (=13)
6. Leviathan	13 seconds	3:13 (=13 forward and backward) (=39; 3 × 13)
7. Mysteries		5:47 (=39; 7 × 5 + 4)

The Tradition of Transgression and the Transgression of Tradition

The analyses of *Necronomicon* and *IAO* provide some sense of the scope and depth of Zorn's interest in matters both magickal and mystical. Without a doubt, more detailed analyses of these and other recent works will yield a number of other formal and organizational techniques based on number symbolisms drawn from a variety of occult sources.

An objection that could be raised against my analyses is that—even by acknowledging the importance of mystical and magickal symbolisms in Zorn's recent compositions—the types and forms of analyses such as those presented above are subjective and variable; that is, the numbers can be manipulated to say/mean almost anything given Zorn's seemingly ad hoc reliance on mystical traditions as diverse as Kabbalah or the thought of Aleister Crowley. Admittedly, the symbolic meanings derived from Kabbalistic/Crowleyian number practices do not lend themselves to typical "musical analyses" and their attendant expectations in musical scholarship. As a result, any rationalized explanation that may be offered via a set of musical axioms or proofs is impossible in the case of Zorn's mystical compositions.

In my opinion, to expect clear-cut, unambiguous, and intersubjectively verifiable analytical claims in this body of music misses the point. Developing Bataille's notions of heterogeneity and base materialism, Zorn's mystical compositions—functioning as heterogeneous objects—actively confront and problematize those deeply entrenched claims and expectations associated with musical analysis (the homogeneous realm). The following quote from Crowley resonates with these Bataillean notions, especially if we relate Crowley's notion of "unmeaning" to Bataille's "nonknowledge":

> The objective can always be expressed in subjective symbols if necessary. The controversy is ultimately unmeaning. However we interpret the evidence, its relative truth depends on its internal coherence. We may therefore say that any magical recollection is genuine if it gives the explanation of our external or internal conditions. Anything which throws light upon the Universe, anything which reveals us to ourselves, should be welcome in this world of riddles.[57]

The "riddles" alluded to by Crowley resemble the "mysteries" described by Zorn in the liner notes to *Magick*. Zorn refers to these "mysteries" and their associated powers as a form of understanding, a "deeper, more intuitive understanding. The understanding that Mysteries, to remain Mysteries, must remain Mysteries, and are not meant to be understood. Unraveled, yes. But never fully, because it is the Mystery itself that is the reality." Zorn then goes on to consider the composition of *Necronomicon* and *Sortilège* (another "mystical" work included on *Magick*) as, at a certain level, unexplainable:

> Because one can never know where the creative spark comes from or why it exists, it must be treasured **as** Mystery. . . . The process of composing music is often at its best when the piece is seemingly writing itself and the composer is merely an observer. These two pieces came about in such an atmosphere, and months of preparation were involved before putting pencil to paper. . . . Both pieces transcended my expectations and my abilities. I cannot explain them. They are part of the Mystery.[58]

By organizing his compositions according to number symbolisms and their various interpretive meanings, Zorn forces the analyst to engage in a "new game of analysis" and forces us to question and reconsider the primary goals of any analytical enterprise. Rather than viewing Zorn's compositions as fixed—like specimens tacked to a board and waiting to be dissected—we should consider them as open, almost *mobile* in how they relate to themselves and how we relate to the works and the works to us.

This openness extends, I believe, to how we can understand these and similar works in relation to Zorn's complex relationship with history and tradition. On the one hand, the use of occult number symbolisms as a basis for musical composition has a long history. In the twentieth century alone, Zorn is certainly familiar with similar compositional strategies in the works of Arnold Schoenberg, Anton Webern, Alban Berg, and George Crumb. However, while Zorn's musical forms and musical language both develop long-standing compositional tendencies, a number of conceptual incongruities in Zorn's "magickal" compositions can create a certain amount of confusion. For example, considering *Necronomicon,* Zorn's decision to base a piece of music that, at first glance, seems to scoff at and profit from unknowing initiates of magick might seem to be an odd choice. If the place of the Necronomicon—both Lovecraft's fictional book and all subsequent "versions"—within "real" magickal practices is suspect, to base a string quartet on such a work might give the appearance that Zorn is not serious in his mystical and magickal pursuits. We could easily dismiss questions of sincerity and degree of belief on Zorn's part by appealing to traditional notions of postmodernist practice whereby items or ideas are used without any concern for their intended use, associated meanings, or historical/cultural contexts. By entitling his piece *Necronomicon,* Zorn—as postmodernist practitioner—uncritically (or uncaringly) drags along this book and everything that it represents within mainstream consciousness (evil, devil worship, sacrifices, ritualistic murders, troubled teens, etc.) into his latest transgressive fascination: magick and mysticism. The *Necronomicon* is *the same as* Crowley's Thelemic practices and writings, or Gnosticism, or Kabbalism, or . . .

That Zorn is not necessarily interested in an "authentic" relationship with these and other occult traditions is evident in one of his earliest mystical recordings, *Zohar* as performed by the Mystic Fugu Orchestra.[59] By entitling his recording after what is arguably the most important work of Jewish mysticism, we might be tempted to believe that Zorn is participating within the larger religio-mystical tradition of Kabbalah. Kabbalah, of course, means tradition, but it would be a mistake to equate "tradition" with "authenticity." As Gershom Scholem points out in relation to Kabbalah and/as tradition, "the very doctrine which centers about the immediate personal contact with the divine, that is to say, a highly personal and intimate form of knowledge, is conceived as traditional wisdom." At the same time, the tradition of Kabbalah (and the forms of "traditional wisdom" imparted or held by practitioners of Kabbalah) exists in a dynamic and contested position with and against "traditional Judaism." Scholem continues by noting how "reverence for the traditional has always been deeply rooted in Judaism, and even the mystics, who in fact broke away from tradition, retained a reverent attitude towards it."[60] Kabbalah, therefore, forms both an integral part of "traditional Judaism" and is often treated as something outside, as a remainder that has been buried and not discussed despite the central place it assumes within more traditional Jewish practices and thought.

The uneasy relationship between traditional and mystical strains of Judaism is reflected in many ways on the Mystic Fugu Orchestra recording of *Zohar*.[61] For example, the liner notes indicate that the performances heard on this recording are by Rav Yechida (vocals) and Rav Tzizit (harmonium). In actuality, *Zohar* is performed by Yamatsuka Eye (the lead singer of the Japanese band The Boredoms and longtime vocalist for Zorn's band Naked City) and Zorn himself. Like the separation between actual and stated performers, a similar type of distancing is present in the music heard on this recording. According to the Tzadik website, the tracks on *Zohar* are "inspired by historical recordings of ancient Judaica." In reality, these tracks are "masquerades" posing as "'newly discovered' recordings from the Mystical tradition of Kabbalah."[62] Any sense of authenticity associated with these recordings might derive from the fact that the vocal and instrumental tracks are buried deep in the mix and are nearly imperceptible given the amount of surface noise (scratches and pops heard on older recordings). However, these noises were added in postproduction and mask the state-of-the-art digital recording technologies available to Zorn and Eye in 1995, the year the tracks were "written" and recorded.

Adding to the many paradoxes and incongruities associated with this recording, Zorn also includes a quote from Gershom Scholem. Zorn's decision to include this quote could be understood as a legitimizing tactic, as if, by including a quote from the renowned Kabbalah scholar, this recording and the intentions that lie behind it are somehow "more authentic." The excerpted quote (in German, no less) only adds to the conceptual difficulties presented by *Zohar*:

> The philology of a mystic discipline like the Kabbala has something ironic in itself. It devotes itself to a veil of mist. . . . An ironic assertion: that the truth . . . is everything other than tradition. It can be perceived but it cannot be handed down, and . . . what is transmittable contains [the truth] no more.[63]

Much like the Mystic Fugu Orchestra's *Zohar*, Scholem's unattributed quotation problematizes the notion of tradition in that he makes a distinction between tradition—presumably including all associated texts and practices—with the claims made by such a tradition. It seems that for Scholem (and probably even Zorn), an appeal to the notion of authenticity *qua* truth is impossible within a tradition as varied and complex as Kabbalah.

A recurring quotation (also from Scholem) that appears on all ten of Zorn's original recordings for his group Masada provides some clues as to how Zorn might conceive of tradition:

> There is a life of tradition that does not merely consist of conservative preservation, the constant continuation of the spiritual and cultural possessions of a community. There is such a thing as a treasure hunt within tradition, which creates a living relationship to tradition and to which much of what is best in current Jewish consciousness is indebted, even where it was—and is—expressed outside the framework of orthodoxy.

To me, this second quote from Scholem suggests a view of tradition that is not necessarily concerned with excavating some sort of truth or authentic relationship with a tradition. Instead, such a relationship is concerned with extending and expanding traditions "outside the framework of [an] orthodoxy." I believe that for Zorn (in both his magickal/mystical compositions and perhaps his recordings and projects often labeled Jewish) this "treasure hunt" involves making connections and uncovering unforeseen or forgotten resonances between a myriad of traditions. More specifically, Zorn is interested in recovering those traditions that have, for one reason or another, been marginalized over time, whether this is Kabbalah, alchemy, or the thought of Aleister Crowley. By letting these traditions speak again (or where he speaks for or within these traditions), Zorn is concerned with what these traditions have to say and what, if anything, we might learn from them. Zorn's interest in various forms of mysticism and magick, therefore, represents an affinity for "traditions of (heterogeneous) transgression" that seek to accomplish a "transgression of (homogeneous) traditions." This is not a tendency specific only to Zorn's more recent music but is, I believe, a defining feature of Zorn's overall poetics of music. The remaining chapters will examine how Zorn identifies with and develops the thought and practices of a variety of marginalized (and not-so-marginalized) artists and traditions in an effort to situate himself within this amorphous "tradition of transgression."

Tradition, Gifts, and Zorn's Musical Homages

In the short biography that appears on the homepage of his publishing company, Hips Road, Zorn lists a number of composers and/or musicians as his "early inspirations," including Charles Ives, Harry Partch, Elliott Carter, Igor Stravinsky, Ennio Morricone, and Carl Stalling.[1] It is a long list of predominantly nonmusicians, however, that appears to have *influenced* crucial aspects of Zorn's musical poetics. Also on this website, Zorn writes how he "learned alchemical synthesis from Harry Smith, structural ontology with Richard Foreman, how to make art out of garbage with Jack Smith, . . . [and] hermetic intuition from Joseph Cornell." As his *teachers*—either real or imagined—all of these individuals *gave* something to Zorn; more specifically, they provided formal and structural strategies to be used in the creation of new artworks as well as more general ideas as to how art interacts with or "fits into" the world.

The transmission and continuation of various ideas associated with Zorn's teachers/influences is evident in many of the composer's musical tributes. Zorn's aim in his dedicated works is, I believe, a conscious musical act whereby he attempts to find some way to translate the ideas associated with these artists and their works (originally formulated often in relation to film, literature, painting, etc.) and to transmit these ideas into and through music. In an attempt to understand the transmission of certain artistic ideas (ideas as diverse as compositional strategies or techniques, aesthetic foundations, or aims), I will consider Zorn's poetics from the perspective of the gift and gift giving. Stated briefly, by considering the materials, ideas, or works of earlier artists as "gifts" that can be passed along, I believe that Zorn is able to enter into a loosely defined yet historically viable artistic tradition. Recognizing certain obligations associated with gifts and gift-giving practices, Zorn receives such gifts and appropriates and manipulates these materials in his compositions, fashioning them in ways that bear not only the mark of Zorn but also that of the giver. As a result, Zorn's musical homages are just as much about him as they are about the giver.

The notion that Zorn has received or assimilated "gifts" that must, in one way or another, be given back is suggested by comments made in an interview for a BBC radio documentary. In the second installment of this four-part interview, Zorn describes how many of the tributes written during the 1980s (for example, *Shuffle Boil* for Thelonious Monk, *Two-Lane Highway* for Albert Collins, and *The Big Gundown* for Ennio Morricone) arose as an attempt "to give back to a tradition that I had taken from."[2] What, exactly, has been given and what could possibly be "given back" is complex. When I asked Zorn about the role of the gift and its place in his musical poetics, he simply said, "Of course, the idea of the gift is key." Elaborating on what types of "things" he has received, Zorn identified "Marcel Duchamp's conceptualism . . . Jean Genet's rough sensuality . . . Marguerite Duras's strong femininity . . . Joseph Cornell's nostalgia for the past."[3] In an effort to acknowledge these gifts received, Zorn's tributes must assimilate and transform certain ideas, techniques, or strategies of earlier artists into his own compositions. By doing so, Zorn acknowledges the artistic visions of his dedicatees and their contributions to his musical poetics. At the same time, Zorn's gift-giving conception of musical influence and, more crucially, the specific individuals to whom he is giving back provide a catalog of influences for Zorn that can be understood from the perspective of tradition, what I will be calling a "tradition of transgression." Functioning within an economy of the gift, Zorn participates within a living (yet partially marginalized and paradoxically constructed) tradition as his works carry on specific ideas and practices set in motion (or continued) by earlier artists.

In this chapter, I will consider Zorn's dedicated works from the perspective of gift theory. I will do this by examining the theoretical practices of two artists and how their ideas have been absorbed and transformed in two works by Zorn: *In the Very Eye of Night* (Maya Deren) and *Untitled* (Joseph Cornell). In the following analyses of these works, I will concentrate on how Zorn is able to transform certain ideas or features associated with each of these "donors" into his music. This will involve some discussion of these earlier artists and their thoughts about their own works. Before my analyses, a bit of theoretical unpacking, untangling, and reconfiguring of "gift theory" is in order, specifically as it relates to the notion of artistic influence.

The Gift, Gift Giving, and Tradition

Any discussion relating to the gift and gift giving must necessarily have as its starting point Marcel Mauss's seminal essay/monograph *The Gift*.[4] Mauss's work has been interpreted in a variety of ways and has been influential for scholars working in fields as diverse as anthropology, sociology, economics, literary and critical theory, and philosophy (not to mention those scholars who operate within or across one or more of these disciplines).[5] For the purposes of this chapter, I will begin by considering Mauss's ideas on the function of the gift and the roles of gift exchange before considering the work of other scholars who have developed and expanded on Mauss's original ideas. These preliminary critical overviews are useful for understanding the ways in which Zorn is able to participate within a certain historical tradition through his dedicated works.

Mauss's essay examines what he considers to be an alternative or premodern form of exchange in "primitive" or "archaic" societies, a form of exchange that differs from the impersonal and calculating economy associated with the market. This form of exchange—a "system of total service" that permeates almost every facet of the society or culture under consideration—centers around the ambiguities, paradoxes, and apparent contradictions associated with the gift and gift giving. The paradoxical nature of the gift arises, Mauss points out, from the "apparently free and disinterested but nevertheless constrained and self-interested" qualities that are attached to the gift. The complex nature of the gift reveals itself when we consider that, when anything is "generously given," there is "in the gesture accompanying the transaction . . . only a polite fiction, formalism, and social deceit, and when really there is obligation and self-interest."[6] Read this way, gift exchange is seen through the lens of a market economy where anything exchanged or given is understood as containing an unspoken expectation of a sort of "tit-for-tat" or *quid pro quo*. As a result, there can be no such thing as a "free gift" (something given freely and disinterestedly, with no expectation of return) because of the imagined self-interest on the part of the donor and the subsequent obligations impressed upon the donee to reciprocate.

To read gift exchange in another way—one not tainted by the lens of the market economy and its associated principles—reveals a more unstable and variable system whose aims differ dramatically from those of the market. The market depends upon the notion of equivalency where an "object" or "service" is assigned some monetary value and where a constant sense of equilibrium is maintained between producers and consumers. (This equilibrium is only momentarily displaced between the time it takes to select an object or service and the moment when it is paid for.) At the same time, the roles of producers and consumers within the market are diminished and are secondary to the object that is being exchanged (or, in this case, bought and sold). As such, the notion of a "free" and autonomous individual is both created and reinforced within a market economy and where social ties are sacrificed to the principles associated with a "restricted economy" such as capitalism. If some form of exchange is perceptible within a market economy, it is a unilateral exchange that consists of only two obligations: to give and to receive.

By contrast, Mauss identifies three obligations within an exchange system predicated on the gift: not only the obligations to give and to receive but also the obligation to reciprocate. It is the obligation to reciprocate—the making of a countergift—that breaks the unilateral, closed structure of a restricted economy and instead develops a "general economy" that, for Mauss, more closely resembles a cycle, or circle, where the initial donee becomes a donor. I will have more to say on Mauss's metaphor of the circle below, but for now it is useful to think of the "system of gift-through-exchange" as forming a sort of network "marked by the continuous flow in all directions of presents given, accepted, and reciprocated." More important for Mauss, this network moves beyond the impersonal relations between individuals associated with a market economy to permeate the entire social fabric of a community or culture not only through the objects exchanged but also by the individuals involved within the system. On the one hand, exchange within a gift system "assumes an aspect that centers on the interest attached to the objects exchanged." On the other hand, these exchanges and the objects exchanged "are never completely detached from those carrying out the exchange." As a result, the "mutual ties and alliance that they establish are comparatively indissoluble."[7] A major feature of the "total system" of "gift-through-exchange" examined by Mauss centers upon the formation of bonds between individuals, groups, cultures, and, ultimately, society itself. As Mary Douglas succinctly notes in her foreword to *The Gift,* the "cycling gift system is the society" and Mauss's "theory of the gift is a theory of human solidarity."[8]

How societies and a sense of solidarity are formed depends on the constant interactions and transformations of Mauss's three obligations: to give, to receive, and to reciprocate. However, it is not just *what* is given away or given back that contributes to these formations but what the thing given or exchanged *contains* or *symbolizes*. In an effort to describe the types of bonds that are formed between individuals and groups, Mauss appeals to the Maori notion of the *hau*, a magical force or spiritual power that resides in objects and that accompanies particular objects through the gift cycle.[9] In receiving a particular object, an individual or group not only receives a material object but also inherits some spiritual "part" or essence of the original donor.[10] The obligation to reciprocate in a gift system has to do with the fact that, in Mauss's words, "what imposes obligation in the present received and exchanged is the fact that the thing received is not inactive. Even when it has been abandoned by the giver, it still possesses something of him. Through it the giver has a hold over the beneficiary just as, being its owner, through it he has a hold over the thief." Mauss concludes that "to make a gift of something to someone is to make a present of some part of oneself. . . . In this system of ideas one clearly and logically realizes that one must give back to another person what is really part and parcel of his nature and substance, of his soul."[11]

Mauss's essay presents a compelling picture of the role of the gift, particularly the inherent tensions and embedded paradoxes associated with gift exchange and its relations/differences to the form(s) and function(s) of exchanges typically encountered within the sphere of the market. Unlike the market, the exchange of gifts emphasizes the roles played by individuals and the various types of social and human bonds that are created and transformed. At the same time, the object exchanged assumes an active role within the exchange between individuals or groups, a feature typically absent from the inactive nature of objects bought and sold in the market. The active nature of the gift arises from a sense that it is imbued with features or characteristics associated with the giver, features that are then absorbed by any and all subsequent receivers.

There remain, however, certain blind spots in a Maussian notion of the gift. First, the three obligations of giving, receiving, and reciprocating are viewed by Mauss as forming a circle. The metaphor of the circle derives, in part, from the reciprocative obligation, an obligation Mauss explains through the transference of a spiritual essence, the *hau*. Because an object contains a "little bit" of the giver, "the giver has a hold over the beneficiary just as, being its owner, through it he has a hold over the thief." The original donor never really gives anything away; instead, because he or she knows that what has been given will be returned (presumably with "interest"), the metaphor of the circle applied to gift exchange may actually mask a form of unilateral exchange commonly associated with "restricted economies." As a result, the communal forms imagined by Mauss appear to be rather circumscribed and would seem to be governed by individual self-interest.[12] At the same time, the circle of exchange imagined by Mauss severely limits the temporal potentialities of the gift and gift giving. If, as the circle metaphor implies, an originary gift must ultimately return to its "rightful owner" (given the drive of the *hau* or some other spiritual essence with which it is imbued), then a system of gift exchange creates a rather limited sense of community that exists within a very small time frame. While the circle can be expanded through an ever-widening system of receivers, who become givers, who become receivers in space, the object itself ceases to move when it is eventually returned to the originator of the gift, presumably within a time frame in which this original giver can reap the benefits of the object's return and the various "extras" it has accrued during its travels. Here, gifts and gift giving still appear to function within a restricted economy where self-interest predominates. This is a severe limitation on our commonsense notion that groups, communities, and society exist *through* extended periods of time.[13]

In their book-length examination of the "modern gift," Jacques T. Godbout and Alain Caillé consider these (and other) apparent limitations of Mauss's original ideas. Like Mauss and other theorists of the gift, Godbout and Caillé consider the human bond(s) formed in gift-giving practices as being just as—if not more—important than the object or objects actually exchanged. For the authors, "society is made up of groups of individuals who are constantly trying to establish their position within the group by breaking and renewing ties with others." It is their opinion that "only the gift can actually—not just in the imagination or ideologically—transcend the opposition between the individual and the collectivity, making individuals part of a larger, concrete entity."[14]

A market economy perpetuates the idea of a complete and irreducible self or individual where social ties (that may extend through time) are replaced by economic obligations (that have a limited temporality but may extend indefinitely in space). Godbout and Caillé consider the ways that gifts and gift giving—with their emphases on human bonds, community, and collectivity—highlight the limited temporalities of the market by focusing on the historically and culturally constructed formation of subjectivity or the "self." A key feature of the market and its inability to form extended communal bonds has to do with its emphasis on equality, where an object is exchanged for another object considered to be of equal value or when a price is affixed to an object or service. Once equality has been reached (object/service performed/paid for), the relationship (if we can use the term) is complete. In contrast to the equalities associated with the market system, the gift thrives on inequalities. As Godbout and Caillé point out, "the gift abhors equality. It seeks alternating inequality." A sense of inequality first arises at that moment when a donor gives something (and thereby has "less") and when the donee receives (has "more"). On the one hand, to give back to the original donor could result in some sort of equivalence (as if by "paying back" someone) or could lead to an escalating cycle of giving and receiving where participants try to outdo one another (where the stakes get higher and gifts are continuously received and given). On the other hand, if we turn our attention away from the object(s) circulating to the process itself, any obligation one perceives when receiving a gift arises not from the object received but rather from a decision to strengthen the bond that has been extended by the donee. Understood this way, the "gift serves the bond, it is not the bond." Furthermore, this bond can extend through time where the inequalities associated with the gift and gift giving are understood as part of a "filiation, establishing a link with the past instead of wiping the slate clean of time."[15]

Within a system of gift giving, the constructed character of the self displaces the notion of an autonomous individual imagined by the market. Echoing the Maori notion of the *hau* utilized by Mauss, Godbout and Caillé believe that "what circulates [with the gift] carries with it [a] personal element—it contains a part of the self. Every gift is a gift of the self, and cannot easily be treated as an object. The gift derives from animist thought."[16]

Extending this idea, not only does every gift carry with it a personal element associated with the donor, but when the gift is accepted and assimilated
by a receiver, this personal element is also passed on and augmented. In other
words, a gradual accrual of characteristics and features associated with individuals associated with a particular gift-giving chain is passed along through time.
This feature—associated with what Godbout and Caillé refer to as "bonding
value"—is viewed not as a circle but as a spiral. The metaphor of gift giving as a
spiral foregrounds not only the motion of the gift through time but also, contra
Mauss, the possibility that elements given may not necessarily return to their
original owner. Instead, the gift is essentially an act characterized by loss for any
participant within the spiral. As such, the giver always "loses" and everyone is
transformed into a "giver" at some point along the spiral. Understood this way,
the gift is characterized by qualities that are far removed from the types of exchanges typically associated with the market: qualities such as utility, accumula-
tion, and equivalence. "In fact," Godbout and Caillé claim,

> the gift is anti-utilitarian, anti-accumulative, and anti-equivalence. It is anti-utili-
> tarian because it seems to thrive on the squandering and sacrifice of useful goods,
> or, at the very least, to turn its back on them. It is anti-equivalence because the gift
> creates an imbalance whose correction must be put off indefinitely, for to settle all
> debts would be to interrupt the obligational cycle. Finally, it is anti-accumulative
> because the wealthiest must not enrich themselves to the point that they have vio-
> lated the social obligation to be a spendthrift and to return in kind.[17]

What, then, is gained by participating within the gift-giving spiral? Again,
the authors emphasize the gift as representing "the most complex social phenomenon" and as an "experience that not only enables the individual to become
part of a collective but that opens up onto a universal network, onto the world,
onto life, onto other states, onto belonging to something greater than oneself."[18]
This thing greater than oneself is described at points within *The World of the
Gift* as tradition and where any discussion of the gift involves a "language that
seems coextensive with tradition, the language of the gift."[19]

The authors illustrate their points relating to characteristics associated
with the gift-giving spiral, community/tradition, and the passage of "personal
elements" by considering art, artists, and artistic communities. The authors describe the artistic world as a "gift system" composed of a "community who share
the same belief, the respect for a certain product." In particular, Godbout and
Caillé locate "avant-garde" artists, practices, and traditions within such a perspective, emphasizing the anti-utilitarian stance often assumed by some artists
in relation to the public at large ("To be successful, for the avant-garde, is proof
of failure") and who value, instead, the formation of bonds or links with other
like-minded artists ("For the avant-garde, all that counts is the appreciation of
other artists, in other words the community of producers"). Finally, it is this

link with other artists associated with a particular community or tradition that gives rise to new works of art:

> The artistic act is the act of receiving and transmitting a gift. The product, the work of art, is the result of inspiration. The work of art, in fact, is not actually a product—it does not fit into the system of modern production. The artist receives something that he passes on, which is a gift. Aesthetic feeling, beauty, whatever name one gives to this supplement, it is essential: without it the work would be only a product and the artist would have long joined the ranks of industrial producers.[20]

We have now reached a point where we can situate Zorn's dedicated works, musical tributes, or homages within a system predicated on the notion of the gift and gift exchange. In such works, key aesthetic/poetic ideas or stylistic/ technical strategies associated with the dedicatee's chosen artistic medium (film, painting, literature, etc.) are received as gifts by Zorn and are then subsequently transformed and assimilated within his own musical compositions. While the work is Zorn's, it depends on specific ideas or techniques passed along from the intended dedicatee and subsequently received by Zorn. The result is a composition that builds on and develops ideas and techniques originally set in motion by the intended dedicatee and then elaborated upon (and transformed) by Zorn; Zorn the recipient becomes Zorn the giver in the completion and transmission of his many dedicated works. However, it would be a mistake to think that Zorn's dedicatees represent a single point along the gift-giving spiral described by Godbout and Caillé. The dedicatees of Zorn's works exist along this same spiral and, as such, must have been—at one point—a recipient themselves. Instead of a timeless originating point as described by Godbout and Caillé— the point of "inspiration"—it is more useful to think of Zorn's individual dedicatees as occupying a single point along a chain or spiral that unfolds much farther back in time. That is, Zorn's "givers" were—at one time—receivers of gifts from those artists or individuals who were givers who were receivers who were. . . . Looked at this way, it is easier to imagine the trajectory of a historical continuum—a sense of tradition—in which Zorn situates himself through his dedicated works.

What, exactly, is the tradition in which Zorn attempts to situate himself through his dedications or homages? In many respects, this tradition is firmly rooted in the practices of musical modernism as exemplified by composers such as Schoenberg, Webern, Berg, Stravinsky, and Boulez. While Zorn has not paid tribute to any of these composers in his own works through explicit dedications, he has often borrowed musical ideas or structural principles developed by these and other modernist composers and applied them to his own works: for example, the oblique reference to Schoenberg's row from the "Sonett von Petrarca" movement from the Serenade op. 24, in his *Chimeras*, the use of Webern's pitch material from the String Trio op. 20 in *Walpurgisnacht,* references to Berg's *Lyric Suite* in *Memento Mori,* and pitch derivations from Boulez's *Le Marteau sans maître* in *Elegy.* At the same time, a number of "noncanonical" composers have made a tremendous impact on Zorn's musical poetics, most notably Edgard Varèse, Henry Cowell, Harry Partch, Charles Ives, and Ennio Morricone. This latter list can be greatly expanded by including jazz musicians and other improvisers, specifically Albert Ayler, Evan Parker, and Derek Bailey. Stylistically, very little seems to relate, say, the music of Ives or Partch with that of Morricone, Ayler, or Bailey. While it is clear that Zorn has gathered and assimilated a variety of compositional skills and performance techniques from artists such as these, Zorn seems to be more interested in how these artists, their works, and, more specifically, their thoughts pushed the limits of what music can be.

These tendencies become clearer when we also consider the many painters, filmmakers, authors, actors, philosophers, and essayists cited by Zorn as contributing to his overall poetics of music. Seen from this perspective, a number of barely visible connecting threads can be perceived between the many artists and thinkers who have significantly shaped Zorn's poetics. Within their respective milieus, all of the influences or inspirations mentioned by Zorn worked at the margins of the dominant styles, trends, or schools prevalent at that time, whether it is the inseparable blending and blurring of high and low culture in the music of Ives and Morricone and the films of Jack Smith, the free jazz infused with a sense of nostalgia in the music of Albert Ayler or the surrealistically nostalgic constructions of Joseph Cornell, the expansion of acceptable sounds and materials in Varèse, Cowell, Partch, Marcel Duchamp, or Hermann Nitsch, or the changing roles of the composer/performer in the works of John Cage, Earle Brown, or Antonin Artaud.

In an interview with William Duckworth, Zorn has mentioned how he sees himself as participating within a tradition that could be described as "experimental" or as a "maverick tradition." The reason, Zorn believes, is that—like the artistic practices and thought of Ives, Ayler, Duchamp, and Genet—he has created his own world, describing it as "multifaceted" and "like a little prism" that "goes off in a million different directions."[21] Developing the points described in the previous two chapters, I will refer to this loose-knit tradition as a "tradition of transgression." All of the artists Zorn admires can be understood as working at the margins of what was considered artistically and/or aesthetically acceptable. However, instead of undermining or destroying many of the dominant practices in which they worked, the artists and thinkers associated with this tradition of transgression acknowledge limits by operating within the spaces carved out by these limitations. Individuals such as Joseph Cornell, Maya Deren, Jean Genet, and Ennio Morricone created works that inhabit a sort of negative, aporetic space that is determined by a set of historical and artistic pressures exerted from without (cultural, disciplinary, etc.), while they question and problematize these very pressures and the assumptions and expectations from which they are formed. Given the provocative aims of those artists and thinkers with whom Zorn aligns himself, the commonsense notion of tradition—as a relatively stable set of features or characteristics that persist through time—is itself decentered. Instead, the tradition of transgression is discernible only when it is successful at revealing the artificial limitations and boundaries of "traditional" structures and formations. In this sense, the tradition of transgression is founded upon an apparent paradox: a tradition of practices and thought that zeroes in on and exploits the spaces or "blind spots" deemed impermissible, unacceptable, and unrecognizable (yet ultimately created) by traditional institutions of art.

By conceiving of the works and any associated techniques, strategies, and practices of earlier artists as gifts, Zorn is able to maintain the sense of instability and inequality associated with the tradition of transgression while avoiding the possibility of being co-opted by more traditional modes of artistic/aesthetic thought. In an attempt to make sense of this continuing spiral of giving and receiving within the tradition of transgression, it may be useful finally to view the traditions and processes enacted and created by gift-giving practices from the perspective of influence.[22] Unlike the agonistic, usurping model proposed by Harold Bloom in his writings on the "anxiety of influence," the gift *qua* influence does not function to "rise above" or "swerve" from certain ideas or practices associated with an earlier figure and his or her works but assimilates, appropriates, and celebrates these ideas and practices.[23] An acknowledged connection, a link in a historical continuum, is celebrated when influence is viewed from the perspective of the gift and gift giving and not from the sense of outdoing or "one-upmanship" characteristic of an anxious conception of influence. Furthermore, the emphasis on originality associated with a particular precursor (Bloom's "strong poet") is set aside in favor of a communal relationship between earlier and later artists that may resemble the relationship that often exists between a teacher and a pupil. Certain features associated with artistic originality—specifically notions of "ownership" as well as a perceived scarcity of viable artistic ideas, strategies, etc.—are overturned within a gift-giving conception of influence. Any perceived aesthetic significance that may have been associated with the notion of artistic "originality" is thrown into question when later artists celebrate their "derivative" or secondary (sometimes tertiary, etc.) relationships with earlier artists. Artistic inheritance is not a burden that must be borne by later artists but is something to be celebrated and continually investigated in the creation of new works. Furthermore, the notion that there may exist a scarcity of viable and/or acceptable artistic practices/topics for later artists to work with and from (determined, in part, by the cult status of "originality" imparted to earlier artists) is rejected in favor of artistic plentitude. The work and thought of earlier artists is viewed instead as a deep well from which later artists may continually draw in a never-ending spiral of development and/or elaboration.[24]

The remainder of this chapter will be devoted to an examination of the role of the gift and gift giving in two tributes or homages by Zorn: *In the Very Eye of Night* (Maya Deren) and *Untitled* (Joseph Cornell). The work of these two artists have exerted a strong influence on Zorn's musical poetics, and I will attempt to describe how Zorn's compositions incorporate key poetic and technical/compositional strategies often associated with the work of Deren and Cornell. For Zorn, certain obstacles must be overcome in these particular works; most notably, he must find a way to translate the work and thought of Deren (a filmmaker) and Cornell (a visual artist) into a musical language. To do so will not only enable Zorn to receive the gift(s) imparted by these artists but also will allow him to participate within a tradition of transgression in which they participate.

In the Very Eye of Night (Maya Deren)

The films of Maya Deren occupy a privileged place in twentieth-century avant-garde art. For many early interpreters, Deren's films—especially *Meshes of the Afternoon* (1943; 1959) and *At Land* (1944)—were viewed as continuing and extending certain practices and modes of thought associated with surrealist filmmakers, especially the films of Luis Buñuel and Jean Cocteau. Film critic Parker Tyler likens Deren's films to the "visions of Cocteau and Dalí," while Richard Lippold compares them to Germaine Dulac's *Seashell and the Clergyman* (on a screenplay by Antonin Artaud), claiming that Dulac's films "might have sprung from the heart of an identical twin of Maya Deren" and that "Jean Cocteau's *Blood of a Poet*, too, is not far from *Meshes of the Afternoon*." Other critics who perceived some sort of affinity with Deren's works and those of surrealism were less than flattering. James Agee explains how "I cannot feel . . . that they do anything . . . which was not done, and done to an ill-deserved death, by some of the European avant-gardists, and especially by the surrealists, of the 1920s."[25] Despite the many historical/stylistic connections critics may have perceived between Deren's work and that of the surrealists, Deren herself constantly fought the label of "surrealist" and any and all of its attendant associations in relation to her films. According to Jonas Mekas, a fellow filmmaker, founder of the Anthology Film Archives, and longtime friend of Deren, the topic of surrealism "was always a very sensitive subject with Maya. . . . Any reference, or in real life discussions, to her work as containing elements of surrealism made Maya mad."[26] For Deren, a fundamental difference between the work of the surrealists and her films has to do with the place and function of reality or separate realities in art and artworks, a topic I will pick up below.

Another feature of Deren's film poetics that is frequently mentioned involves her position as a woman filmmaker, particularly the tensions brought about between her own avant-garde/underground films and contemporary mainstream Hollywood productions and practices. From this perspective, Deren's films are often interpreted as a critique of the place of women in western culture in general. Lauren Rabonivitz notes how Deren's films "represent a position of refusal while still being defined by the very sexual terms against which they rebel. There is ultimately a corollary between Deren's difficult position as a woman filmmaker-activist in postwar America and the ways in which her films rework existing film language to inscribe a place for female subjectivity."[27] In the early history of American avant-garde cinema, Deren carved out a space for later women directors and fostered a deeply personal style of filmmaking that highlights the fluid boundaries of the self in general and female subjectivity in particular. This aspect of her work is clearly recognizable in her *Meshes of the Afternoon,* where Deren plays three "characters," all representing portions of her (conflicted) self.[28]

In addition to her films, Maya Deren's writings on film theory represent some of the most important early writings on the topic in the English language. Drawing upon and developing the theories of writers/filmmakers such as Rudolf Arnheim, Jean Epstein, and Sergei Eisenstein, Deren's own poetics of filmmaking has been characterized as modernist. At the heart of Deren's modernist poetics lies what Renata Jackson has called a "core assumption of medium specificity: the two-pronged belief that art forms are differentiated from one another by virtue of their distinctive formal or structural capabilities, and that there is a direct connection between these structural characteristics and each art form's 'proper' expressive realm."[29]

Deren's medium specificity, or medium essentialism, is rigorously described in her *Anagram of Ideas on Art, Form, and Film,* her most extensive theoretical writing on film. Here, Deren considers how the "process of creative art is twofold: the experience of reality by the artist on one side, and his manipulation of that experience into an art reality on the other. In his person he is an instrument of discovery; in his art he exercizes [*sic*] the art-instrument of invention."[30]

As an example of these various forms of reality—as experienced and as created—Deren considers photography and cinematography:

A photograph will serve as proof of the "truth" of some phenomenon where either a painting or a verbal testimony would fail to carry the weight. In other art forms, the artist is the intermediary between reality and the instrument by which he creates his work of art. But in photography, the reality passes directly through the lens of the camera to be immediately recorded on film, and this relationship may, at times, dispense with all but the most manual services of a human being, and even, under certain conditions, produce film almost "untouched by human hands."[31]

Although she admits that photography can be manipulated so as to appear "arty," photography is better equipped for representing a sort of immediate reality. Deren believes, however, that the true work of art should strive to manipulate reality according to the capabilities of a specific artistic medium. In cinematography, for instance, these manipulations involve certain editing procedures or techniques. According to Deren, "The proper form of film is accomplished only when the elements, whatever their original [i.e., real] context, are related according to the special characters of the instrument of film itself—the camera and the editing—so that the reality which emerges is a new one—one which only film can achieve and which could not be accomplished by the exercize [sic] of any other instrument."[32] The new emergent reality is therefore one of artifice, a synthetic reality.[33]

For Deren, the unique manipulative possibilities associated with film involve the medium's ability to alter or rearrange both time and space, individually and simultaneously. In her opinion, the "dynamic manipulation of the relationships between film-time and film-space (and potentially, film-sound) can create that special integrated complex: film form."[34] While painting can disrupt or alter our perception of space, it is less successful in dealing with time, as it is often constrained by the frame. The theater can alter our perception of time, yet is ill-suited in regard to matters of space.[35] On the manipulative possibilities of time inherent in filmic form, Deren provides an example from her film *Ritual in Transfigured Time* (1945–46):

> A running leap has, with slight variations, a given tempo; slow-motion photography creates of it a reality which is totally unnatural. But a use of slow-motion in reference to a movement which can, in parts, be performed at a variable tempo can be even more creative. That is, one can shake one's head from side to side at almost any rate of speed. When a fast turning is reduced, by slow-motion, it still looks natural, and merely as if it were being performed more slowly; the hair, however, moving slowly in the lifted, horizontal shape possible only to rapid tempos, is unnatural in quality [see figure 3.1]. Thus one creates a movement in one tempo which has the qualities of a movement in another tempo, and it is the dynamics of the relationship between these qualities which creates a certain special effectiveness, a reality which can only be achieved through the temporal manipulation of natural elements by the camera as an art instrument.[36]

Concerning possible spatial manipulations in film, Deren uses as an example a shot from her *Study in Choreography for the Camera* (1945):

Figure 3.1. Still from *Ritual in Transfigured Time* (1945–46) depicting an "unnatural quality" possible through multiple tempos (tempo of Deren's hair and the tempo of her hands and head moving as filmed in slow motion). *Photo courtesy of Anthology Film Archives, all rights reserved.*

In the film dance which I have made, the dancer begins a large movement—the lowering of his extended leg—in a forest. This shot is interrupted at the moment when the leg has reached waist-level, and is immediately followed by a close-up shot of the leg in a continuation of its movement—with the location now the interior of a house [see figures 3.2a and 3.2b]. The integrity of the time element—the fact that the tempo of the movement is continuous and that the two shots are, in editing, spliced to follow one another without interruption—holds together spatial areas which are not, in reality, so related. Instead of being destructive to a dramatic integrity, the mobility of the camera and the interruption and resumption of action, here creates an integrity as compelling as that of the theater, but of a totally different quality.[37]

With its emphasis on the manipulative possibilities associated with space and time, Deren's poetics of film reflects a more primary aesthetic regarding the purpose of art and artworks. For Deren, the "invisible," the "emotional," and the "metaphysical content" of a work of art "creates experience." In her *Anagram*, Deren explains how "*the distinction of art is that it is neither simply an expres-*

Figure 3.2a. Dancer's leg being lowered in one location . . .

sion, of pain, for example, nor an impression of pain but is itself a form which creates pain (or whatever its emotional intent)."[38] Elaborating on this particular passage, Renata Jackson remarks that "true art," in Deren's opinion, "is the embodiment of an idea or emotion which, like a hypodermic needle, is powerful enough to inject that idea into or affect directly the reader/observer."[39] Deren's "directly communicative" understanding of art leads her to consider "a work of art [as] an emotional and intellectual complex whose logic is its whole form."[40] The logic Deren speaks of derives from her own understanding of Gestalt psychology where "the parts are so dynamically related as to produce something new which is unpredictable from a knowledge of its parts. It is this process which makes possible the idea of economy in art, for the whole which here emerges transcends, in meaning, the sum total of the parts. The effort of the artist is toward the creation of a logic in which two and two may make five, or, preferably, fifteen; when this is achieved, two can no longer be understood simply as two. This five, or this fifteen—the resultant idea or emotion—is therefore *a function of the total relationships, the form of the work.*"[41]

The *type* of art form suggested by Deren is not a mimetic, naturalistic conception nor is it one of autonomy, where the meaning—and by extension, value—of a work of art resides in its internal relationships and/or its internal

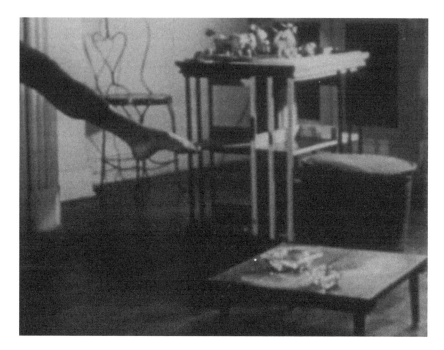

Figure 3.2b. . . . only to come down in another location. Consecutive
stills from *A Study in Choreography for Camera,* 1945. *Photo
courtesy of Anthology Film Archives, all rights reserved.*

logic. Instead, Deren conceives of a "ritualistic form" which "reflects . . . the
conviction that . . . ideas are best advanced when they are abstracted from the
immediate conditions of reality and incorporated into a contrived, created
whole, stylized in terms of the utmost effectiveness." Ritualistic form—"*a conscious manipulation designed to create effect*"—"treats the human being not as
the source of the dramatic action, but as a somewhat depersonalized element
in a dramatic whole."[42] The ritualized artwork places the creator within a larger
collective consciousness that departs from the reality of the specific or particular to a reality composed of myth.

As a tribute to Deren, Zorn's *In the Very Eye of Night* can, on the one hand,
be understood as an attempt on the part of the composer to situate himself
within a particular artistic tradition, a tradition devoted to a continual critique
of well-entrenched limits and assumptions concerning the roles and functions
of works of art.[43] On the other hand, when viewed from the perspective of the
gift system described above, it is clear that for Zorn to create a musical work that
expands upon and develops many of the key features associated with Deren's
aesthetics of film (particularly her ideas relating to the manipulative possibili-

ties of space and time), he must get past Deren's essentialism. In other words, Zorn must find a way to translate the central place occupied by sight and vision in Deren's poetics of film into his own chosen sound medium.

Zorn's title is drawn from Deren's last completed film, *The Very Eye of Night* (1952, music added in 1959). Although this film is not granted the same type of prestige enjoyed by many of Deren's earlier films—such as *Meshes of the Afternoon* and *At Land*—it still exhibits and relies upon many of the key ideas that Deren described in her writings on film and film-form.[44] The film depicts various celestial movements enacted by dancers (choreographed by Antony Tudor) in negative imagery. The photographic negative images of the dancers are superimposed against a starry sky, a backdrop that is continually changing throughout the film. Given this elusive and ever-changing background, a referential spatial "ground" is absent for the viewer. The dancers move horizontally, diagonally, and vertically across the screen with no stable point of reference to relate their movements. At other times, dancers enter the frame, hover, and move off in a completely unexpected direction. Of course, the manipulative capabilities relating to space in film are (along with time) a central component of Deren's poetics. With this film in particular, Deren has commented on how the "sleepwalker"—one of the main characters of the film, identified as "Noctambulo" in the film's credits—"travels in three directions at once: down into the abyss, up into the heavens, and inwards to the self. The direction is of no consequence. The three are all in the same place. It is his travel in the interior."[45]

At the same time that the dancer's movements and motions on the screen exploit certain spatial possibilities associated with the film medium, a new reality emerges in *The Very Eye of Night* through Deren's decision to film the dancers in a negative imagery.[46] Furthermore, a sense of "unreality" in the dimension of time is manifested in a number of ways. Most noticeably, various gestures associated with individual dance sequences appear to occur in "real time." However, a close examination of the dancers' clothing—specifically the scarves wrapped around their bodies—reveal that many of these sequences have been slowed down. The unnatural flow and motion of the scarves (and, at other moments within the film, the motion of the women's hair) provide the only evidence for these slow-motion segments as the bodies appear to be moving naturally. These juxtaposed temporal configurations give *The Very Eye of Night* an almost trancelike quality that draws the viewer out of a real-time viewing experience. Confronted by the fluid and evolving spatial and temporal qualities of Deren's film, the starry background provides the only sustained point of reference for the viewer that, as stated above, is itself in constant motion.

Zorn's *In the Very Eye of Night* was created entirely in the studio utilizing the recording software Pro Tools. Given this fact, *In the Very Eye of Night*—indeed all of the tracks included on *Songs from the Hermetic Theater*—is unlike most of Zorn's music in that its existence depends entirely upon the manipulative capabilities offered by recording technology. For Zorn, it seems, the recording studio allowed him to realize certain temporal and spatial manipulations associated with Deren's film poetics in a musical context. As such, Zorn is able to continue the gift-giving spiral bequeathed to him by Deren and is able to create a new sonic reality, a reality that emerges from a variety of recording and performance techniques and the transformation of these sounds through the use of certain manipulative effects.

Approximately twenty tracks were utilized in constructing *In the Very Eye of Night,* including cricket sounds, electric bass, wooden flute, dripping water, bass drums, piano, and many others. Many—if not all—of these tracks were subsequently altered and transformed in various ways in the studio. For example, the bass guitar never actually *sounds* like a bass guitar as we might expect to hear it. Instead, this part was subjected to a number of effects, including distortion and pitch/octave displacement (lowered). As a result of the pitch displacement, the bass guitar part of *In the Very Eye of Night* more closely resembles a low, thunderlike rumbling or a continuous band of low frequency static (with occasional peaks as we will see). For Zorn, the electric bass guitar was chosen not for its standard uses (such as providing a harmonic anchor defined by clearly recognizable pitches) but for its sonic potential when subjected to a variety of digital effects. Much the same can be said about Zorn's use of the piano in this work. Throughout the entire piece, the inside of the piano functions solely as a surface upon which a glass bowl is rotated. The result is a complex collection of high frequency pitches that serves to balance or offset the low rumbling produced by the bass guitar.[47] The registral space that will define *In the Very Eye of Night* is formed as the piano and bass guitar define the upper and lower sonic boundaries.

From the beginning of the piece until approximately 1:25, the listener is confronted by the sound of Deren's voice, presented prominently in the center of the stereo field.[48] The recorded excerpt chosen by Zorn for his work is significant, especially with regard to her views of time and what she understands as a woman's conception of time:

> What I do in my films is very, oh, I think very distinctively . . . I think they are the films of a woman and I think that their characteristic time quality is the time quality of a woman. I think that the strength of men is their great sense of immediacy, they are a "now" creature and a woman has strength to wait, because she's had to wait. She has to wait nine months for the concept of child. Time is built into her body in the sense of becomingness. And she sees everything in terms of it being in the stage of becoming. She raises a child knowing not what it is at any moment but seeing always the person that it will become. Her whole life, from her very beginning—it's built into her—is the sense of becoming. Now in any time form, this is a very important sense. I think that my films, putting as much stress as they do upon

the constant metamorphosis—one image is always becoming another—that is, it is what is happening that is important in my films, not what is at any moment. This is a woman's time sense, and I think it happens more in my films than in almost anyone else's.

Deren's voice is accompanied by irregular strikes on the bass drum. Initially, these bass drum strokes appear only on the right side of the stereo field and very deep in the mix, almost imperceptible. Beginning at :22, as Deren emphasizes the word *immediacy*, another bass drum enters, here occupying the left channel. With this move, Zorn has effectively "opened up" the left and right spaces that *In the Very Eye of Night* will occupy. At the same time, the bass drum heard on the left channel is qualitatively different in a number of ways from the bass drum sound that opens the work (on the right side). For instance, the bass drum on the left is a bit softer in volume, and it appears to have been muffled, as the mallet articulations are less defined than those that can be heard on the right side. The left side can be said to be "wet" in contrast to the "dry" sound on the right. Shortly after Deren completes the phrase "in the stage of becoming," another bass drum part enters, now in the middle of the stereo field and heard underneath Deren's voice. From :40 until 1:00, the three bass drum tracks threaten to overtake the total sound of *In The Very Eye of Night* as the individual strokes give way to a nearly continuous rumbling and a slight increase in volume and overall activity. At 1:00, however, the bass drum tracks reduce down to just those heard directly down the middle and on the right-hand side. The left-hand side of the stereo field now appears empty, and the sonic configuration of the track seems lopsided.

The sound of rippling water replaces Deren's voice (along with its place in the center of the stereo field) at 1:25. However, almost as soon as we get accustomed to the sound of the water, it, too, gives way to another timbre, this time a sound that resembles the chirping of crickets. This "cricket sound" bounces back and forth between the left and right channels in a hypnotic rhythmic ostinato. At the same time, it occupies a level that sits comfortably in the middle of the overall volume range. Because it persists (it is still present even when extreme changes in volume render it inaudible), this cricket sound serves as a sort of reference sound, or ground, that relates various aspects of the entire spatial field of *In the Very Eye of Night*: the left and right channels through the use of panning as well as a sense of depth and the sonic impression of "near" or "far" relations achieved through volume, microphone placement, compression, and/ or equalization. In this respect, the cricket sound functions in a manner analogous to the celestial backdrop of Deren's film.

The entrance of the cricket sounds at 1:30 is accompanied by more strokes on the bass drum. The decay of this particular bass drum stroke quickly transforms (or "metamorphoses") into the low rumbling of the bass guitar. This guitar track gradually takes over the entire sonic field, spreading out from the center to "infect" the left and right channels; as a result, the clearly defined sonic spaces of the opening are replaced by a singular space. This effect is compounded by the introduction of the breathy sounds of the wooden flute at 3:08, a sound that combines with the bass guitar part and begins in the center of the stereo field.

At 3:23, the sound of the glass bowl being rotated on the strings of the piano enters for the first time, beginning in the center and then slowly shifting to the right. As stated above, the dense harmonics associated with this track introduce the uppermost pitch boundaries of *In the Very Eye of Night*. The entrance of the glass bowl is a startling moment in this work, a work that has, up to this point, been dominated by low-pitched sounds. At the same time, the appearance of the piano/glass bowl track provides the final element in the three-dimensional spatial boundaries explored by *In the Very Eye of Night*: the left/right motion achieved through panning, the impression of depth (e.g., the nearness of Deren's voice/the rippling water versus the distance of the bass drum parts), and the high/low boundaries created by the low sounds of the bass drums and electric bass and the high frequencies of the glass bowl, both of which are balanced around the cricket sounds in the middle register.

Up until about the six-minute mark, no single track seems to predominate over any of the others; instead, the individual tracks bleed into one another, fusing into a single complex timbre. At the same time, they emphasize the center and the right side of the stereo field. While quiet, distant strokes on a bass drum can be picked out on the left side, this side is mostly unoccupied. Beginning at 5:59, the overall density of the entire track thickens as the electric bass guitar and the piano begin to dominate. At 6:13, for example, these two parts each try to take over the entire track. Beginning around 8:20, the piano sounds begin to move from their place in the center/right-hand side of the stereo field by gradually entering into the left side. This is an important moment in *In the Very Eye of Night* as it marks the first appearance of a high-pitched sound on the left. At the same time, the right-to-left motion of the piano at this moment reactivates the left-hand side of the stereo field, a side that—aside from some intermittent and irregular bass drum strokes—has not played an important role in the temporal "becoming" of Zorn's piece since the opening. Zorn emphasizes the appearance of the piano/glass bowl on the left side with short bursts on the wooden flute, heightening our awareness of the newfound importance of the left channel (listen especially at 9:07 and following). The sounds produced by the piano/glass bowl now dominate both the left and right channels while the bass guitar, cricket sounds, and lapping water are still in the center. In effect, the piano sounds have assumed a greater role in the work: it not only defines—through its vertical function—an upper registral boundary; it also functions horizontally as it envelops the left and right sides of the track as a whole.

By 9:35, the sounds of the piano have faded away from the track, leaving only the rumbling bass guitar part, the lapping water, and the cricket sounds (still in the center). At this point, the dramatic narrative associated with the left and right channels can be understood as having been neutralized by the central stereo placement of these remaining tracks. The bass guitar part gradually fades away, leaving only the middle ranges of the cricket sounds and rippling water. As this part recedes from the track, bass drum strokes—beginning around 10:30—can be heard on the left- and right-hand sides. These textures and timbres recall the opening of *In the Very Eye of Night* and, as a result, provide a sense of return and closure to the track as a whole. From 10:48 until the final stroke at 11:07, the bass drum appears only on the left-hand side of the stereo field.

While the reappearance of the bass drum parts at the end can be understood as a recapitulation, the fact that the left-hand side is emphasized near the end (in contrast to the emphasis on the right side at the opening of the piece) creates a "similar-yet-different" experience. Despite the textural/timbral similarities between the work's beginning and ending, these are not the same "places." Instead, the slow and deliberate motion from the right side at the beginning to the left side at the close of the work realizes the concept of "becoming" articulated by Deren in the recording that opens Zorn's *In the Very Eye of Night*. While this "becoming" necessarily takes place in and over the time of the entire track, it is a time that appears to fold back onto itself. Sound images heard on *In the Very Eye of Night* gradually and almost imperceptibly metamorphose into one another over time and are, by the end of the work, subtly transformed in terms of their spatial locations. In these respects, Zorn's work is a fitting sonic analogue to the film poetics of Maya Deren.[49]

Untitled (Joseph Cornell)

In his book *Joseph Cornell: Gifts of Desire,* Dickran Tashjian succinctly describes the many paradoxes and seemingly irreconcilable contradictions associated with the life and works of the American artist/sculptor/filmmaker/packrat Joseph Cornell. Cornell, Tashjian writes, "was anomalous in many ways: middle-class in his daily life yet intensely interested in New York's avant-garde; without college education and self-taught as an artist yet formidably knowledgeable about film, dance, music, and literature."[50] In many ways, Tashjian's description of Cornell applies to Zorn and his diverse interests and background. Adding to these resemblances is the fact that Zorn's childhood home in Queens was very close to Cornell's studio/home at 3708 Utopia Parkway. Always fascinated by the innocence and purity of childhood as well as perhaps the irrational (or "pre-rational") thought processes of children, Cornell would often have parties for children at his house. Cornell even held exhibitions of his work in rather unlikely places, including the Children's Room of the New York Public Library.[51] Growing up, Zorn did have personal contact with Cornell, explaining to me how he "used to see him in the neighborhood" and the two would share "egg creams at Manny's candy store."[52] In retrospect, given the close, personal connections between the two, it seems that Cornell's position as a "major influence" on Zorn's poetics was unavoidable.

Cornell's art—whether we consider his collages, boxes, or films—routinely involves the manipulation of found objects and their reorganization into a context that can sometimes seem baffling for anyone hoping to find some sort of implied meaning. The found objects can include items as disparate as newspaper clippings, film stills, small decorated boxes, seashells, glass pipes for blowing soap bubbles, marbles, costume jewelry, pieces of wire or wood, statuettes, cordial glasses, and innumerable other objects. His *Untitled* (c. 1956–58), for example, is a box construction with a map of the stars attached to the back wall with three pieces of wood suspended from the top edge of the box (see figure 3.3). Flanking the interior of the box are two cordial glasses (each containing a blue marble) surrounding a piece of driftwood that is decorated with map tacks and a flag that resembles some sort of putting green on the moon. A long drawer is hidden below the box. On the base of this drawer is another celestial map, covered with sand, seashells, and small silver ball-bearings. Except for the map, none of the items in the drawer are securely fixed to the bottom. If you tilt the box with the drawer open, the items float across the fixed night sky, resembling stars and other celestial bodies in motion. What is most remarkable is the work's dimensions: the entire box construction is just over twelve inches tall, seventeen inches wide, and less than four inches deep. The entire infinite universe—as conceived by Cornell—can be held in your hands.

Of course, the importance of collage and the manipulative potential of found objects have long been recognized as two of the major conceptual innovations of twentieth-century art. In this regard, it is important to mention that Cornell's earliest artistic influences can be traced to surrealism, especially the works of Max Ernst (recognizable in Cornell's early collages) and Duchamp (compare Cornell's "penny arcades" and other box constructions with Duchamp's *Box in a Valise*).[53] Even though he greatly admired the works of a few surrealist artists, Cornell often expressed his misgivings about certain tenets of the movement, particularly what he perceived as an overt emphasis on sex and sexuality and perhaps the misogynist tendencies he perceived in many of their works.[54]

While Cornell may be considered a latecomer, even an unwilling participant, to surrealism, it is also possible to understand him as a forerunner to postmodernism. Lynda Roscoe Hartigan, for example, has commented on how "Cornell's elastic interpretation of found materials and quotation set the stage

Figure 3.3. Joseph Cornell, *Untitled* (c. 1956–58). *Art* © *The Joseph and Robert Cornell Memorial Foundation/licensed by VAGA, New York, N.Y.*

for the postmodern concept of appropriation."[55] As Richard Vine reminds us, the appropriation of found objects or materials in postmodernist practices typically function as

> a commentary not on the relation between past and present (since the distinctness of the past is largely ignored) or between the worldly and the divine, but an all-in-the-present sport played with signifiers. The very purpose of the game [i.e., the postmodern moment] is now to show that all vehicles of verbal or visual language (including those supposedly freighted objects and images that once enraptured Cornell) are actually neutral, devoid of inherent qualities, since they acquire their meaning only relationally.[56]

The rejection of both history and meaning in certain strains of postmodernist thought would not have appealed to Cornell at all. It is certainly the case that Cornell's works often incorporate elements whose historical associations and implications are great. What emerges in his works, however, is not some sort of ironic distance generally associated with postmodernism and its treatment of history. Instead, as Diane Waldman explains, "Cornell, preoccupied with the past, brings it into the present by formal means. In referring back to the past—

whether using a Pinturicchio portrait, rare old books or weathered driftwood, dime store trinkets or recent issues of *Scientific American*—Cornell orients all of his objects, old or new, toward history—a dream history."[57]

As for postmodernism's dissolution of meaning, Cornell might have granted the difficulty in discovering an object's singular meaning, but this was only because the object—any object—is inextricably linked to any number of other objects in a vast network of symbolization. The appearance of disparate and seemingly unrelated objects in his art should not be understood as a collection of random, empty signifiers but as elements within a potentially infinite network of relations designed to reveal some sort of transcendental meaning or significance, a sense of meaning that Cornell had difficulty capturing and articulating in his works. Lindsay Blair has written how Cornell constantly "struggled to communicate his wishes" in his works and that this difficulty in communicating "lay in the very nature of what he wanted to speak about—visions, revelations, moments of inspiration, the 'rarified and spiritual,' the 'sense' of things . . . , the metaphysical aspect ('the metaphysical aspect of this expectancy,' the 'something that might have happened')."[58] Cornell's abiding faith in history and his spiritual metaphysics of meaning would surely make any card-carrying postmodernist cringe.

Cornell's poetics of art derives from his nearly lifelong adherence to the principles and beliefs of Christian Science. For Sandra Leonard Starr, Cornell's art is inseparable from the Christian Science doctrine that "physical matter is a delusion of mortal perception and that true substance is reflected only in spirit and cannot be perceived in matter." Given this close dependency between his works and his faith, Starr understands Cornell's artistic output as "striving to eliminate art as material object and our perception of it as such, by gradually replacing it with 'The substance of things hoped for, the evidence of things not seen.'"[59] In his constructions, individual objects do not necessarily represent themselves as they appear to us in the real world but as the appearance of their associated essences. This corresponds to Cornell's idea that his objects were not simply objects per se but what he called "metaphysical ephemera." As Richard Vine has noted in his examination of the close relations between Cornell's work and Christian Science beliefs, to make sense of Cornell's objects and their place(s) within specific artworks, we must "study [their] oblique relations, [their] contraries" for the "fundamental nature of being is best conveyed by what is least substantive and least permanent."[60] Elsewhere, Dina Waldman explains how:

> By wrenching things from their naturalistic form and forging them together with anomalous surroundings, by stripping away conventional associations and a conventional perspective on things Cornell made nature come to life and instilled in

it a new energy. In borrowing things from apparently dissimilar worlds a charge is created, the meeting of opposites becomes the source for a new chemistry. Cornell subjugated natural elements to his own code of classification.[61]

When discussing his own works, Cornell often stressed the associative potentialities of disparate elements. Such associative potentialities arise not only from the objects and their place within a larger work but also from the viewer/ spectator who attempts to "make sense" of the disparate elements and features that constitute the primary materials of Cornell's works as a whole. For Sandra Leonard Starr, Cornell's art "begins with the finite reality of the object, proves the unreality of it and our seeing it as such, and arrives at a statement of aesthetic experience, as a manifestation of spirit."[62] For the viewer, therefore, an emergent unity or "mysterious congruity" is gradually formed through a sort of "association through synchronicity."[63] Cornell's sense of unity is not causal or developmental but associative; the task of his art, therefore, is to recognize and try to make as clear as possible the many associations he perceived in everyday objects, not only in their relation(s) to items around them (temporally, spatially, and/or functionally) but also to their relation(s) to the past.[64]

Such far-reaching associations, combined with Cornell's abiding faith in a metaphysical unity, have helped to create the image of Cornell as some sort of modern alchemist. "All I want to perform," Cornell once remarked to gallery owner Julien Levy, "is white magic."[65] According to Blair, Cornell's attempts at "white magic" are most apparent in his box constructions:

> He tried to imbue that which is concrete with magical properties. There is an extreme realization, in physical terms of objects, and then by association he made his objects resonate with a spiritual electricity. The process involved drawing from physical things their energy, turning an idea (mental energy) into a physical thing (an object), and then trying to make that object "live" again so that it would transmit its energy in its relation to other objects.[66]

The alchemical features of Cornell's work derive from his attempt to construct a sort of grand unity out of everyday experiences. This could be achieved, he believed, by stripping away the apparent reality of everyday objects to reveal their inner essence(s). Whereas Deren manipulated real objects in the hope of creating a new reality in her films, Cornell dispensed with the idea of an external reality altogether (a belief directly related to his Christian Science views). In relation to Cornell's films, P. Adams Sitney has remarked how "all of Cornell's work speaks of the aesthetic mediation of experience. To encounter anything in its fullness was to come into nearly tangible contact with its absolute absence, its unrecoverable pastness, its evanescence."[67]

If the Surrealists practiced free association to uncover the repressed schemata of the mind, Cornell utilized some of the same principles of association to emphasize the false corporeality of images and to help substance become nothingness in order to make the reflection of "the central light of being" the focus of his art.[68]

For the viewer, Cornell's artworks offer a momentary glimpse into the "Grand Design of Being" often associated with Christian Science metaphysics, a design in which his artworks participate.

Complex and nearly imperceptible associations emerge in the work of Joseph Cornell through his alchemical combinations and juxtapositions of seemingly random materials and references. For Cornell, such relations point to the false corporeality of everyday objects and reveal the associative unity that binds together all essences. Cornell's artistic practices and poetics serve as a guide for how we can view Zorn's *Untitled* for solo cello, a work dedicated to Cornell. For Zorn, I believe, *Untitled* functions as a sort of "countergift" that "continues the spiral" according to the principles (and in the interests of) the gift, influence, and tradition outlined above. Before turning to Zorn's work, however, I will briefly consider features of one of Cornell's constructions that, I believe, will provide us with certain correspondences and resonances between Zorn's *Untitled* and its relations to Cornell's artistic practices and visions.

Cornell's *Untitled* ("Dovecote" American Gothic, ca. 1954–56, shown in figure 3.4) consists of thirty boxes (or "birdhouses"), some of which contain balls that are painted white that are free to roll around. Some, but not all, of these "rooms" include arches. But, like the placement of balls, there is no easily recognizable or discernible pattern or reasoning behind which boxes contain or do not contain arches or balls. Each box, however, contains a circular, unpainted form on the back wall, perhaps symbolizing former placements of the accompanying balls or the "shadow or memory of occupants past or present."[69] Lacking some sort of equation or symbolic meaning for this arrangement, the viewer constructs relationships from a variety of perspectives: symmetries, ordering of the balls, vertical and/or horizontal similarities, etc.[70] As I hope to show, Zorn's *Untitled* resembles Cornell's work in that it invites a close, analytical reading where we might expect to uncover some sort of hidden logic or patterning. As with Cornell's construction, there is no discernible large-scale patterning or system that governs the types of relations that are perceivable amongst the musical materials that form Zorn's *Untitled*. Instead, momentary and localized mini-systems or patterns participate within a larger form where we recognize similarities, associations, and resonant relationships between musical gestures and shapes.

Zorn characterizes *Untitled* as "Nostalgia, romance, and a touch of surrealism [filtered] through a set of very private obsessions."[71] The work is in two parts with a short coda, yet as we listen to the work, we do not necessarily perceive these formal divisions. The music flows seamlessly from one section to the

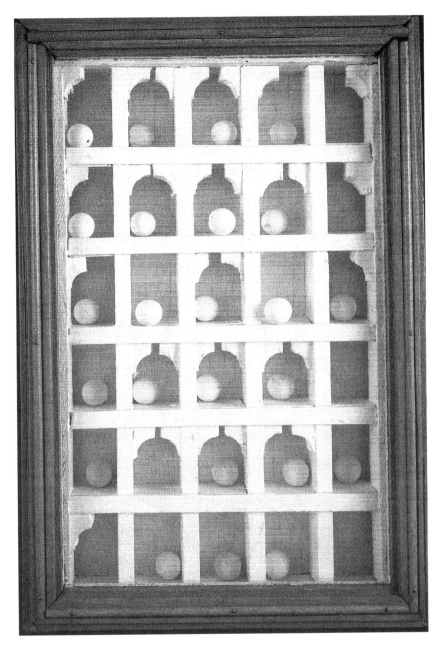

Figure 3.4. Joseph Cornell, *Untitled* ("Dovecote" American Gothic, c. 1954–56). *Art © The Joseph and Robert Cornell Memorial Foundation/licensed by VAGA, New York, N.Y.*

next without any remarkable changes in texture, musical material, or dynamic variation that might possibly assist in identifying the formal boundaries. Even the fermatas in the score that mark the ends of Parts 1 and 2 lack any strong formal delineating functions, perhaps due to the abundant use of silences and fermatas throughout much of the work. At the same time, a sense of formal continuity or seamlessness is achieved by a somewhat limited set of recurring musical ideas—chords, rhythmic or melodic gestures—that are heard throughout the work as a whole. The two-part background takes a backseat to the gradual unfolding and reworking of musical ideas and connections that emerge on the musical surface.[72]

Occupying only six score pages, the tempo and pacing of *Untitled* proceeds very methodically with the work lasting around sixteen minutes. Although numerous repetitions of a small number of musical ideas (both exact and varied) give the work an almost static quality, Zorn gives the listener ample opportunity for absorbing, remembering, and recognizing the various combinations and transformations undergone by these ideas. Consider the opening of the work. As shown on the first system of example 3.1a, *Untitled* begins with a minor/major seventh chord on D that moves to an E minor triad before returning to the original sonority, a progression that is repeated two times and that strongly suggests D as a referential pitch center. This focus on D as a pitch center can also be perceived at other points within the work (example 3.1b). At the same time, the opening minor/major seventh sonority reappears (with variations and on other pitch centers) at other places within the work. Table 3.1 identifies other occurrences of this sonority.[73]

The many varied or exact repetitions of this sonority enables the listener to make some sense of this long work while, at the same time, revel in the slightly changing and emergent quality of its constituent ideas. In no traditional sense of the word can this be piece be described as "developmental"; instead, the various combinations of recognizable gestures, harmonies, textures, and timbres work together to create an emergent work, one whose possibilities may or may

Example 3.1a. Opening two systems (0:00–0:34) (*Untitled*).

Page 3, Systems 7-8 (5:06-5:36)

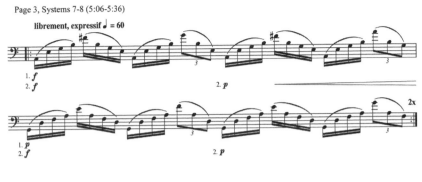

Page 4, System 7 (8:12-9:03)

Example 3.1b. Later passages implying D as a tonal center.

not be fulfilled within the temporal frame of the composition. This same quality has been recognized in Cornell's own works, where "repetition and variation stage the culminating duality [of the work]" and where "the dynamic tension of an open-ended scenario of possibilities . . . [conjures] a harmonious ensemble of form, effect, and idea."[74]

The tonal implications present in the opening system becomes less clear in the second system (also shown in example 3.1a). Here, a pentachord composed of the pitches D-F♯-G-G♯-A retains certain elements of the opening sonority (notably the pitches D and A shifted up an octave) while "confounding" the issue with a chromatic tetrachord (F♯-G-G♯-A). This "confounding sonority" (at this original pitch level) returns at the end of the fourth system on page 4

Table 3.1. Other instances of the minor/major seventh sonority

Page 3, beginning of the fourth system (on D)—3:05
Page 4, end of the first system (on D)—7:08
Page 4, beginning of the eighth system (on E♭)—9:41
Page 5, first two systems (arpeggiations in "4/2" position on C♯, D, D♯, E, F, F♯)—9:49–9:57
Page 6, end of the fourth system (on D—return of opening)—12:04
Page 6, end of seventh system (on E)—13:03
Page 7, end of second system (on G)—13:41

(7:48–7:52) and at the beginning of the second system on page 6 (11:32–11:36). Modified forms of the confounding sonority also appear over the course of the entire work; see, for example, the middle of seventh system on page 5 where the upper voice G♯ is replaced by F♯ (10:55–10:59).

The sonorities in the opening two systems give way to a group of quintuplet figures beginning in the third system. This passage exhibits a number of interesting pitch and intervallic properties as shown in example 3.2. First, a portion of this passage forms a pitch class palindrome around the low B♭ sounded as part of the second quintuplet figure. This palindrome breaks off with the D5, the third sixteenth-note of the third quintuplet grouping. Second, the intervallic makeup of this brief palindromic gesture is rather limited where overlapping trichords are members of either (012) and (016) set classes, shown below the score example.[75] These trichordal segments can be understood as being related to intervallic properties heard in the "confounding" chord in the second system: particularly, the chromatic trichord associated with the chromatic tetrachord and the (016) trichord related to the sustained tritone (D-G♯). As seen in example 3.3, ordered pitch class segments derived from these quintuplet gestures recur at various points in the work: the section marked *agité* at the end of the first system on page 3 (where this retrograded segment is rudely interrupted by a *sforzando* chromatic tetrachord that is possibly related to the "confounding sonority") and the beginning of the fifth system on page 4 (a segment that is also interrupted, now by an augmented fifth (C-G♯).[76]

Referring back to example 3.2, we see that the final note of the quintuplet passage (E♭), when combined with the grace note F♯ and sustained G form a (014) trichord. Admittedly, this collection is probably very difficult to hear, not only in its immediate context but also in relation to all of the music that has come before it. If we do recognize it as a familiar sonority, we might relate it to the opening minor/major seventh sonority (0148). It is this very sound that Zorn latches onto in the music that immediately follows the quintuplet figures (see example 3.4). Here, the entire (012456) segment is divided evenly

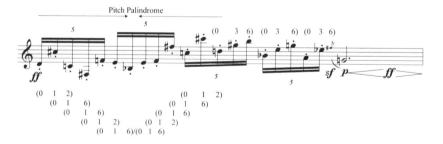

Example 3.2. Quintuplet figures, page 2, beginning of system 3 (0:35–0:38).

Page 3, end of 1st system (2:23)

Page 4, beginning of 5th system (7:52)

Example 3.3. Varied/repeated occurrences of pitch class material from quintuplet figures (compare with example 3.2).

into two three-note segments, both of which project a (014) trichord. Zorn repeats this figure thirteen times as if reinforcing this sound in our ears and, as if thirteen times weren't enough, a transposed version (at the tritone) appears shortly thereafter in a passage marked *sous un charme* (also shown in example 3.4). Emphasizing this moment, this passage is repeated for thirty seconds with gradual crescendos and decrescendos.

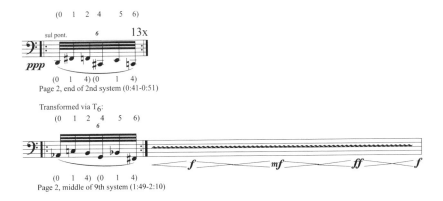

Example 3.4. Intervallic content of transformed sextuplet gestures.

Toward the close of the first part, repeated five-note figures act almost like a varied reminiscence of these sextuplet figures. The sextuplet's (012456) structure is contracted to a (01245) collection in the section marked *égal* (example 3.5). The 3+2 division of these five-note gestures allows us to relate this figure to sounds associated with the sextuplets; for example, the opening three-note idea is (014), the primary trichordal collection exploited in (012456) earlier as discussed in relation to example 3.4. The final dyad forms a (04) pair. In the section marked *innocent* that follows (also shown in example 3.5), the five-note idea returns (arranged, again, as 3+2) where the (04) dyad is retained at the end but where the opening trichord is replaced by a (036) collection. Clearly, this last idea is derived from the tail end of the quintuplet figure on the opening page of the score (refer back to example 3.2). Again, both of these short passages are repeated a number of times as if Zorn wants us to recognize and ruminate upon these emerging interrelationships.

The beginning of Part 2 continues to explore various combinations of many of the recurring sounds presented in Part 1. As shown in example 3.6, five-note figures reappear, but instead of five equal sixteenth notes, the cello plays three quarter-note triplets followed by two half-notes, retaining the prominent 3+2 organization of the *égal* and *innocent* moments described in relation to example 3.5. At the same time, the overall sound of the collection is new: (01368). While this collection clearly contains the distinctive (036) heard in the *innocent* section and the end of the quintuplet gestures from page 2, our ear is not drawn to this "diminished" sound because it appears over the 3+2 division (where the pitches

Page 3, beginning of 6th system (4:20-4:50)

Page 3, end of 6th system (4:53-5:04)

Example 3.5. Five-note figures appearing at the close of Part 1.

Page 4, beginning of 1st system (6:32-7:09)

Example 3.6. Opening of Part 2.

G-C♯-B♭ would have to be heard across the registral and rhythmic designs of this five-note figure). However, the opening three-note segment is familiar (016) as first emphasized in the quintuplet gestures on page 2. Again, Zorn retains one element while altering another by closing this idea not with a (04) dyad but a falling perfect fourth. The music that opens Part 2 of *Untitled* repeats (either literally or in some sort of varied form) elements previously heard while drawing our attention to new(er) ideas giving rise to more and more connections.

Six-note gestures similar to those shown in example 3.4 reappear on page 5 (sixth system) where a 4+2 organization is indicated by the articulation markings (see example 3.7). The entire collection (012567) includes a (04) dyad at the end (like the *égal* and *innocent* sections on page 3) along with a (0157) tetrachord.[77] For registral/gestural reasons, the six-note idea can also be parsed 3+3, resulting in a (016)+(014) arrangement (shown in example 3.7). Here we have, for the first time, the motivically prominent (016) and (014) trichords grouped together as part of a recurring gesture. Zorn drives this point home in the last system of page 5 (example 3.8a). Here, the sustained G from the preceding C minor triad becomes the opening pitch of a short melodic fragment. This segment—extending from the held G to the C♯ forms a (012367) hexachord where the discrete trichords are arranged (016) and (014). A more subtle connection emerges if we focus on only a portion of this segment, specifically the opening

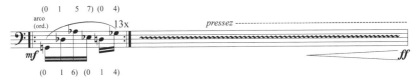

Page 5, 6th system (10:32-10:46)

Example 3.7. Reappearance of six-note gesture (compare with example 3.4).

Page 5, 7th and 8th systems (10:54-11:17)

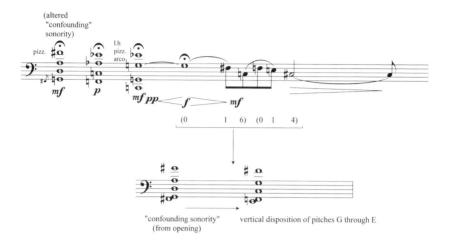

Example 3.8a. *Brutal* section followed by long melodic gesture.

G through the E♮ (disregarding the final C♯) that forms a version of the original "confounding" sonority, arpeggiated and transposed down a second.

The passage just discussed is recalled on the following page where another long note G initiates a melodic line (example 3.8b). The passage (marked *au coeur brisé*) also resembles the string of quintuplets heard near the opening of the work in that the passage is symmetrically formed around B♭. This connection is further strengthened by the fact that the point at which the rhythms begin to be retrograded is accompanied by the pitches F, E, and B♭, the same unordered pitch segment that marks the pitch palindrome in the third system of page 1 (refer back to example 3.2). Rhythmically, the passage shown in example 3.8b is also retrogradable around a B♭. In terms of the pitches, however, what might appear to be either an inversion or a retrograde inversion around B♭ is inexact. In addition, what appears to be a transposition (beginning with the E-E♭-B fragment) disintegrates as the melodic line continues downwards to the G♮. Although the two halves of the rhythmic palindrome shown in example 3.8b lack nice and tidy pitch correspondences, we most certainly hear this passage as some sort of varied "reminiscence" of the melodic gesture shown in example 3.8a.

Near the end of the second part, the opening chordal figures are recalled (example 3.9). A series of perfect fifths leads to a chord that recalls the mysterious (0157) collection described earlier in relation to example 3.7 and that is followed by a pizzicato (0156) tetrachord; this chordal passage finally comes to rest on a transposed version of the opening minor/major seventh sonority. The

Page 5, 7th and 8th systems (10:54-11:17)

Page 6, 6th system (12:27-12:51)

Rhythms Retrograded

Example 3.8b. Comparison of *brutal* melodic passage and a varied "reminiscence."

(0156) collection, a relatively new sonority, is immediately elaborated upon in the *fluide* section.

The coda that follows functions as a summation, or distillation, of many of the primary (and not-so-primary) gestures/motives discussed up to this point (example 3.10a). The coda begins with a solitary pizzicato (016) trichord repeated four times (*isolé*) followed by a long tremolo on the low F (*séloignant*). Of course, we have become very familiar with this particular collection over the course of the work, particularly the quintuplet gestures from Part 1 and the material that introduces Part 2. Next, a series of harmonics played glissando is followed by a low pizzicato fifth, E♭-B♭. This passage is reminiscent of a gesture from page 4 where a series of harmonics lead to a long note perfect fourth

Page 7, 2nd and 3rd systems (13:24-14:23)

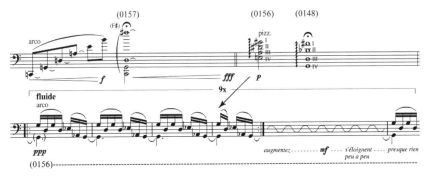

Example 3.9. Varied return of opening chords (on G).

Page 7, 4th-6th systems (14:27-15:12)

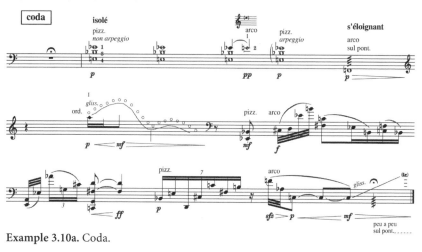

Example 3.10a. Coda.

(also E♭-B♭) played vibrato and marked *tendre* (example 3.10b). The following arco passage in the coda shares a number of contour relations with gestures first heard in the *vite* section of Part 2 (example 3.10c). Next, the (0157) tetrachord heard at the end of the second section reappears at the same pitch level along with the sustained F♯-D dyad. A pizzicato septuplet is clearly derived—in terms of its pitch material—from the quintuplet passage near the opening of the work (refer back to example 3.2). Finally, the work ends with a long glissando from C3 up to the high C♯, marked "peu a peu sul point" with a decrescendo. This clearly resembles the end of Part 1, where the final sound is the high C♯ harmonic played *pp* (example 3.10d). As the work drifts away, we can imagine the ascent continuing upward even after the cello has faded.

The coda can be understood as a summation of *Untitled* but not, I would stress, a synthesis; the coda is not characterized by some sort of grand Beetho-

Page 5, 4th system (10:05-10:11)

Example 3.10b. Passage from Part 2; compare with harmonic glissando passage from coda.

Page 4, 8th system (9:41-9:49)

Example 3.10c. *Vite* section; compare contours with arco passage from coda.

Page 3, end of 10th system (6:09-6:28)

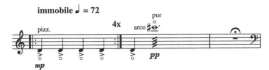

Example 3.10d. Conclusion of Part 1;
compare with conclusion of work.

venian *pronunciomento* where certain ideas left hanging in the body of the work
are resolved. Instead, ideas from the body of the work are restated, modified,
evoked, or suggested. Even with all of the connections discussed in my analysis,
there is no grand narrative that ties all of these gestures together. There are definitely similarities, recollections, and reminiscences, but no "key" to the work.
In lieu of any grand synthesis, *Untitled* just fades away, leaving us to make sense
of all of the connections presented to us by the work. This sense of "ungraspa-
bility" is dramatically portrayed at the work's conclusion as the cello disappears
upward. This sense of "fading from sight" is remarkably similar to Cornell's
"gift" for Emily Dickinson, his "Toward the Blue Peninsula (for Emily Dickinson)," reproduced in figure 3.5. Here, the gridlike work of the cage represents a
rational Cartesian coordinate system where objects can be plotted, related, and
contained. This grid, however, has been burst apart, opening up into a beautiful blue "beyond." As Walter Hopps has noted, the "cage both confines and
releases: the wire grid opens to allow us to enter from the front, experience our
earthly boundaries, then escape through the window in the back of the box to
a limitless world beyond."[78] The end of Zorn's *Untitled* mimics this release from
reason, relations, and connections, leaving the listener to draw his or her own
conclusions from the work. At the same time, the ending of the work seems to
poke fun at the "rationalistic" analysis pursued above as all of the sets and numbers ultimately give way to something that cannot be assimilated. The disap-

Figure 3.5. Joseph Cornell, *Toward the Blue Peninsula (for Emily Dickinson)* (c. 1953). *Art © The Joseph and Robert Cornell Memorial Foundation/licensed by VAGA, New York, N.Y.*

pearing ascent of the cello at the end of *Untitled* carries both the listener and the analyst *beyond* the perceived frame that we wrongly imagine confines a closed work.[79]

* * *

The compositions examined in this chapter represent, in one form or another and to varying degrees, musical responses by Zorn to the work and thought of individual artists. It has surely not gone unnoticed that this discussion makes no mention of Zorn's conception of the gift, gift giving, and tradition in relation to other musicians, especially composers. This is not to say, of course, that composers or musicians are ignored or are not granted the same type of treatment afforded to individuals such as Maya Deren or Joseph Cornell. In fact, compositions that explicitly or implicitly draw upon works by other composers—be they tributes, or memorials, or simply musical quotations—often evince a much more involved and developed sense of appropriation and integration of materials than those works dedicated to nonmusicians. In the next chapter, I consider Zorn's large-scale work *Aporias* and the various ways he integrates and modifies aspects of an earlier composition, in this case, Igor Stravinsky's *Requiem Canticles*. As I hope to make clear, those compositions that are either based on or derived from the works of other composers can and should be understood according to the perspective of the gift system outlined in the present chapter and, specifically, Zorn's continuing efforts to situate himself within a particular artistic tradition.

FOUR

Continuing the Spiral: *Aporias* and the Prisms of Tradition

> Divine or poetic apprehension is on the same level as the empty
> apparitions of the saints, in that we can, through it, still
> appropriate to ourselves that which exceeds us, and,
> without grasping it as our own possession, at least
> link it to us, to that which had touched us. In this
> way we do not die entirely: a thread—no doubt
> tenuous—but a thread links the apprehended
> to me.
> —Georges Bataille, *Inner Experience*

In much of Zorn's concert music from the late 1980s, barely concealed musical quotations alert the listener to a particular musical source and its function as a tribute or homage. In *Cat O' Nine Tails,* for example, the collage blocks that form such an integral part of the work's design consist of quotations drawn from the tradition of what Zorn has described as "the great string quartet composers" and include quotes from Carter, Xenakis, Schoenberg, and Berg.[1] A similar approach to the use of preexisting musical materials can be heard in works such as *Carny, Angelus Novus,* and *Forbidden Fruit.*

In more recent works such as *Elegy* (a piece that draws much of its pitch material from Boulez's *Le marteau sans maître*) and *Walpurgisnacht* (based on Webern's String Trio op. 20), direct or even slightly disguised quotations give way to a method of composition where works by other composers are integrated into the overall fabric of Zorn's own compositions. With his more recent practices, the referential piece is subsumed and manipulated in the interest of the piece at hand. In other words, a variety of musical features—melodic lines, chords, rhythms, etc.—are used as source material whose compositional end is to serve and satisfy the individual logic, unity, and coherence of Zorn's *own* work. With these works, the listener may not even recognize any surface similarities between the "original" work and Zorn's own composition, as the two are seamlessly blended together.

This distinction may not be as neat as I make it out to be. Even in his earlier collage or pastiche compositions, it is clear that Zorn is not interested in a "name that tune" game of listening (or, for that matter, analysis). Instead, the close musical and/or extramusical interconnections between earlier works and their new context function in a sort of give-and-take fashion. That is, the newly composed work—Zorn's "own" piece of music—is designed to stand on its own and any quotations or references that are included contribute to the structure of the "new whole." As Tom Service perceptibly notes, in many of Zorn's works we are confronted with the seemingly paradoxical predicament whereby "the reference has lost its allusive power and has become [something] to be manipulated by Zorn; or, in other words, the referential has become material." Even in the solo piano piece *Carny,* a work that seems to wear its postmodern/collage credentials on its sleeve, Service recognizes how Zorn—by reworking a chord from Stockhausen's *Klavierstück IX*—is able to "manipulate a continuum of referentiality" and where the "changes wrought to Stockhausen's chord reveal that the 'referential' is always part of *Carny*'s 'material'—and vice versa. This doubleness stands as a metaphor for the parallel universes inhabited by the whole piece. The materials of *Carny* simultaneously belong to the piece and to the outside world. Zorn's critical relationship with all of the different musics in the piece is responsible for this rich but perilous situation. . . . *Carny* might be said to reimagine autonomy by its insistence on world and work, reference and originality, interpretative openness and notational fixity. These complex negotiations account for the piece's situation between the total fragmentation of the postmodern text and the ideological confines of the musical work."[2]

Developing Service's suggestive insights, I believe it is possible to conceive of these processes of assimilation and manipulation from the perspectives of the gift and gift giving. The ways in which many of Zorn's works absorb and then subsequently present preexisting musical material positions these works in the type of gift-giving spiral described in the previous chapter. Understood this way, an earlier work—the "gift received"—is assimilated into Zorn's own music, which is then transformed into a gift that must be "given away." This spiraling process of receiving and giving—a process that enables Zorn to participate in a particular historical continuum or tradition—creates an intimate relationship between Zorn and his model(s).

In this chapter, I will examine two movements from Zorn's *Aporias: Requia for Piano and Orchestra,* a work that draws on and develops a variety of musical ideas, features, and characteristics originally presented in Igor Stravinsky's *Requiem Canticles*. I hope that my analytical comments on the "Misterioso" and "Drammatico" movements will satisfy multiple ends. First, the myriad ways Zorn manipulates and reconfigures another composer's musical materials and ideas has not been examined in the few analytical essays that address his music. At the same time, my analyses will incorporate and interpret certain features and ideas included with Zorn's working, or reference, materials for this work and how they eventually found their way into the finished composition. These materials provide not only a number of interesting insights into *Aporias* but also aspects of Zorn's compositional and precompositional practices or tendencies. Finally, Zorn's reliance on Stravinsky's source work expands on the notion of a composition as a gift, an idea that plays out on multiple levels in *Aporias*. In this respect, the following analytical comments serve to refine many of the theoretical ideas developed in chapter 3.

Formal and Topical Correspondences

In a short essay that appears in Ann McCutchan's book *The Muse That Sings*, Zorn provides us with what is perhaps his most detailed description of how (and why) he integrates works by other composers into his own "classical" compositions:

> One of the things that I do to give each classical piece structural integrity is use another composer's work from which to derive pitch information. With [Aporias], I used the Requiem Canticles by Stravinsky. I mirrored the basic structure (several movements with a prelude and postlude) in a certain way, and then I took certain phrases or chords and wrote out the pitches, just in letters. Sometimes it would be as many as twenty-five pitches, all the pitches in one large chord. I'd write them out and create melodies out of them. Or I'd take a melody and create a chord out of it. Or I'd copy out an actual viola part and compose other parts on top of it. Using someone else's work as source material gives a piece a kind of unity. Everything's coming from one place.[3]

Table 4.1 offers a formal comparison between these two works. Except for the concluding Coda that appears in *Aporias*, the formal design of the two works are identical. Since the Coda blends seamlessly into the preceding Postlude, this single formal dissimilarity is not evident when listening to the work in performance.

In addition to the formal correspondences between Zorn's work and Stravinsky's *Requiem Canticles*, *Aporias* reveals a deeper design constructed from a conglomeration of mini-memorials (what Zorn describes as "tributes" or "requia") to those who have, in complex and subtle ways, influenced his own

Table 4.1. Formal comparison of *Requiem Canticles* and *Aporias*

Stravinsky, *Requiem Canticles*	Zorn, *Aporias*
I. Prelude	I. Prelude (Ebollimento)
II. Exaudi	II. Impetuoso (John Cassavetes)
III. Dies Irae	III. Con Mistero/Misterioso (Francis Bacon)
IV. Tuba Mirum	IV. Languendo (Elias Canetti)
V. Interlude	V. Risentito (Camarón de la Isla)
VI. Rex Tremendae	VI. Freddamente (John Cage)
VII. Lacrimosa	VII. Religioso (Olivier Messiaen)
VIII. Libera Me	VIII. Drammatico (Marlene Dietrich)
IX. Postlude	IX. Postlude (Flebile)
	X. Coda (Cantando)

compositional thought.[4] Most of the interior movements of *Aporias* (Movements II–VIII) are dedicated to individuals who died around the time the work was being written (also shown in table 4.1). The painter Francis Bacon, the composers Olivier Messiaen and John Cage, the musical and film icon Marlene Dietrich, and the Spanish Flamenco singer Camarón de la Isla (José Monge Cruz) all died in 1992 (the year Zorn began the work), and the writer Elias Canetti died in 1994, the year *Aporias* was completed. The death of filmmaker John Cassavetes in 1989 lies outside of the time Zorn spent working on *Aporias* and possibly points to an earlier date of the conception of the work or to another work dedicated to Cassavetes that was eventually absorbed into *Aporias*.

As revealed by his reference materials for this work, Zorn spent a considerable amount of effort in determining the final ordering of these individual movements.[5] Figure 4.1 reproduces a page from Zorn's reference materials. Quite a bit of information is present in this single page; for example, the generic title of "Piano Requia" suggests that this is one of the earliest pages dedicated to the work that would become *Aporias* (notice that the provisional title of "Illuminations" is crossed out).[6] In addition, Zorn includes numerous textural, timbral, and orchestral models/associations for each movement: for example, the "Jazz shapes" of "Cassavetes," the "Full Orchestra" indication for the "Interlude," and the reference to the fifth movement of Busoni's Piano Concerto for the Dietrich movement. As can be seen in the lower right-hand side of figure 4.1, the textures and timbres associated with "23 solo strings" of the "Postlude" is conceived in relation to Richard Strauss's *Metamorphosen* as well as Arnold Schoenberg's *Verklärte Nacht* (presumably the string orchestra version of 1917). Finally, the few musical shapes that do appear on this page can be traced to

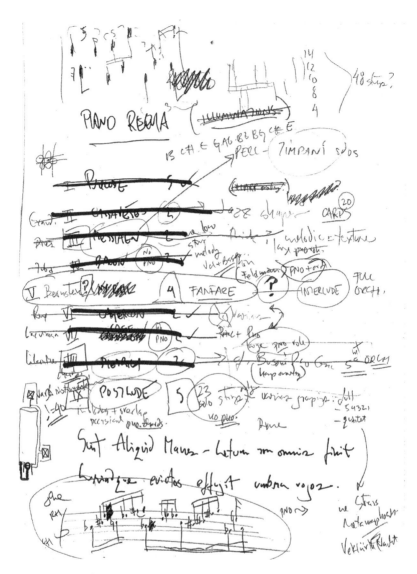

Figure 4.1. Page from Zorn's reference materials for *Aporias*.

various moments in Zorn's completed score. The angular rhythmic idea at the top of the page appears in measure 37 of the "Cassavetes" movement as part of a piano cadenza, while modified forms of the pitch-rhythmic gesture circled at the bottom of the page appears (in the piano) in measure 5 of "Camarón" and measure 26 of "Dietrich" (where the parts are inverted) as well as the celeste figures in measures 18–20 of the "Messiaen" movement.

The ordering of movements that form the center of figure 4.1 also point to a preliminary, or working, conception of the work. At the same time, the information presented here provides a key to the source(s) of pitch relations that exist between Zorn's work and Stravinsky's *Requiem Canticles*. Recalling the ordering of movements in Zorn's completed composition (as shown in table 4.1), figure 4.1 reveals an earlier ordering (visible under Zorn's strikeouts): (1) Prelude, (2) Cassavetes, (3) Messiaen, (4) Bacon, (5) "Interlude," (6) Camarón, (7) Cage, (8) Dietrich, and (9) Postlude. At this early stage, there is no indication of a final coda. Furthermore, Zorn appears to have been undecided about the "Interlude" and to whom it should be dedicated. As seen on this page, Zorn considers the possibility of dedicating this particular movement to either Leonard Bernstein/the New York Philharmonic (Bernstein died in 1990) or Morton Feldman (who died in 1987). Given that the movement would eventually be dedicated to Elias Canetti, it is probable that Zorn did not resolve this issue until sometime close to the completion of the work (according to the score, the work was completed on "Yom Kippur, 1994"). Figure 4.1 also reveals the specific derivations/relations between Zorn's movements and those of Stravinsky's work. As seen here, the names of the individual movements from *Requiem Canticles* appear to the left of Zorn's movements where Zorn's "Prelude" is based on the pitch material of Stravinsky's "Prelude," the "Cassavetes" movement on the "Exaudi," and so on.[7] Table 4.2 represents Zorn's earliest ordering of *Aporias*'s movements and the correlations to Stravinsky's work.

Extending the close interrelationships between these two works, *Aporias*—conceived as a set of mini-memorials—corresponds to a similar topical concep-

Table 4.2. Original ordering of movements in Zorn's *Aporias* with correlations to Stravinsky's *Requiem Canticles*

Stravinsky, *Requiem Canticles*	Zorn, *Aporias* (original ordering—from figure 4.1)
I. Prelude	I. Prelude
II. Exaudi	II. Cassavetes
III. Dies Irae	III. Messiaen
IV. Tuba Mirum	IV. Bacon
V. Interlude	V. "Interlude" (Leonard Bernstein?/ Morton Feldman?)
VI. Rex Tremendae	VI. Camarón
VII. Lacrimosa	VII. Cage
VIII. Libera Me	VIII. Dietrich
IX. Postlude	IX. Postlude

tion of *Requiem Canticles*. Robert Craft has suggested that Stravinsky may have conceived of the individual movements of *Requiem Canticles* as a series of "Requiems" for friends who had passed away. Craft's conjecture derives from the fact that "pasted-in obituaries" of figures close to the composer—including Edgard Varèse, the sculptor Alberto Giacometti, and the novelist Evelyn Waugh—are included with the sketch materials of this work. Craft has described how:

> The sketchbook of the Requiem Canticles is also a necrology of the friends who had died during its composition. The composer once referred to these pasted-in obituaries as a "practical commentary," and, in fact, each movement seems to relate to an individual death. Stravinsky denies that it really does, but the framing of his musical thoughts by the graves of friends . . . exposes an almost unbearably personal view of his mind.[8]

At the same time, Vera Stravinsky has confided how both "[Stravinsky] and *we* knew he was writing [the *Requiem Canticles*] for himself."[9]

Conceptually, Zorn's *Aporias* can also be understood as a sort of "passing away" (although not as dramatic as Stravinsky's conception of his own work). In many respects, *Aporias* marks the end of certain compositional practices common to much of Zorn's concert music from the late 1980s and early 1990s. Works from this earlier period often feature choppy, disjunct musical surfaces, a characteristic typically associated with Zorn's music. At the same time, the quick and manic pace with which musical ideas pass before our ears imparts a frantic quality to this music. As a result, it is very difficult to process, absorb, or investigate individual musical ideas for any length of time as we do our best to simply hang on to the barrage of musical information that these works present.

Beginning around 1992, however, the tone of Zorn's music changed as these hyperactive tendencies gave way to a form of presentation that fosters a listening experience that can best be described as "perspectival." Beginning with the string quartet *Memento Mori,* the chamber work *Elegy,* and *Aporias,* musical ideas are presented to the listener in ways that allow them to be examined from a variety of viewpoints or angles in real time. Instead of the apparent two-dimensionality and left-to-right processing of his earlier works, a certain depth and space opens up before us in many of Zorn's works written at this time. It is interesting, therefore, that the three works from 1992 that signal this "new way" each refer to some sort of passing away: *Memento Mori* (where Zorn puns on a traditional "remembrance of death" by dedicating the work to the multi-instrumentalist and artist Ikue Mori), *Elegy* (dedicated to Jean Genet), and *Aporias: Requia for Piano and Orchestra.*[10]

While Zorn's presentational practices changed dramatically at this time, certain long-standing compositional concerns are still present in these later works. For instance, the block formations and formal designs common to so much of Zorn's music still dominate these more recent works. At the same time, Zorn's interest in incorporating/employing music or musical processes associated with other composers and their works persists in his more recent compositions. Unlike the many types of references that exist close to the musical surface in earlier works, in works composed after 1992, Zorn strives to assimilate these sources in ways that render the original(s) almost unrecognizable. By submerging his sources, the original becomes much more integrated into the fabric of the (newer) whole. The original source, therefore, is understood as being necessary both *to* the formation of and *for* any possible musical developments or extensions unique to the newer work.

In the following analyses of two movements from *Aporias,* I will show how Zorn assimilates certain features of Stravinsky's *Requiem Canticles.* At the same time, by viewing the *Requiem Canticles* as a repository of possibilities, I hope to show how *Aporias* emerges as a self-contained and somewhat independent composition that exists in an almost epiphenomenal relationship to Stravinsky's work. This sense of quasi-independence from the source is, I believe, a result of Zorn's desire to reflect and impart certain aesthetic features or emotional responses associated with the work or image(s) of the individual dedicatees that dictate the formal design of *Aporias. Aporias* can be understood as a sort of musical kaleidoscope where Stravinsky's *Requiem Canticles* is manipulated by Zorn's own musical logic and that is then refracted once again by Zorn and his desire to reflect the nature(s) of his dedicatees.[11] Drawn from a variety of sources and intentions, the peculiar musical continuities that emerge over the course of *Aporias* are the (not necessarily logical) result of all of these compositional concerns.

"Misterioso" (Francis Bacon)/"Tuba Mirum"

The third movement of *Aporias* ("Misterioso") is a short musical memorial to the British painter Francis Bacon.[12] Bacon's worldview (reflected in his paintings) was a combination of his conflicting conceptions of religion (he was an atheist, yet many of his paintings depict "religious" figures or scenes), his violent and extreme lifestyle (a lifelong drinker who was fascinated by homosexual S/M practices), and his nihilistic views on life and existence.[13] As one of the most prominent postwar painters, Bacon's work, much like Zorn's, fits uncomfortably in relation to contemporary artistic practices. He was an "expressionist" thirty years after expressionism's heyday who distrusted abstract art and its inability to reflect the struggles and pains of existence. In many ways, Bacon can be considered a "realist" when realism in art was passé. However, Bacon's version of realism was a bit too real for many viewers who were shocked by his screaming popes, the tortured and horrific figures at the base of a crucifix, or the slabs of

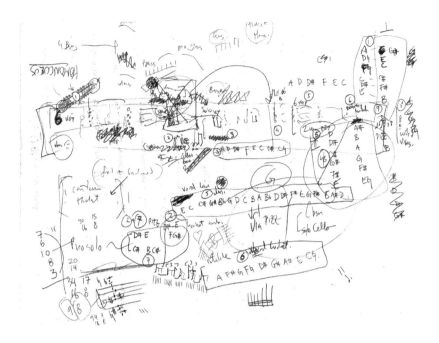

Figure 4.2. Formal outline of "Misterioso" (Francis Bacon) from Zorn's reference materials.

---

meat that enclose many of his figures. In short, Bacon—his work and thought—is analogous to what Zorn has been doing in music for the last thirty years. Bacon's painting practices, particularly his use and assimilation of found materials, correspond to Zorn's own compositional concerns. I will return to these correspondences at the end of this section; for now I will examine how this particular movement derives from and expands on Stravinsky's source material.

Figure 4.2 reproduces a formal outline of this movement from Zorn's reference materials.[14] This page presents an early sequential outline of many of the events, rhythmic gestures and figures, instrumentation and orchestration decisions, and sources of pitch material that would find their way into the completed score. Two systems are present on this page where each system is grouped by a brace on the left-hand side of the page. Zorn's preferred method of composing in and with blocks can easily be seen in this example, as individual moments are notated with encircled arabic numerals. In the analysis that follows, I will parse the surface of "Misterioso" according to the "block" formations present in figure 4.2. At the same time, I will attempt to clarify many of the difficult-to-read annotations on this page by describing how Zorn's blocks are derived from Stravinsky's *Requiem Canticles*.[15]

"Misterioso" is the only movement that includes a small vocal ensemble of six boy sopranos, augmenting the large orchestra and piano textures present in the rest of the work. The voices (who sing wordless vocalises throughout) open the movement with two sustained harmonies. The opening block "1" in figure 4.2 identifies these sustained chords with an indication that they are to be sung by six voices ("6 vox"). Also, in the top right-hand corner, Zorn has realized these opening sonorities and a possible voice-leading strategy connecting them (also identified with an encircled 1). Ultimately, however, Zorn abandons the dispositions of these two harmonies and their voice-leading connections in his completed score (the first page of this movement is reproduced in example 4.1).[16] Zorn does, however, maintain the pitch class content of these two harmonies and where, with a bit of work, it is possible to hear the opening sonority as possessing certain tonal or tonal-centric implications. Here it is possible to hear D as a possible tonal center and where the E♮/E♭ pairing can be understood as the 9th and ♭9th extensions coloring the minor seventh chord, D-F-A-C. With the resolution of the chord in this same measure and the rumbling cello and

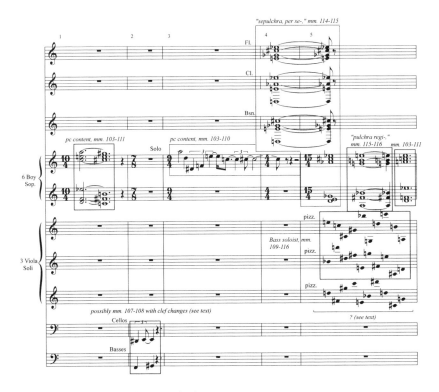

Example 4.1. First page (mm. 1–5) of Francis Bacon movement ("Misterioso," 0:01–0:45, *Aporias*).

bass interjections in measure 2, hearing D as some sort of tonal center becomes more difficult to sustain, particularly with the presence of the C♮/C♯ pairing in the voice parts and the D♯ in the cello.

To better understand the precise pitch derivations from Stravinsky's score in Zorn's block 1, we need to look ahead to block 3. The melodic line sung by the soloist in measure 3 (block 3 in figure 4.2) is derived from the first seven discrete pitch classes heard in the "Tuba Mirum" movement of *Requiem Canticles* (I have reproduced the score to Stravinsky's movement in example 4.2). Beginning with the trumpet's oscillating A-D dyad that opens this movement, the vocal soloist in Zorn's work dips down to grab the D♯ from trumpet 2 and then back up to the E♯ (F♮) of trumpet 1. The three remaining pitches are drawn from the E-C dyad in the first trumpet and first trombone and the opening three pitches sung by the bass soloist (E-C-C♯). It is possible to see how this solo vocal line is derived from the two six-note sonorities that open this movement and their source in the "Tuba Mirum." The first sonority in measure 1 of *Aporias* is formed from the first six pitch classes heard in the "Tuba Mirum": A-D-D♯-E♯ (F)-E-C. The second sonority is derived from the first four pitch classes of the bass solo up to the "-rum" of "mirum" in measures 110–11 (E-C-C♯-G♯)

Example 4.2. Stravinsky, "Tuba Mirum" (*Requiem Canticles*). © Copyright 1967 by Boosey & Hawkes Music Publishers Ltd. Reproduced by permission of Boosey & Hawkes Music Publishers Ltd.

Example 4.2, cont. Stravinsky, "Tuba Mirum" (*Requiem Canticles*). ©
Copyright 1967 by Boosey & Hawkes Music Publishers Ltd. Reproduced
by permission of Boosey & Hawkes Music Publishers Ltd.

and the last three pitch classes played in measure 110 (B-C#-F#). As seen in figure 4.2 (near the middle of the first system), Zorn has extracted and encircled this string of pitch classes from Stravinsky's score and identified them with the numeral 3.

Referring back to figure 4.2 and in particular block 2, it seems that Zorn wrestled with this moment as evidenced by the many cross-outs and scribbles. He eventually decided on a short musical fragment played by pizzicato strings (indicated as cellos and basses—see the markings that accompany the encircled 2 in the first system of Zorn's reference materials). Zorn identifies the pitch material of this short musical idea in the area devoted to the second system on his reference page, just to the left and slightly below the long string of pitch classes in the middle of the page. Here, the D#-E idea heard in the cello corresponds to the ordered pitch classes played by the first trumpet in measure 116 of Stravinsky's score. However, the accompanying F-G# heard in the basses does not appear as an ordered pair in the "Tuba Mirum," at least before measure 116. The melodic figure D#-E-E# (F)-G#, again played by the first trumpet, does appear in measures 119–21; it is possible that the music of measure 2 in the "Misterioso" movement of *Aporias* is the result of Zorn's decision to break up this short melodic fragment and then superimpose the two halves. An alternative method for explaining the derivation of the cello and bass ideas in measure 2 is possible if the pitches of trumpet 1 from measure 107 in Stravinsky's score is read in the bass clef; this would reproduce the pitches sounded in the basses of measure 2 of Zorn's score. The pitches played by the cellos in Zorn's score can perhaps be derived from Stravinsky's score if the C#s in measure 108 are shifted to the bass clef and where the first pitch is notated enharmonically.[17]

Sustained harmonies that recall the opening of the movement return in measures 4 and 5. Block 4 of figure 4.2 corresponds to measure 4 of the score. In his reference materials, Zorn chooses to orchestrate the first sonority with three flutes, clarinets, and bassoons before the return of the six voices in measure 5 (block 5). In these measures, Zorn appears to skip over the pitches Stravinsky uses to set the text fragment "spargens sonum" (measures 112–13) and proceeds directly to the pitch material in measures 114 and 115. The dense chord heard in the woodwinds in measures 4 and 5 of *Aporias* is formed from the pitches used to set "sepulchra, per se-" (D-D#-F#-E) and the C#-G# dyad sounded in the first and second trumpets. In figure 4.2, the pitches associated with the rhythmic shape of block 4 are shown under block 5 (shown by the encircled area marked by a roman numeral II where a "4/5" marking indicates two sets of six-note sonorities). The remaining pitches included in Zorn's woodwind chord are doublings of these pitch classes. The return of the boys' choir in measure 5 begins with the same sonority just sounded by the woodwinds and quickly moves on, picking up where Zorn left off in Stravinsky's score. The second six-note sonority heard in measure 5 (A-F#-Bb-G-B-E) is formed from the melodic fragment that sets the text "-pulchra regi-" in measures 115–16 and the A-B dyad in the trumpets in measure 115. This is the six-note sonority that appears under block 6 in figure 4.2 (A♯-B-A-G-F♯-E from top to bottom). This chord then resolves to the sonority that opened the work (D-F-E♭-A-C-E), a return to the material associated with block 1, a feature not indicated in Zorn's reference material.

A group of arrhythmic pizzicato figures played by three solo violas accompany the chords heard in the vocal parts in measure 5. In Zorn's reference materials, this area appears to have been originally conceived as being scored for two solo violins marked "pizz." Still referring to figure 4.2, Zorn identifies the source of pitch material as 5, but instead of the material associated with block 5 described above, this 5 refers to the string of pitches that begins E-C-C♯, etc. highlighted in the middle of the page and identified by the notes "vocal line" and "vlns." This indication of 5 actually includes the pitches associated with blocks 4 and 5 heard in the woodwinds and vocal parts described above but also includes the E-C pairing associated with the pitches in block 3. In effect, this newer block 5 includes and subsumes pitch materials associated with blocks 3, 4, and the "other" 5. Beginning with the uppermost viola part in measure 5, these pitches duplicate the ordered pitch classes sung by the bass soloist from measure 109 up to the B-A dyad that sets "so-" of "sonum" in measure 113.[18] The second violist picks up where the first left off, beginning with the pitches A♯ (B♭) and D that set "-num Per-" and continue until the end of the vocal phrase in measure 116 (also A♯-D). Although playing at the same time as the first viola, the pitch material heard in the second viola forms a sort of harmonic counterpoint that is derived from a linear melodic gesture in Stravinsky's score. Zorn's appears to have notated the first viola part and then the material associated with the second viola where Stravinsky's source material is "spiraled" from the end of one part to the beginning of the next.[19] These two solo viola parts account for the gap in Zorn's derivations described above (the "absence" of source material from the end of the solo vocal part in measure 3 into the woodwind chords in measures 4 and 5) and are based on the string of pitch classes identified as 5 (albeit the second block 5) in Zorn's reference materials.

For the most, the pitch material of the first page (measures 1–5) of the Francis Bacon movement is derived from Stravinsky's "Tuba Mirum" up to measure 116. However, the source of the material heard in the third solo viola part in measure 5 is unclear. It does not correspond to any ordered pitch class material found at any point in Stravinsky's movement, nor is it clearly derived from any of Stravinsky's vertical sonorities. I have been unable to determine the source of this viola part in any of Zorn's reference materials for this movement or materials devoted to any of the other movements.

Continuing on in Zorn's score, example 4.3 reproduces measures 6 through 10 of "Misterioso." The melodic line that is passed between the six vocal soloists in measures 6 and 7 is drawn from the pitches Stravinsky uses to set the text

Example 4.3. Second page (mm. 6–9) of Francis Bacon movement ("Misterioso," 0:46–1:03, *Aporias*).

"Coget omnes ante thronum" in measures 117–19 where the E♮ sung by the first boy soprano corresponds to the last pitch of the first trumpet in measure 116. This string of pitches is indicated as being associated with block 6 in Zorn's reference materials where it is described as "solo vox hocket" and, near the bottom of the page, simply as "vocal hocket." (The A♯ that Stravinsky uses to set "-te" of "ante" is present in Zorn's reference materials but does not make it into the completed score.)

In measure 8, tutti cellos and basses interject a short musical idea that recalls a similar gesture heard in measure 2. In fact, Zorn groups together both of these blocks—blocks 2 and 7—in his reference materials. In measure 8, the unison melodic idea D♯-E-C♯-B is formed from the trumpet gestures heard in measures 119–20 of Stravinsky's score. The oscillating D♯-E idea played by the first trumpet in measures 116 and following of Stravinsky's score is supported by the second trumpet's C♯. Zorn rearranges these pitches and continues to the

B♮ that temporarily resolves the second trumpet's static C♯. Referring to the reference page in figure 4.2, we can see how Zorn has extracted these pitches from Stravinsky's score (identified as block 7 to the left and slightly below the string of pitches that begins E-C-C♯). Returning to the completed score, the D♯-E fragment is then repeated at the end of measure 8 by some of the basses and is accompanied by a G♯-D figure in the divisi cellos. While we certainly recognize the source of the D♯-E gesture, the G♯-D idea is not entirely clear. These two pitches do not appear successively at any point within Stravinsky's "Tuba Mirum" movement, nor do they correspond to any vertical sonorities in measures 116 and following, the measures that appear to be the primary source for Zorn's pitch material in measures 6 through 9. At the same time, this particular pitch pairing is not part of block 7 as it appears in Zorn's reference materials.

The vibraphone and woodwind harmony in measure 9 corresponds to block 8 in Zorn's reference materials, a block that, in terms of pitch content and registral disposition, is the most consistent musical idea between his reference materials and the completed score (see the dense chord on the staff fragment in the lower left-hand corner of figure 4.2).[20] Zorn derives the pitch material for this harmony from the pitches sung by the bass soloist up to and including the setting of "sonum" in measure 113 and, therefore, the string of pitches indicated as block 5.[21] While some pitch class duplications are omitted (for example, the repeated E-C figure that sets "Tuba"), others are retained (notably the two A♯'s in Stravinsky's passage that appear as both an A♯ and as a B♭ in Zorn's chord). There appears to be no systematic process by which Zorn extracted the pitches present in this chord.[22]

Following the breathy timbres of the voices and the percussionists' handslaps at the end of measure 10 (not shown in my examples), a legato melodic line played by a solo violin enters in measure 12.[23] As seen in example 4.4, this melodic line is constructed from the ordered pitch classes beginning with the bass soloist in measure 117, dipping down to the trumpets (measures 121–24), reaching back to the bass soloist's E-C melodic fragment heard in measures 124 and 125, and finally returning to pick up the melodic gesture left dangling at the end of measure 119.

Initially, the final entrance of the voice parts in measure 14 suggests a large-scale formal return, recalling the solo vocal line in measure 3 (see the top two

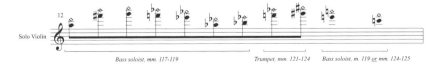

Example 4.4. Solo violin, m. 12 ("Misterioso," 1:23–1:50, *Aporias*).

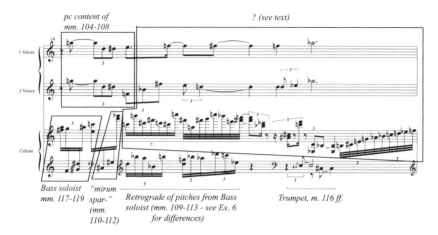

Example 4.5. Closing section, m. 14 ("Misterioso," 2:18–2:26, *Aporias*).

staves of example 4.5). Following the E-F dyad formed between the voice parts on beat 3 of measure 14, however, the music begins to veer away from its source in Stravinsky's score. The B♭ to F♯ motion that appears within the triplet figure of beat 3 of the lower voice parts does not correspond to any obvious pitch class sequence or simultaneity in the opening measures of the "Tuba Mirum." Instead, the pitches emphasized at this point within the measure seem to focus around the D-F pairing reminiscent perhaps of the oscillating D-E♯ figure played by the first trumpet in measure 107 of Stravinsky's score.

A similar progression of clarity moving to uncertainty involving Stravinsky's source material appears in Zorn's celeste part in measure 14 (lower staves of example 4.5). Like the voices it accompanies, the first two beats of the celeste are clearly derived from familiar spots in Stravinsky's score. The opening quintuplet and the first sixteenth-note of beat 2, for example, are formed from the pitches used to set the phrase "Coget omnes ante thronum." The pitches that appear with the three remaining sixteenth-notes of beat 2 are drawn from the pitches that set the text fragment "mirum spar-" of measures 110–12. Throughout much of this measure, the left hand continues to draw its pitch material from Stravinsky's score; the D♯-E-C♯ figure that appears on beats 6 and 7, for example, comes from the familiar trumpet figure that first appears in measure 116. With beats 3 and 4, however, Zorn employs a technique he has not used up to this point, as the pitch classes that make up the quintuplet and sextuplet groupings in the left hand are drawn from the solo bass part in measures 109–13, albeit in retrograde. There are a few differences as I show in table 4.3.[24]

With the right-hand part of the celeste, Zorn seems to be intentionally obscuring the specific source material that has served as the basis for this movement. The disjunct melodic line spanning beats 3 through 7 of the right hand

Table 4.3. Variant pitch classes between piano left hand, m. 14, beats 3 and 4 (Zorn, "Misterioso") and the retrograde of the bass solo, mm. 109–13 (Stravinsky, "Tuba Mirum")

Zorn's piano part:	D	B♭	A	B♭	B	D	G	B♭	A♭	D♭	C	E♭
Stravinsky's bass solo:	D	A♯	A	B	C	F	G	A♯	G♯	C♯	C	E

cannot be derived from the "Tuba Mirum" by any of the techniques described thus far. While there are a few moments within this passage that seem to hint at spots from Stravinsky's score—for example, the oscillating F♯-A gesture on beat 4 (possibly a reference to "Coget omnes") or the C-E dyad at the end of beat 6 (familiar from the pitches of the bass soloist at measures 109 and 125)—none of these moments materialize into any clear extended references. Of course, it is quite possible that the right hand is presenting newly composed material. As Zorn has mentioned regarding the composition of this piece, he would some-times copy out a part from the source score and "compose other parts on top of it." This passage seems to be a clear example of this latter technique given the obvious references that occur in the left-hand part in this measure.

It is clear that the closing moments of this movement are designed to be ambiguous. Acting as a sort of dissolution, the material in the right hand of the celeste part in measure 14 is sandwiched between material whose source is obvious (the left hand of the celeste) and music that has strong associative reso-nances with portions of the "Tuba Mirum" (the vocal parts). The dissolution is complete in the closing measures of "Misterioso" as the voices, celeste, and five solo basses sound a harmonic cluster which suggests either an A♭ or D♭ major collection. (The final harmony and the quintuplet that precedes it in measure 14 lacks either the G or G♭ that would clarify the specific major-mode collection.) If—or even *how*—this final sonority can be derived from Stravinsky's "Tuba Mirum" is unclear (see example 4.6).

Example 4.6. Final sonority, m. 15 ("Misterioso," 2:26–2:36, *Aporias*).

Figure 4.3a. Francis Bacon, *Study after Velázquez* (1950). *© 2008 Estate of Francis Bacon / Artists Rights Society (ARS), New York / DACS, London.*

The closing moments of Zorn's "Misterioso" blur the relations and connections between this movement and Stravinsky's referential source. Measure 14 is like looking through various superimposed images where we recognize the similarities, connections, and overlaps. At the same time, we also recognize an emergent image: an image that shares features with the original but that also projects newer, unforeseen characteristics. This musical quality of the final measures of "Misterioso" is analogous to the working methods and techniques of the movement's dedicatee, Francis Bacon. Photographs, film stills, pictures clipped from newspapers, and images from medical or instructional manuals all functioned as primary resources for much of Bacon's work.[25] While such items might have sometimes functioned as inspirations for aspects of his paintings, Bacon typically sought to effectively integrate these and other images into his works through superimposition and allusion, forging a dense web of subtle (and not-so-subtle) suggestions and associations. Often the end result is a highly disturbing image that seems both entirely foreign yet strangely familiar.

Study after Velázquez exhibits many of the features common to Bacon's poetics of painting (see figure 4.3a). Dating from 1950, this is one of Bacon's many paintings based on Velázquez's portrait of Pope Innocent X. In his life-

Figure 4.3b. Velázquez,
Pope Innocent X (c. 1650),
Galleria Doria Pamphilj.

time, Bacon completed over thirty paintings that are, in some way, based on Velázquez's portrait (collectively referred to as "screaming popes"). Although Bacon had every opportunity to see the original portrait in Rome, Bacon intentionally avoided seeing the work in person until two years before his death in 1992, preferring to model his own paintings after photographic reproductions of Velázquez's portrait; figure 4.3b reproduces one of the photographs found in Bacon's studio. Velázquez's portrait of Pope Innocent owes much to the work of Titian; indeed, a possible model for Velázquez's work may have been Titian's *Portrait of Cardinal Filippo Archinto* (figure 4.3c). In addition to the postures of both men, the stark contrast created by a narrow range of colors (red and white) in both portraits is strikingly similar.

Even if Titian's portrait did not serve as *the* model for Velázquez's work, Bacon did make the connection; furthermore, he extended these connections to his own painting. In his *Study after Velázquez,* Bacon latches on to certain features of Velázquez's portrait (notably the posture and angles of the pope along with certain articles of clothing) and combines them with the white, wispy curtain that obscures half of the cardinal in Titian's portrait. In Bacon's work, this "curtain" extends across the entire surface and—like the railing that surrounds him—distances the viewer from the seated subject as if by a fog or a row of lights shining down from above.

The open mouth of Bacon's "pope" can be understood as expressing either extreme terror or mocking laughter. While I do not believe we have to decide on the precise meaning, Bacon most likely adapted this expression from an image

Figure 4.3c. Titian (Tiziano Vecellio), *Portrait of Cardinal Filippo Archinto* (1558). John G. Johnson Collection, Philadelphia Museum of Modern Art.

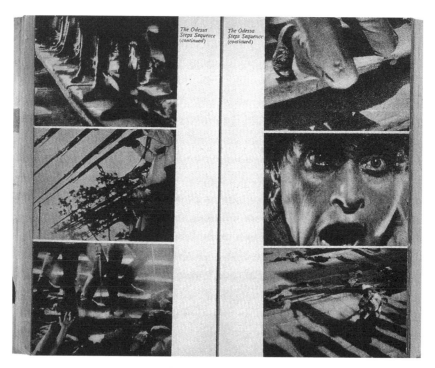

Figure 4.3d. Eisenstein, film stills from *The Battleship Potemkin* (1925).

from Sergei Eisenstein's film *The Battleship Potemkin.* Figure 4.3d reproduces six of these stills (again, a page ripped from a paperback book found in Bacon's studio) from the famous "Odessa Steps" sequence. The image of the screaming nurse (middle still on the right) served as the model for many of Bacon's "Screaming Pope" images (as well as other paintings).

When viewing Bacon's painting, we are, in essence, looking through at least three borrowed sources: the portraits of Velázquez and Titian and the image from Eisenstein. At the same time, we perceive a variety of conflicting semantic resonances from these sources, resonances formed by the expressive ambiguity of Bacon's subject (and its connection to the dread and horror of Eisenstein's image), the enigmatic religious piety of Pope Innocent X, and the veiling effect of Bacon's/Titian's curtain. The sense of "strange familiarity" described above arises from these superimpositions, a technique that, perhaps not coincidentally on the part of Bacon, is reminiscent of Eisenstein's own "theory of montage" and its cinematic uses and functions.[26]

Returning to *Aporias,* it is worth recalling that Zorn's poetics of music is heavily influenced by aspects of film, particularly the thought and practice of experimental filmmakers such as Eisenstein (see the discussion in chapter 2). In fact, Zorn has described his music as "put together in . . . a very "filmic" way, [like] montage. It's made of separate elements that I compose completely regardless of the next, and then I pull them, cull them together."[27] We can clearly recognize this approach to composition in this movement from *Aporias* with its juxtaposed, superimposed, and stratified block structures. Although based on Stravinsky's "Tuba Mirum," the specific techniques Zorn enacts on Stravinsky's source result in a range of references that are sometimes very clear to those that are, it seems, entirely unclear. As we saw in the case of measure 14, for example, the variety and range of such associations often exist simultaneously in musical space over a short span of time. The result perhaps is a sort of musical analogue to Eisenstein's "stereoscopic three-dimensionality."

While this movement exhibits many of the compositional features that have been explored and developed by Zorn throughout much of his compositional career, the overall goal of creating a new, resonant musical space has much to do with the movement's dedicatee, Francis Bacon. While the pitch language of the movement owes a great deal to Stravinsky's source, the aim of the movement owes just as much to Bacon, Zorn's admiration for the artist, and the curious point of contact represented by the thought of Sergei Eisenstein.

"Drammatico" (Marlene Dietrich)/"Libera Me"

As we have seen, a variety of features associated with film and cinema have contributed to Zorn's musical poetics, features ranging from specific films, directors, film theories, film composers, editing techniques, and the numerous narrative designs specific to the medium. At the same time, actors and actresses often inspire individual compositions, a practice evident in "tribute" works such as *Forbidden Fruit* (for the Japanese film star Ishihara Yujiro), the game piece *Xu Feng* (named after a Chinese actress), and the three works that appear on his *New Traditions in East Asian Bar Bands* ("Hu Die," "Hwang Chin-ee," and "Qûê Trân"). Zorn continues this practice in *Aporias,* whose eighth movement, "Drammatico," is a tribute to Marlene Dietrich.

In terms of the specific appropriative/manipulative compositional strategies between *Aporias* and *Requiem Canticles,* many of the same techniques described in "Misterioso" are also employed in "Drammatico." Because of this, I will not present a similarly detailed and exhaustive analysis of this movement. Instead, I will highlight those techniques that appear to be unique to this movement and their relation to its primary source in terms of pitch material, the "Libera Me" from *Requiem Canticles.*

Stravinsky's "Libera Me" movement is curious in many respects. First, the text is delivered simultaneously by both an ensemble of four soloists who sing in a metronomic and monotonous chantlike fashion and by the rest of the choir who sing-speak fragments of the text. The end result resembles the "rhubarb" technique often used in crowd scenes in films where, to give the impression of numerous, independent conversations, the movie extras repeat the word "rhubarb" over and over again.[28] Second, this movement is scored in a four-part chorale style (with quintessentially Stravinskian harmonies) and where the vocal soloists are doubled by four horns throughout. Of course, it is not uncommon to find extended passages of pure harmony in Stravinsky's scores; what is curious about the "Libera Me" movement is how Stravinsky derives his tetrachordal harmonies from the hexachordal structures that form the basis of the work.[29] Example 4.7 provides a reduction of this movement.

The labels below the reduction identify the hexachordal forms from which Stravinsky derives his four-note sonorities.[30] In some instances, single, complete hexachordal collections are present over a span of one or more measures; see, for example, measures 267–69 (IR_3b), 270–72a (the first part of measure 272, I_4a where the E-F# dyad in the treble clef is carried over to 272b), 274–75 (I_3a), and measures 278–79 (I_4a). In other instances, multiple hexachordal collections can be identified given specific pitch class collections. This can be seen in measures 272b (the second part of measure 272) through measure 273 where the pitch classes can be related to either IR_2a or I_4b (where "o.p." identifies the order positions of the specific pitch classes) and in the multiple hexachordal forms hinted at as the Ia/IR_1b collections slowly unfold in measures 280a–84. Stravinsky overlaps two hexachordal collections in the movement's closing measures by exploiting the D#/D♮ pitch class invariances that exist between R_2b and R_3b. Finally, incomplete hexachordal collections are also present in this movement. In measure 266, the pitch classes from order positions 1–4 of IR_4b are present while measures 276–77 include five of the six pitch classes associated with both I_3b and IR_3a.[31]

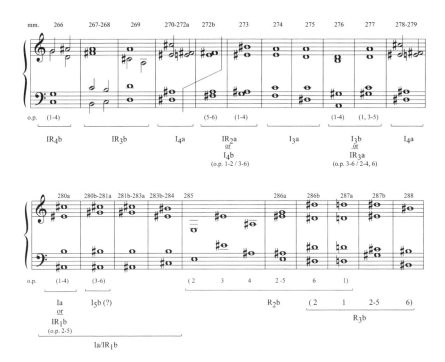

Example 4.7. Reduction of "Libera Me" with hexachordal derivations (Stravinsky, *Requiem Canticles*).

The individual moments of the "Libera Me"—the successive, overlapping, and juxtaposed hexachords—do not appear to be the result of any systematic technique on Stravinsky's part. It is tempting, therefore, to view the hexachordal, serial design of the "Libera Me" as secondary to what Stravinsky wanted to achieve with his sonorities and where, as Stephen Walsh has argued, the "real function of the rows is to generate notes."[32] While I do not wish to engage in the messy (and irresolvable) particulars of any debate regarding Stravinsky and the "logic of the ear" and/or "the logic of the mind," it is clear that Zorn—in the "Drammatico" movement—is more interested in what can be done with and to Stravinsky's harmonies and not necessarily the harmonies' serial sources and derivations.[33]

Example 4.8 reproduces the harmonies from the "Libera Me" one more time. Here, I have affixed a series of chordal labels (A, B, C, etc.) that identify individual four-note sonorities based solely on their pitch class content. (The octave unisons in measures 286b, 287a, and 287b break from this labeling scheme and are identified by their pitch names; also, the soaring E-E♯-A♯ melodic fragment in measure 285 is identified simply as the "alpha" gesture.) Example 4.9 is a reduction of the first sixteen measures of Zorn's "Drammatico"

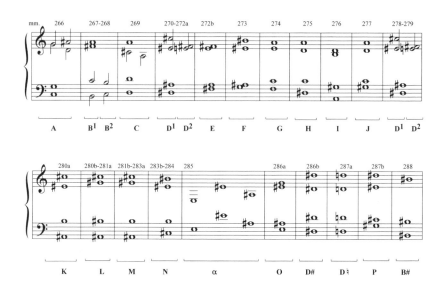

Example 4.8. Reduction of "Libera Me" with chordal labels (Stravinsky, *Requiem Canticles*).

where a melodic line is gradually unfolded before splintering into the sustained sonority of measure 15. The solitary C held throughout the first three measures picks up where Stravinsky's score left off by enharmonically transforming the sustained B♯ that concludes the "Libera Me." As the melodic line begins to take shape with the entrance of the C♯ in measure 4, Zorn begins to draw from the sonorities of Stravinsky's movement, transforming the vertical tetrachords into linear configurations.

As seen in example 4.9 (and compared to example 4.8), Zorn begins with the chord I have labeled D¹. As Zorn's music moves forward in time, he draws

Example 4.9. Reduction of opening sixteen measures with chordal labels ("Drammatico," 0:01–1:24, *Aporias*).

from Stravinsky's score by moving backwards to C, B², and B¹, all the while starting from the uppermost note of Stravinsky's collections and proceeding down through the voices. The sustained sonority in the cellos and violas in measures 15 and 16 completes this backwards progression by returning to Stravinsky's opening sonority, the incomplete (enharmonic) "ninth chord" I have identified as A. The quasi-cadential F-F♯ motion in measures 14 to 15 is not clearly derivable from Stravinsky's opening four-part simultaneities. While these two pitch classes are both contained within I₄a, they do not appear together vertically. It is possible that the F♯ is a copying mistake on Zorn's part, misreading the E♮ that is grouped together with F♯ in D². Whatever the case may be, the F-F♯ half-step creates an interesting parallel with the B-C motion that concludes the first phrase in measures 8 and 9, creating a sense of formal balance to these opening measures (see connecting line in example 4.9).

Zorn modifies and reworks Stravinsky's verticals throughout this movement. In measures 29–30, for example, the piano presents its own short chorale where the harmonies are drawn from the end of the "Libera Me" (see example 4.10). Here, Zorn skips over the unison pitches that occur toward the end of the "Libera Me" and follows the chordal progression N-α/O-P before wrapping back around to the "ninth chord" that opens Stravinsky's movement (A). The triplet quarter-note gesture at the end of measure 29 and the sonority on the downbeat of measure 30 cannot be derived in any clear manner from Stravinsky's source sonorities.

Example 4.10. Piano, mm. 29–30 with chordal labels ("Drammatico," 2:15–2:19, *Aporias*).

Beginning in measure 38, a frantic passage in the piano is drawn from the middle of Stravinsky's progression, presenting H-I-J-G-H before skipping forward to what appears to be O. In this passage, Zorn picks up on certain pitch class invariances between sequential sonorities, specifically the A♮ that is shared between the gestures that occupy beats 1 and 2 of measure 38 (overlapping collections H and I) and the two collections that make up the sextuplet on beat 2 of

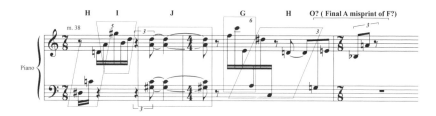

Example 4.11. Piano, mm. 38–40 with chordal labels ("Drammatico," 2:57–3:03, *Aporias*).

measure 39 (collections G and H). In example 4.11, I have represented the final gesture as possibly being related to O. To be O, however, the concluding pitch A would have to be understood as a misprint for the F♯ that appears in Stravinsky's score. While a misprint is certainly a possibility (think of the D/F misreading that occurs throughout the Francis Bacon movement described above), I am not entirely convinced that this is the case here. The question mark in example 4.11 serves to reflect my uncertainty.

The conclusion of this movement contains one of Zorn's most nostalgic and touching moments (see example 4.12). In measure 60, the celeste, harp, and chimes (not shown) sound the familiar ninth chord that opens the "Libera Me" (A), which then resolves to an unidentifiable sonority (unidentifiable in that its relation to the "Libera Me" is unclear). Beginning in measure 61, the pianist plays a slow-moving jazz progression that is accompanied by an erratic

Example 4.12. Measures 60–64 ("Drammatico," 4:18–4:51, *Aporias*).

and jagged line played by the solo violin. Focusing first on the solo violin part, we recognize a transformation of the melodic line that opens this movement. In fact, Zorn has simply retrograded this line beginning with the F-F♯ first heard in measures 13–15. As a result, the chordal progression that is unfolded follows Stravinsky's score exactly: where A (in the harp and celeste) is presented in measure 60 followed by B^1, B^2, C, and D^1 in measures 61 and 62 (up to the C♯ grace note in measure 62) in the solo violin.

Initially, the E♭ tonality of the progression in the piano seems anomalous within the context of the rest of this movement, a movement lacking in any clearly identifiable tonal center or centers. (I have provided jazz chord symbols above the piano part in example 4.12.) Zorn has related to me that this progression is derived from the Burt Bacharach/Hal David song "I'll Never Fall in Love Again."[34] The upbeat and lively tempo of the original song is obscured in Zorn's movement by the piano's slow-moving chordal progression. Furthermore, Zorn extracts only selected portions of Bacharach's original progression. In example 4.13 I have reproduced the opening of this tune where the harmonies in measures 3–6 and 9–10 (the sources of Zorn's progression) are highlighted. Comparing examples 4.12 and 4.13, we can recognize a few slight variations between Zorn's score and the original progression, notably the 4-3 motion over a stationary G in the bass and the resolution to a V^7 of C in measures 61–62 and the C minor chord (with an added seventh) in measure 63 as compared to the C major chord (also with an added seventh) of the original. Lastly, the striking A♭ chord with an added minor seventh in measure 9 of example 4.13 is replaced by the more docile A♭ major seventh chord with an added ninth in Zorn's progression (m. 63).

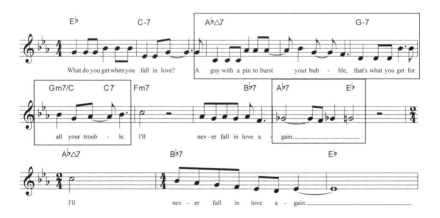

Example 4.13. "I'll Never Fall in Love Again," from *Promises, Promises.* Lyrics by Hal David. Music by Burt Bacharach. *Copyright © 1968 (Renewed) Casa David and New Hidden Valley Music. International Copyright Secured. All Rights Reserved.*

For Zorn, this concluding chordal progression functions as a personal tribute to Marlene Dietrich by reminding us that Bacharach was her accompanist and arranger in the 1950s and 1960s. At the same time, Zorn's progression serves as a poignant farewell to Dietrich by subtly evoking what was perhaps her most recognizable song: "Falling in Love Again." Marlene Dietrich's death in 1992 may not have silenced her voice (a voice that will live on in numerous films and recordings), but it did put an end to the song's personal sentiment and meaning, a fact that—in Zorn's context—David and Bacharach's "I'll Never Fall in Love Again" makes clear.

The Ninth Chord as a Referential Sonority in *Aporias*

Stravinsky's *Requiem Canticles* offers a rich yet entirely preliminary source for Zorn's *Aporias*. I say preliminary because Zorn must still make decisions as to what he is going to do with Stravinsky's source material, just as Stravinsky had to decide what to do with his two twelve-tone rows and his rotated hexachords. After deciding on the *Requiem Canticles* as a primary source for his work, the question for Zorn then becomes: what musical features will emerge from Stravinsky's source that will then function as defining features of *Aporias*?

Throughout much of *Aporias,* various forms and types of ninth chords function to create a sense of continuity both between movements and in relation to the whole. Given the work's reliance on Stravinsky, it is perhaps not surprising that Zorn would choose a referential sonority as a sort of sonic thumbprint for his own work. For Stravinsky, of course, referential sonorities are not uncommon; think, for example, of the "Petrushka" chord, or the "motto chord" heard in the "Augurs of Spring" from the *Rite,* the "Psalms" chord, and many others. In contrast to these and other examples of referential sonorities found in Stravinsky's *oeuvre*—chords that are relatively consistent in regard to their instrumentation and pitch or pitch class content—Zorn's harmonies are more malleable and variable, particularly in terms of their intervallic content. However, seen through a tonal lens, the types of referential sonorities found in *Aporias* can be understood as belonging to a special class of chord formations, a class I will be referring to simply as "ninth chords." Before describing some of the more prominent ninth chords in selected passages from *Aporias,* a bit of explanation is in order regarding certain features of these chords as well as my rationale for ascribing to them any degree of significance in Zorn's work.

First, by ninth chord, I mean any harmony constructed in thirds that extends up to a pitch class that can be understood (either visually or aurally) as forming some sort of interval a ninth above a root. For example, in the previous section, I consistently referred to the opening sonority of Stravinsky's "Libera Me" as a ninth chord where the sonority C-G-D-A♯ is built on the root C, the D forms the ninth, and the A♯ can be heard as a B♭. While some of the ninth chords I will describe below do not contain a pitch or pitch class that forms a seventh in relation to the root, they all contain a root, a pitch, or a pitch class that can be understood as forming the interval of a perfect fifth above the root and, of course, the ninth (or multiple forms of the ninth). While it would have been possible to identify an enormous number of sonorities that meet these criteria, I have limited my discussion to only those ninth chords that contain a perfect fifth. My reasoning behind this limitation has to do with this interval's ability to impart a sense of centricity or referentiality to the pitch lying a perfect fifth below. Except for possibly those ninth chords that appear in the piano's jazz progression at the end of "Drammatico," none of these sonorities exist within a larger context of functional tonality. While Zorn is certainly exploiting the tonal implications of these harmonies and the expectations they carry with them, his ninth chords exist as pure harmonies that function as aural, associative signposts that allow the listener to make connections and forge pathways through *Aporias.*

Example 4.14 reproduces—in reduced versions—a number of significant ninth chords heard throughout *Aporias.* Zorn draws the listener's attention to

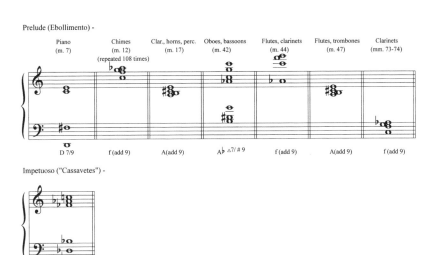

Example 4.14. Instances of ninth chords (*Aporias*).

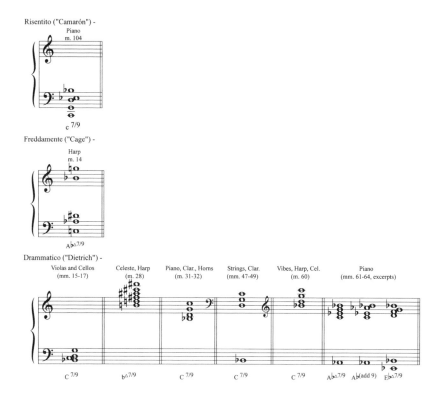

Example 4.14, cont. Instances of ninth chords (*Aporias*).

Example 4.14, cont. Instances of ninth chords (*Aporias*).

these sonorities through a variety of means. For example, an f minor chord with an added ninth is sounded in the chimes in measure 12 of the Prelude and is repeated one hundred and eight times in succession. The same sonority is also heard in the flutes and clarinets in measure 44 and in the clarinets alone in measures 73 and 74. Given the importance of this particular sonority and its centering around f in the Prelude, it is not insignificant that a similar sonority (now with an added seventh) reappears in the Postlude, played by the harp in measures 25–28 and repeated seventy times. The reappearance of this sonority in the Postlude connects back to the repeated sonority of the Prelude, creating a sort of circular form to the work as a whole.

Certain compositional decisions on Zorn's part point to a deeper structural significance of the ninth chord and not just the many surface manifestations of this class of chords. As shown in example 4.15, the long note values and slow tempo of the "Dietrich" movement allow us to hear the composing-out of a ninth sonority over the opening nineteen measures. A sustained C in the strings frames the opening eight-measure phrase as described above after which the pitch A is added in the clarinets beginning in measure 10. The C gives away to a sustained A in measure 11 before Zorn picks up again with the arpeggiated material derived from the "Libera Me" movement (the wavy lines indicate that I have excised the intervening pitch material between certain phrase markers and boundaries). The arrival on the F♯ in measure 15 signals the close of the balanced phrase structure of the opening, a fact signaled by the timbral shift effected by the divisi string harmonies in measures 15 through 17. As the music appears to be moving away from the opening ideas, the harp, celli, and basses provide one final element of this gradual unfolding by continuing the unison motion first down to a E♭ in measure 18 and finally to a B in measure 19. The sonority formed by this unison line is heard as a B seventh chord with an added ♭9 as shown in the lower staff.

An examination of Zorn's reference materials reveals the significance of this class of sonorities in *Aporias*. Figure 4.4 provides details from the refer-

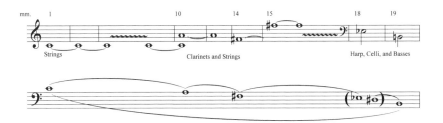

Example 4.15. Composing-out of B$^{7♭9}$ (reduction of mm. 1–19, "Dietrich").

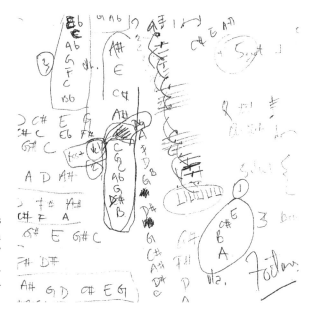

Figure 4.4a. Details of ninth chords from Zorn's "Prelude" reference materials.

ence materials relating to three movements: the "Prelude," "Cassavetes," and "Dietrich." As shown in figure 4.4a—materials relating to the "Prelude"—Zorn has circled and identified three significant forms of a ninth chord, where label 1 identifies the A add 9 sonority that appears in measures 17 and 47, label 2 the A♭ major seventh chord with an added ♯9 (B) in measure 42, and, finally, a collection whose pitches include the recurring F add 9 and/or F minor seventh with an added ninth chords (identified as 3) heard throughout the "Prelude" and again in the "Postlude."[35] In figure 4.4b, the G♭ major seventh chord with an added ninth heard in the "Cassavetes" movement is also circled. Referring back to example 4.14, it is possible to see how this specific background harmony was subsequently transformed in the completed score with the addition of the sustained C forming the ♯11 encountered in measure 9 of this movement. At the same time, we can locate this particular harmony and its specific aural characteristics and features to an earlier stage of the work's development given the "Messiaen" indication that can be seen to the right and slightly above the

Figure 4.4b. Details of ninth chords from Zorn's "Cassavetes" reference materials.

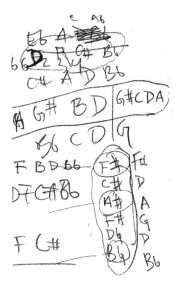

Figure 4.4c. Details of ninth chords from Zorn's "Dietrich" reference materials.

encircled harmony in figure 4.4b. As described above, this second movement was originally conceived as a tribute to Olivier Messiaen and later changed to John Cassavetes. Still, the musical material associated with this movement and its location within the overall design of *Aporias* is clear given the written note "segue into Bacon" that appears to the left of this harmony. Finally, figure 4.4c identifies the B minor chord with an added major seventh and ninth heard in the harp and celeste in measure 28 of the "Dietrich" movement (seen in the lower right-hand corner, circled). This harmony is interesting, as it combines certain linear as well as vertical musical ideas heard earlier in the movement, specifically music heard in measures 18 and 19 (including the harp, bass, and cello parts shown in example 4.15) while evoking the harmony that is composed out over the opening nineteen measures as described above.

Conclusions

I hope that the analytical points presented above offer not only a "way into" *Aporias* but also other similarly conceived works, works such as *Elegy, Rituals,* and *Walpurgisnacht,* which derive much of their pitch materials from a single musical source.[36] At the same time, a great deal of analytical work remains to be done, specifically on the "Prelude," "Interlude," and "Postlude" movements of *Aporias,* a fact made evident by the many pages of notes devoted to these movements in Zorn's reference materials. Given the close musical connections that exist between Zorn's work and Stravinsky's *Requiem Canticles* as well as the specific resonances and/or correlations between Zorn's music and the thought and practices of the individual dedicatees, it is worth considering, in conclusion, the meaning(s) of the title and how *Aporias* can be understood as encapsulating many of the key features I have identified with Zorn's poetics of music, notably aspects of transgression as well as his complex relationship to history and tradition.

It is clear from an examination of the reference materials for *Aporias* that Zorn struggled with the title of the work (see figure 4.5). Buried in this page is the earlier ordering of movements also shown in figure 4.1, the relation of the individual movements to the *Requiem Canticles* (on the left-hand edge of the page), as well as textural, formal, and orchestral outlines for these movements. Most of this page is devoted to possible titles for the work as a whole, including the names of works by other individuals, such as Walter Benjamin's *One Way Street* (above the description of the "Messiaen" movement, underlined) and Walt Whitman's *Leaves of Grass* (on the right-hand side of the page directly opposite the "Cage" movement). Most of the proposed titles suggest praise or respect; for example, the various forms of "Paeans"—"Piano Paeans," "Paean Tableaux," "Paean Requia"—as well as "Accolade," the various titles that utilize the words "Encomium" or "Eulogy," "Letters of Praise," and, what may have been an early working title, "Latrias for Piano and Orchestra."

Ultimately, Zorn chose the title *Aporias* after the work was completed, a title inspired by Jacques Derrida's book of the same name.[37] As a title, "Aporias" lacks the strong sense of tribute, remembrance, or influence that is evoked by many of the proposed titles included in figure 4.5. Whereas many of Zorn's early titles clearly draw attention to the sense of tribute and praise that lies at the heart of *Aporias,* Zorn has intentionally obscured and concealed the individual references present in this work. In the liner notes to *Aporias,* Zorn writes that "these requia are not for any particular artist or group of artists: they are dedicated to *all* artists and to the indomitable spirit of creativity itself." The individual dedications of *Aporias,* therefore, are only revealed to someone who has seen the score or Zorn's references to this work in his writings/interviews.

This type of concealment could be related to the composition and conception of another work written a year before *Aporias: Elegy,* a work dedicated to Jean Genet. Zorn has written how he had grown tired of simply calling his dedicated works after the name of the intended dedicatee: "Enough of this *Spillane* shit, you know what I mean? I'm just going to do an abstract piece called *Elegy.* I know it's about Genet, but I'll tell nobody else. Then it came out that it was about Genet, and everyone was talking about it. But I don't even think I'm going to put Genet's name on the outside; I'll just put *Elegy* and maybe a picture of him on the inside or a quote from [*The Thief's Journal*]."[38]

Deciding to call his work *Aporias* could be understood as an attempt on Zorn's part to conceal not only the immediate panegyric nature of the work but

Figure 4.5. Formal outline and possible titles from Zorn's reference materials.

also the more far-reaching function of the work, that is, Zorn's attempt to situate himself within a certain artistic tradition or traditions. However, by settling on the title of "Aporias," Zorn is able to place this work within his overall poetics of music and his long-standing concerns for not only a sense of tradition but also the insights afforded by working and composing within certain negative, or transgressive, spaces. A brief examination of Derrida's text will reveal the importance it may hold for Zorn in terms of tradition and transgression.

Derrida's short text *Aporias* is, not surprisingly, a dense and very difficult one, and it is probable that Zorn latched on to certain ideas from this book while leaving others behind (notably the detailed and exhausting analysis of the interdependent necessities between death, dying, perishing, and *Dasein* in Heidegger's *Being and Time,* an analysis that takes up nearly two-thirds of Derrida's text). The ideas presented in Derrida's book that probably appealed to Zorn should be clear from much of the terrain covered in previous chapters. For example, the very notion of an "aporia" resonates with the idea of "transgressive space" and Zorn's long-standing concern to reveal the possibility of such spaces through his compositions. The negative, transgressive spaces in which Zorn's music and thought operate are translated, in Derrida's text, as aporia. As conceived and used within the skeptical tradition associated with Sextus Empiricus in particular and Pyrrhonism in general, aporia describes a condition arising from "a set of individually plausible but collectively inconsistent propositions."[39] In Derrida's text, the aporetic condition is developed and expanded so as to resemble a certain space in which thought (and possibly actions) can move and take place. Such a space, Derrida writes, is characterized as "the impossible, passage, the refused, denied, or prohibited passage, indeed the nonpassage, which can in fact be something else, the event of a coming or future advent . . . which no longer has the form of the movement that consists in passing, traversing, or transiting."[40]

What, then, prohibits the types of movement (passing, traversing, transiting) described in this quote? For Derrida, it is the "indivisible line," the constructed and unquestioned/unquestionable limits or borders that constrain thought by limiting/constructing what is possible and what is impossible. By reaching back to the more traditional conception of the term, Derrida recognizes how aporias—both as space and as condition—are paradoxically beneficial and that "where the identity or indivisibility of a line is compromised, the identity to oneself and therefore the possible identification of an intangible edge—the crossing of the line—becomes a *problem*." In an existence where limits are conceded, ignored, or unquestioned, problems don't exist; or, better, problems that may appear can be resolved without crossing over the "indivisible line." Aporias, therefore, function as the possibility and the potential site of/ for problems: "There is a *problem* as soon as the edge-line is crossed."[41]

For Derrida, the emergent problems that result from the crossing of lines or boundaries are exemplified most forcefully with death. "What, then, is it to cross the ultimate border? What is it to pass the term of one's life? Is it possible? Who has ever done it and who can testify to it?" The only one who can answer such questions is the subject who is no longer a subject, leading Derrida to ask: "Is my death possible? Can we understand this question? Can I, myself, pose it? Am I allowed to talk about my death?"[42] Speaking of death or, more specifically, speaking of *my own* death relates, within Derrida's critique of Heidegger, to the "possibility of the impossible": "This nonaccess to death as such—but this access only to the aspect of the border that can only be the threshold, the step, as one says of the approach to the border—is also what Heidegger calls the impossible, the access to death as nonaccess to the nonborder, as the possibility of the impossible." Following Heidegger's belief in the undying nature of *Dasein,* Derrida proclaims, "I am, if not immortal, then at least imperishable: I do not end, I never end, I know that I will not come to an end."[43]

If we transport the undying and imperishable nature of *Dasein* to the tributes/memorials of Zorn's *Aporias,* we begin to recognize key features of Zorn's poetics, notably those of transgression and tradition. The persistence of ideas or practices associated with Zorn's dedicatees connect across historical, artistic, stylistic, and conceptual boundaries and ultimately contribute to the formation of a tradition, a tradition in which Zorn aligns himself. *Aporias*—like so many of Zorn's dedicated works—attempts to bridge the gaps or to find the passageways that connect one artist to another. At the same time, Zorn's compositions inhabit the aporetic or transgressive spaces that emerge when certain conceptual or epistemological limits, barriers, and boundaries are problematized.

In his liner notes, Zorn acknowledges these spaces, describing *Aporias* as being "about those mysterious and spiritual passages separating life from death." At the same time, he attests to the possibility of traversing such passageways by spiritual or mystical means, reproducing a quote from Sextus Propertius (also included, in Latin, on the front page of the score to *Aporias* as well as his reference materials; refer back to figure 4.1):

> Spirits **do** exist; death does not end all things and the pale ghost, victorious, escapes the flames.

With *Aporias*/aporias—the work, the concept, and the condition—Zorn seeks to open up an aporetic and transgressive space that draws from and depends on the works and ideas of others while, at the same time, forging a newly emergent whole. *Aporias* highlights the mystical and spiritual qualities that are able to survive death and that persist in Zorn's own works and the tradition in which he seeks to situate himself. *Aporias,* therefore, functions as a microcosmic instance of Zorn's macrocosmic poetics of music.

Epilogue

In every era the attempt must be made anew to wrest tradition
away from the conformism that is about to overpower it.
—Walter Benjamin, "Theses on the Philosophy of History"

John Zorn is a number of things: composer/improviser, saxophone player, producer, club proprietor, and record label owner. Among the many other descriptions that could be included on this list, at least one more must be added: John Zorn, historian. The place(s) and function(s) of history and tradition within Zorn's poetics of music have been a theme running throughout the preceding essays. For those readers who may uncritically accept the image of "Zorn-as-postmodernist," this side of Zorn (which is not really a "side," since it seems to occupy all aspects of his work and thought) problematizes many of the assumptions often associated with such a view. Combined with Zorn's historicism/traditionalism, his interests in structure and unity—which, as we have seen, can be manifested in a variety of ways—only add to the dissonance. On the other hand, for those who have read the many interviews Zorn has given or who have carefully considered the subtle and often not so subtle historical resonances that form such an integral part of his compositional output, the image of "Zorn-as-historian" is not a particularly groundbreaking premise. For these individuals, perhaps the only thing "new" to appear in my essays may be the uncovering of various organizational and structural principles in (admittedly, only a handful of) his works.

In many respects, the image that has emerged in this book is that of Zorn as traditionalist or—dare I say it—as modernist. While it has not been my intention to organize these essays around some sort of "bait and switch," I have been struck by just how off base the popular image of Zorn as the quintessential postmodernist composer really is. At the same time, certain paradoxes relating to Zorn, history, and tradition have revealed themselves, specifically my heuristic of a "tradition of transgression" and Zorn's views on (and his perceived relationship with) the avant-garde. While I do not believe I can fully resolve certain historical/conceptual incongruities that exist between these overlapping and codependent categories, I will conclude by considering some of the practical and theoretical problems presented by Zorn's poetics of music, his deep sense of tradition and history, and the viability of the concept of the "avant-garde" in America in the late twentieth century and the dawn of the twenty-first century.

In chapter 3, I defined the tradition of transgression as a tradition that zeroes in on and exploits the spaces or "blind spots" deemed impermissible, unacceptable, and unrecognizable (yet ultimately created) by traditional institutions of art. Furthermore, I believe that the tradition of transgression is discernible only when it is successful at revealing the artificial limitations and boundaries of "traditional" structures and formations. Therefore, the tradition of transgression can only exist paradoxically: as a tradition (as the concept is typically understood) it can only be an antitradition that speaks to and against more stable, reified traditions. Given these features, the tradition of transgression can include Dadaists and their revolt against the bourgeois tradition of art and all that this tradition represented in the first decades of the twentieth century (the separation of art from life, the assumed redemptive or transcendental qualities believed to be associated with "good" art) to the margins of the margins (e.g., Antonin Artaud and Georges Bataille and their uneasy relationship with André Breton and other individuals associated with surrealism in France).

The notion of a tradition of transgression is my own formulation and not Zorn's. He prefers to identify with a tradition much more familiar to us but no less paradoxical: the avant-garde. The first thing one reads when visiting the home page for Tzadik (www.tzadik.com), for example, is that "Tzadik is dedicated to releasing the best in avant-garde and experimental music." In an e-mail communication to me in December 2007, Zorn was more explicit, describing how he considers the "the avant-garde as a tradition in itself . . . and even more than that, it is a lifestyle, a world view, a philosophical stance, a moral standard, a responsibility, a sacred trust . . . reaching back to Harry Smith, Ives, Laurence Sterne, Biber, Heraclitus, and even further."

I touched upon the category of the avant-garde in the introduction, especially a theory of the avant-garde as formulated by Peter Bürger. For Bürger, historical avant-garde movements such as dada and surrealism exemplified an authentic avant-garde praxis in that both movements sought to integrate art with life in an effort to undermine the entrenched aesthetic that considered art as autonomous and separate from "real-world" concerns. "The intention of the historical avant-garde movements," writes Bürger, "was defined as the destruction of art as an institution set off from the praxis of life."[1] The possibility of realizing such an integration of art and life occurs when our attention is shifted from what a work "means" to its affective potential. For the viewer/listener/recipient, the truly avant-gardiste work of art (what Bürger identifies as "nonorganic") "neither creates a total impression that would permit an interpretation of its meaning nor can whatever impression may be created be accounted for by recourse to the individual parts, for they are no longer subordinated to a pervasive intent."

> This refusal to provide meaning is experienced as shock by the recipient. And this is the intention of the avant-gardiste artist, who hopes that such withdrawal of meaning will direct the reader's attention to the fact that the conduct of one's life is questionable and that it is necessary to change it. Shock is aimed for as a stimulus to change one's conduct of life; it is the means to break through aesthetic immanence and to usher in (initiate) a change in the recipient's life praxis.[2]

Ultimately, Bürger believes, the historical avant-garde's intention to integrate art within the "praxis of life" failed. Such a lofty goal "cannot occur . . . in a bourgeois society unless it be a false sublation of autonomous art." Considering pulp fiction and other items associated with what he calls "commodity aesthetics," Bürger identifies forms of literature "whose primary aim it is to impose a particular kind of consumer behavior on the reader [which] is in fact practical, though not in the sense the avant-gardists intended. Here, literature ceases to be an instrument of emancipation and becomes one of subjection. . . . In late capitalist society, intentions of the historical avant-garde are being realized but the result has been disvalue."[3] Nowhere has this "disvaluing" of the intentions of the historical avant-garde been more apparent, Bürger believes, than with the art and artists identified as "neo-avant-garde." Given the institutionalization of the historical avant-garde (avant-garde "works" displayed in museums and exhibitions, commercial appropriations of avant-garde techniques and/or styles, etc.), neo-avant-garde artists contribute to the institutionalization of the "*avant-garde as art* and thus negate genuinely avant-gardiste intentions." "Neo-avant-gardiste art," Bürger argues, "is autonomous art in the full sense of the term, which means that it negates the avant-gardiste intention of returning art to the praxis of life. And the efforts to sublate art become artistic manifestations that, despite their producers' intentions, take on the character of works."[4]

It is here that we return to Zorn and his place within some sort of avant-garde tradition. Following Bürger, it would seem that Zorn's belief that he is participating within a tradition set in motion by the historical avant-garde is false; indeed, such a belief would appear to be an impossibility if we subscribe fully to Bürger's theory.[5] As a "neo-avant-garde" artist, Zorn can only ape the techniques and/or intentions of artists associated with dada, surrealism, or

Russian constructivism. Read from this perspective, Zorn's traditionalism—as exemplified by the gift-giving spiral described in chapter 3—amounts to name-dropping in an attempt to forge some sort of historical context or lineage for himself and his works. Like Marx's "old mole," Zorn's historical repetition of the avant-garde emerges as a farce that ultimately diminishes the strength and shock of the historical avant-garde.[6] As Hal Foster has written, such a repetition reduces the "anti-aesthetic [of the historical avant-garde] into the artistic, the transgressive into the institutional."[7]

A problematic component of Bürger's theory—one recognized by critics such as Foster and Benjamin Buchloh—is its appeal to historical origins (*the* "historical" avant-garde) and any and all subsequent repetitions (the various neo-avant-gardes) as degenerative or pale imitations of this "authentic" origi-nal. Bürger's reliance on a causal understanding of history makes it nearly im-possible for any post-avant-garde movement or artist to participate within any sort of tradition and where the neo-avant-garde "which stages for a second time the avant-gardiste break with tradition, becomes a manifestation that is void of sense and that permits the positing of any meaning whatever."[8]

In an effort to overcome Bürger's historicism and to salvage the possibility that any number of postwar artistic movements that might identify with the avant-garde have any sort of validity, Benjamin Buchloh suggests that, instead of viewing the avant-garde project as one of failure without any possibility for renewal, an understanding of avant-garde practices proceeds from a "continu-ally renewed struggle over the definition of cultural meaning, the discovery and representation of new audiences, and the development of new strategies to counteract and develop resistance against the tendency of the ideological ap-paratuses of the culture industry to occupy and to control all practices and all spaces of representation."[9] Following Buchloh's plea, Hal Foster has proposed that we view neo-avant-garde movements as participating within a "complex relation of anticipation and reconstruction." In contrast to Bürger's causal view of history, Foster proposes an atemporal view of the avant-garde that involves a "continual process of protension and retension, a complex relay of anticipated futures and reconstructed pasts—in short, in a deferred action that throws over any simple scheme of before and after, cause and effect, origin and repetition."[10] For Foster, the avant-garde is an ongoing, interminable project that not only critiques more mainstream artistic movements and/or styles but also critiques itself. This critique by neo-avant-garde movements and artists is carried out both *within* the forms of institutionalization which have subsumed the histori-cal avant-garde and from *without* as later artists attempt to forge and carry on a tradition that, at its core, was highly skeptical—even antagonistic—toward artistic traditions. This last point highlights a fundamental paradox facing all neo-avant-garde artists and movements. Zorn's relationship and involvement with what I have been calling a "tradition of transgression" exists within a paradoxical conceptual space that is similar to the types of tensions and paradoxes that are aroused by his compositions. In this respect, Zorn's musical works can be understood as individual symptoms of a much more serious affliction facing any number of contemporary artists: that is, the manner in which claims or appeals regarding the place and function of artistic/historical traditions are understood in a time when such historical narratives are viewed with suspicion.

Describing the stylistic and organizational strategies employed by artists associated with the historical avant-garde, Bürger, in his critique of Adorno, questions the place of the "new" as a viable indicator when considering avant-garde praxis, preferring instead to emphasize the radical breaks or ruptures affected by the historical avant-garde:

> But since the historical avant-garde movements cause a break with tradition and a subsequent change in the representational system, the category [of the "new"] is not suitable for a description of how things are. And this is all the less when one considers that the historical avant-garde movements not only intend a break with the traditional representational system but the total abolition of the institution that is art.[11]

Like Bürger, Andreas Huyssen is skeptical of the role of the stylistic innovation when considering avant-garde/neo-avant-garde/postmodern artistic praxis. Contra Bürger, however, Huyssen is just as skeptical of narratives that appeal to historical ruptures or breakthroughs. Instead, Huyssen has drawn our attention to the pervasive tensions relating to history and tradition within a number of postwar avant-garde movements and artists, including those that can be labeled "postmodern." By looking past certain structural or representational novelties associated with neo-avant-garde or postmodern works, Huyssen believes that a "search for tradition combined with an attempt at recuperation seems more basic to postmodernism than innovation and breakthrough." Similar to Foster's belief in the interminable and ongoing project of the avant-garde, Huyssen prefers to highlight the paradoxes facing neo-avant-garde and postmodern artists described above (a move that turns Bürger's argument on its head) and where "the postmodernist search for cultural tradition and continuity, which underlies all the radical rhetoric of rupture, discontinuity, and epistemological breaks, has turned to that tradition which fundamentally and on principle despised and denied all traditions."[12]

For Huyssen, a concern for recuperating and revitalizing certain aims, practices, and/or ideals associated with the avant-garde is the central paradox that is worked through and worked out again and again in contemporary avant-garde circles. This tradition of an antitradition serves both as a backdrop and a barrier for artists such as Zorn who choose to operate within the ongoing, "incomplete" project of the avant-garde:

The recuperation of history and the reemergence of story in [postmodern art] are not part of a leap back into pre-modern, pre-avantgarde past, as some postmodernists seem to suggest. They can better be described as attempts to shift into reverse order to get out of a dead-end street where the vehicles of avantgardism and postmodernism have come to a standstill. At the same time, the contemporary concern for history will keep us from lapsing back into the avantgardist gesture of totally rejecting the past—this time the avantgarde itself.[13]

Zorn's project—if this word can be used—is a revitalization/restoration of the avant-garde. As I have shown throughout many of the preceding chapters, Zorn's musical poetics resonate strongly with a number of "historical" avant-garde movements and individual artists. While I have focused on art, artists, and thinkers predominately associated (rightly or wrongly) with surrealism, a passage from Hugo Ball's "Dadaist Diary" quite nicely captures many of the aims and intentions that drive Zorn's contemporary practices:

People who live rashly and precipitately easily lose control over their impressions and are prey to unconscious emotions and motives. The activity of any art (painting, writing, composing) will do them good, provided that they do not pursue any purpose in their subjects, but follow the course of a free, unfettered imagination. The independent process of fantasy never fails to bring to light again those things that have crossed the threshold of consciousness without analysis. In an age like ours, when people are assaulted daily by the most monstrous things without being able to keep account of their impressions, in such an age aesthetic production becomes a prescribed course. But all living art will be irrational, primitive, and complex; it will speak a secret language and leave behind documents not of edification but of paradox.[14]

Many of the ideals envisioned by Ball in this quote have been encountered in the preceding chapters: the fantasy/reality tensions (chapter 1), complex and structurally significant secret musical languages (chapter 4) against the backdrop of mysteries and magickal irrationality (chapter 2), while the many paradoxes associated with a Bataillean concept of transgression have been described throughout. Finally, Zorn's desire to revitalize many of the goals associated with "historical avant-garde" movements represents the ultimate paradox: he believes in the continued significance of the avant-garde as a viable—indeed necessary—artistic category/project in a time when many critics view the avant-garde—although historically significant—as ultimately irrelevant given certain cultural/artistic concerns associated with our specific historical location.

In one final effort to show how Zorn's works participate within certain conceptual spaces carved out by the avant-garde, I wish to consider how notions of the gift and gift giving can also be read in relation to the paradoxes described above by Ball, Huyssen, and others, especially the ways in which the notion of

the gift intersects with that of transgression. More specifically, I want to consider how a certain type of shock experienced by viewers/listeners of Zorn's music
may bring about a "change in the recipient's life praxis." Therefore, as a way of
concluding, I will consider Zorn's record *The Gift* and how the total package
represented by this recording (music and artwork) reminds us of certain "dangers" that might arise when we accept gifts from others.

In an interview for the *Japan Times* from 2003, Zorn explains the idea of
the gift in the context of what might appear to be a rather startling confession
on the tone or "message" of his music:

> I want to create something that adds to the positive energy in this world, that there
> is not enough of [positive energy], there should be more of [it]. I believe in love.
> It's not about anger and anarchy and nihilism. . . . I've dealt with different elements
> that touch on those areas at different times in my life and worked through different
> things. But those were things that I worked through in my work. In that sense, they
> were 100 percent honest. . . . And all along I've believed that music is love and that
> the world needs positive energy.

In addition to describing his belief in "love" and the ability for music to impart
"positive energy" into the world, Zorn relates what might appear to be a rather
old-fashioned, almost quaint concept of the artist by identifying musicians such
as Bill Laswell and Ikue Mori as "saints" who are "giving, giving, giving and often
don't get that much back."[15] Zorn's comments here obviously resonate with many
of the claims put forth in chapter 3.

Zorn's remarks concerning love, "positive energy," and unlimited generosity
seem to situate him in some sort of hippie aesthetic commonly linked with the
counterculture of the 1960s, an image not usually associated with the composer.
At the same time, his characterization of composers or performers as saints carries with it romantic associations of the artist as seer or prophet. Given these
comments, we might be tempted to think that Zorn has turned over a new leaf,
so to speak, and where a kinder and gentler aesthetic has replaced the dark and
"dangerous" image that has often preceded him. Zorn's emphasis on the unlimited generosity and unselfishness of so many of his fellow musicians would
seem to support such a view. Given the many positive and uplifting sentiments
expressed in this one interview, however, it is worth considering whether or not
the notion of transgression—a concept that, to varying degrees, has played a
critical role in all of the preceding chapters—can still be considered an integral
component of Zorn's musical poetics.

In April 2001, John Zorn released an enigmatic recording simply entitled
The Gift.[16] Along with Zorn, who plays piano and theremin on selected tracks,
The Gift is performed by a number of musicians who have been frequent col-

laborators on many of the composer's projects. For instance, *The Gift* features the entire lineup that forms Masada (Joey Baron on drums, Dave Douglas on trumpet, and Greg Cohen on bass), as well as Marc Ribot on guitar, Jamie Saft on keyboards, Jennifer Choi on violin, and Mike Patton on vocals. Given the diverse lineup, the casual record buyer might expect *The Gift* to be composed of numerous stylistic or generic references, perhaps similar to the eclecticism of Naked City or the chamber music from the mid- to late 1980s. Instead, the listener of *The Gift* is confronted with music that is, for the most part, consistent throughout the entire record and, if a stylistic or generic label had to be attached, "lounge" might seem to fit the bill. According to the "obi strip" accompanying this release (the removable black strip included on many of Tzadik's releases), *The Gift* is a "beautiful and lyrical exploration of surf, exotica, easy listening, and world beat."[17] Unlike the "darker" aura that generally precedes Zorn and his music—described in chapter 1—*The Gift* seems more suited for a relaxing evening on the beach, watching the sun set while enjoying an exotic drink ("Makahaa") or browsing the shops in some mysterious far eastern bazaar ("Samarkan"). Also included on the obi strip is the explanation that "*The Gift* is an honest and heartfelt offering to music lovers the world over: an invitation to forget about the worries and cares of the world; to sit back and relax."[18] Zorn's record, it seems, is a gift to us, the listener, presented in a CD slipcase that features a prominent, inviting red bow.

While the music of *The Gift* might evoke exotic locales and carefree nights spent in a tiki bar, the accompanying artwork (six images by the British artist Trevor Brown) seems to tell a different story. When the buyer removes the disc from the purple cardboard slipcase (with its red bow), she is immediately confronted with a picture of a Japanese girl in a school uniform sitting in a chair, legs spread, with her hands behind her back. Looking closely, we see that she is holding a gun behind her back, which protrudes below her dress. The phallic associations are, of course, undeniable as the girl's alluring and seductive gaze arouses a taboo sexual desire for youth, innocence, and purity. At the same time, the danger associated with such desires (or at least acting upon them) is driven home by the gun and the bright red "X" that covers much of the background. The excitement aroused by the original idea of a gift gives way to something darker and more sinister.

Knowing our weaknesses before temptation, we cannot resist going forward and past the painting on the cover to see what awaits us inside. The remaining paintings all depict Japanese girls in different—but no less disturbing—scenarios. An inability for subjects to see is a theme that runs throughout the images included on *The Gift*. One shows a topless prepubescent girl who appears to be drugged, her eyes closed in front of a mushroom. In another image, a girl suffers from a black eye while her other eye is covered in a bandage as male hands (from more than one man) grasp and claw at her face and mouth. In yet another, a blindfolded girl is shown as an insect with wings as a beam of light (urine?) shoots from (into?) her vagina.

The layout of the images creates an interesting progression, one, perhaps, not necessarily recognized by the listener/looker. Such a progression contains within it interesting implications for how we read/hear *The Gift*—its music, artwork, and "meanings." As noted above, the first image that presents itself to us is of the young girl on the cover holding a gun behind her back, with her seductive half-grin, wide eyes, and head slightly tilted as if she is interested in the viewer. There seems to be some sort of shared knowledge, perhaps an unspoken secret, between the girl and the viewer. When we open the CD case and remove the disc, we are confronted by an image of another young girl, here standing in front of a urinal with her skirted hoisted up and her stockings pulled down just above her knees. Looking back at us, her expression indicates knowledge that she has been caught. Her mouth is open—possibly a gasp at being discovered ("Ohh!") or an expression of release ("Ahh!")—as she relieves herself. No matter how we interpret her reaction(s), the unspoken secret recognized in the first picture appears to be out in the open now as her (possibly feigned) expression of surprise mingles with—becomes inseparable from—her relief/release.

As the music of *The Gift* begins to play in the background, the tension aroused by these two pictures carries over into the interior images. The liner notes are not arranged as separate pages, but as a fold-out with more images and recording information included on the front and the back. When the listener/viewer first opens the fold-out, notes relating to production, recording, and engineering credits appear on the left-hand side. On the right-hand side of the page, the picture of a young girl, topless, drugged behind a large mushroom, stares out at us. The psychedelic connotations of the mushroom represent a world beyond everyday reality, where societal conventions, norms, rules, or laws are not applicable. The girl in her drugged state is part of this world, one that exists in our minds yet is difficult to attain, as represented by the brambles that intrude upon the painting.[19] The young girl in this image is behind the treacherous and thorny branches, more difficult to reach than the mushroom that stands closer to the viewer.

As we continue to examine the fold-out for *The Gift*, we are now confronted by a choice: the layout of the notes can be flipped to the left or the right. If we flip open the notes to the left, we encounter the young girl made up like some sort of insect. The mythic, almost transcendental quality of this painting— her translucent wings and her ability to float in space—seems to have more to do with the mushroom of the previous painting and its associated seductive possibilities. That is, we are still in the "unreal" symbolic world—the world of our mind—where the girl is part of us yet separate at the same time. Her eyes are covered with a cloth, rendering her identity uncertain. If we flip open the booklet to the right, however, we encounter a more disturbing picture: that of a young girl beaten and mauled by male hands. The seduction developed over the course of the artwork has degenerated here into the real world, where the seduced has acted upon his desires by making the symbols "real." As such, the "seductive economy"—which Jean Baudrillard describes as a "spiritual economy" where neither party has the upper hand—has been debased into an economy predicated on power. It is this allure of the unreal, the imaginary, and the mysterious that the seductive powers of the young girls can provide for the (male) viewer.

> To seduce is to die as reality and reconstitute oneself as illusion. It is to be taken in by one's own illusion and move in an enchanted world. It is the power of the seductive woman who takes herself for her own desire, and delights in the self-deception in which others, in their turn, will be caught. . . . The strategy of seduction is one of deception. It lies in wait for all that tends to confuse itself with reality. And it is potentially a source of fabulous strength. For if production can only produce objects or real signs, and thereby obtain some power; seduction, by producing only illusions, obtains all powers, including the power to return production and reality to their fundamental illusion.[20]

As we experience the paintings included with *The Gift*, it is possible to understand a set of options. On the one hand, the unreality of the floating blindfolded girl represents a seductive relation where nonsense rules, where our imagination is free to roam, and where nothing is expected and nothing (real) is gained. On the other hand, the painting of the beaten girl depicts desires acted upon, where seduction has turned base, vulgar, and dangerous; that is, real. The truth of the matter, however, is that the "choice" is illusory. As we encounter the images included within *The Gift*'s liner notes, once we arrive at the middle picture (the girl and the mushroom) there is no reasonable expectation to choose one of the final images—the insect girl or the beaten girl—over the other. Instead of the "choose-your-own-adventure" scenario I present above, the next painting we encounter is simply a matter of chance.[21]

Given the close connections Zorn perceives between the music and accompanying artwork on all of his recordings, our initial sense of gratitude at his "gift" might be construed as premature. In other words, this might be a gift we don't want to receive or acknowledge. Our image of a "kinder, gentler" Zorn has, perhaps, proven to be false. Instead—and depending upon our earlier opinions regarding Zorn (the man, the composer, his opinions, ideas, etc.)—it is quite possible that what we have here is the same old Zorn: the darker Zorn who forces us to confront things in the world (and things about ourselves) that we try to keep hidden away. It is difficult to know exactly what we might upset at—the fact that he tricked us (that we are upset with him for presenting us with these images) or that we continued to look at these images (upset with *him* for presenting these images or upset with *ourselves* for continuing to look). We might feel duped or suckered for falling into the trap laid out by Zorn.[22]

The Gift, therefore, might be seen as a "poisoned gift." For all of the positive features associated with the gift-giving spiral described in chapter 3, an inherent tension accompanies the giving and/or receiving of gifts. As Marcel Mauss points out, there is a certain "danger represented by the thing given or handed on," a danger, he recognizes, in "ancient Germanic law and languages." Mauss goes on to explain "a double meaning of the word *Gift* in [Germanic] languages—on the one hand, a gift, on the other, poison."[23] Despite (or perhaps because of) the latent semantic paradox of gift/poison, the social formations Mauss and others perceive within gift exchange are strengthened. The obligation to reciprocate/react is present when a gift is received graciously or with trepidation or suspicion. Both reactions force the recipient to acknowledge the communal/personal ties that accompany the gift-giving act, for, as Godbout and Caillé point out, "in the beginning, nothing exists but isolated individuals who, as such, are concerned only with their own interests. Then the gift appears on the scene, whether too good to be true or modest and insidious. But it creates a sense of obligation."[24]

Zorn's gift/*The Gift*—received willingly or under false pretenses—forces the recipient to react. The combination of the complex and uncertain narrative trajectory associated with the artwork and the perceived laid-back, carefree sentiments of the music creates an impression of paradox or incommensurability. The shock we perceive when we experience Trevor Brown's artwork or as we attempt to reconcile the apparent incongruities between artwork and music on *The Gift* resonate with the intentions often attributed to works of historical avant-garde movements. At the same time, when understood as a gift that we have no choice but to receive, Zorn's work compels the recipient(s) to acknowledge this shock, an acknowledgment that results in a self-reflexive examination of the recipient's "life praxis." Zorn's works force us to reconsider the various political/ideological/aesthetic lenses through which we view art and its place(s) and or function(s) in the world. Expanding this ocular metaphor, Zorn accomplishes this task by creating works that draw our attention to the scratches that affect our view; that is, the (nearly) imperceptible assumptions/limits/aporias that are built into our various ways of seeing.

The extreme reactions engendered by Zorn's music arise, I believe, from the basic fact that his music does not participate within an aesthetic tradition in which art is considered "redemptive." Recalling Ball's formulation above, Zorn's is an art of "paradox" and not one of "edification" and where, like Bataille's "big toe," Zorn's music reminds us that, despite man's elevated aspirations, "human life entails . . . the rage of seeing oneself as a back and forth movement from refuse to the ideal, and from the ideal to the refuse—a rage that is easily directed against an organ as *base* as the foot."[25] The persistent modernist dogma of the elevated status of art and its ability to "correct" lived experiences is intimately connected to the art for art's sake aesthetic associated with high modernism and, as such, is entirely foreign to Zorn's poetics and the avant-garde tradition within which he participates. Describing this "culture of redemption," Leo Bersani has written how the

> redemptive aesthetic asks us to consider art as a correction of life, but the corrective virtue of works of art depends on a misreading of art as philosophy. . . . A redemptive aesthetic based on the negation of life (in Nietzschean terms, on a nihilism that invents a "true world" as an alternative to an inferior and depreciated world of mere appearance) must also negate art.[26]

As I have tried to show throughout the preceding chapters, Zorn is not concerned with uncovering some sort of "true world" beyond experience. Instead, he has always been interested in exposing the many forms of experience that are normally hidden from view, including the transgressive experiences associated with S/M practices or the complex place of *ero manga* in Japanese society and culture (as described in chapter 1) or the persistence of magickal/occult forms of thought (chapter 2). Finally, Zorn's deep respect for history and tradition—whether this is conceived as a "tradition of transgression" or neo/late/post-avant-garde/postmodern—attests to Zorn's own experiences when confronted by the work and thought of earlier artists. These experiences are passed along to us—the recipients of his music—in a way that almost guarantees that experiences of shock, frustration, anger, wonder, and beauty will be passed along for some time to come.

Discography/Filmography

Select Discography

Naked City

Naked City. Elektra/Nonesuch 979238-2, 1990.
Grand Guignol. Avant Avan 002, 1992.
Leng Tch'e. Toy's Factory TFCK 88604, 1992.
Black Box. Tzadik TZ 7812-2, 1996.
The Complete Studio Recordings. Tzadik TZ 7344-5, 2005.

Painkiller

Rituals: Live in Japan. Toys Factory TFCK 88627, 1993.
Talisman: Live in Nagoya. Tzadik TZ 7342, 2002.

Zorn, various

Spillane. Elektra/Nonesuch 9 79172-2, 1987.
Elegy. Tzadik TZ 7302, 1995.
Aporias. Tzadik TZ 7037, 1998.
The String Quartets. Tzadik TZ 7047, 1999.
Taboo and Exile. Tzadik TZ 7325, 1999.
The Gift. Tzadik TZ 7332, 2001.
Madness, Love, and Mysticism. Tzadik TZ 7065, 2001.
Songs from the Hermetic Theater. Tzadik TZ 7066, 2001.
IAO: Music in Sacred Light. Tzadik TZ 7338, 2002.
Chimeras. Tzadik TZ 7085, 2003.

Magick. Tzadik TZ 8006, 2004.

Moonchild: Songs without Words. Tzadik TZ 7357, 2006.

From Silence to Sorcery. Tzadik TZ 8035, 2007.

Rav Yachida and Rav Tzizit (John Zorn and Yamantaka Eye). Mystic Fugu Orchestra, *Zohar.* Tzadik TZ 7106, 1995.

Zorn, Film Scores

Filmworks IV. Tzadik TZ 7310, 1997.

Filmworks VII: Cynical Hysterie Hour. Tzadik TZ 7315, 1997.

Filmworks X: In the Mirror of Maya Deren. Tzadik TZ 7333, 2001.

Filmworks XV: Protocols of Zion. Tzadik TZ 7345, 2005.

Select Filmography

Anger, Kenneth. *The Films of Kenneth Anger: Volume 1.* DVD. Fantoma Films FAN7048DVD, 2007.

Deren, Maya. *Maya Deren: Experimental Films.* DVD. Mystic Fire Video 76493, 2002.

Notes

Introduction

1. Zorn as quoted in Cole Gagne, *Soundpieces 2: Interviews with American Composer* (Metuchen, N.J.: Scarecrow Press, 1993), 530.

2. See Jonathan D. Kramer, "Beyond Unity: Toward an Understanding of Musical Postmodernism," in *Concert Music, Rock, and Jazz since 1945,* ed. Elizabeth West Marvin and Richard Hermann (Rochester, N.Y.: University of Rochester Press, 1995), 11–34; Tom Service, "Playing a New Game of Analysis: John Zorn's *Carny,* Autonomy and Postmodernism," *BPM Online* 5 (June 2002): http://www.bpmonline.org.uk/bpm5-playing .html; Susan McClary, *Conventional Wisdom* (Berkeley: University of California Press, 2000), 145–52; Ellie Hisama, "John Zorn and the Postmodern Condition," in *Locating East Asia in Western Art Music,* ed. Yayoi Uno Everett and Frederick Lau (Middletown, Conn.: Wesleyan University Press, 2004), 72–84; Kevin McNeilly, "Ugly Beauty: John Zorn and the Politics of Postmodern Music," *Postmodern Culture* 5, no. 2 (1994–95): http://muse.jhu.edu/journals/postmodern_culture/v005/5.2mcneilly.html.

3. Renée T. Coulombe, "Postmodern Polyamory or Postcolonial Challenge? Cornershop's Dialogue from West, to East, to West . . . ," in *Postmodern Music/Postmodern Thought,* ed. Judy Lochhead and Joseph Auner (New York: Routledge, 2002), 185.

4. Kramer, "Beyond Unity," 22.

5. Admittedly, a number of other characteristics or concepts often invoked when describing the "postmodern" artwork—for example, those relating to authenticity, originality, the function/role of the composer, etc.—could be cited in discussions relating to Zorn's music. By focusing on aspects relating to musical unity and history as I do here, I do not imply that these and other features are not important. Such avenues of investigation could offer any number of interesting insights into Zorn's music, musical thought, and reception.

6. On the topic of the postmodern and/in music, Timothy Taylor has explicitly questioned the usefulness of inferences that move from "style" to "label." Taylor notes:

> In discussions of music, by far the most frequently used sense of "postmodern" refers to style, and many authors compile lists of stylistic traits, lists that include some well-worn words in cultural theory: intertextuality, interreferentiality, pastiche, bricolage, fragmentation, depthlessness, the fragmentation of the subject, and more. . . . Such representations can lead (and have led in discussions of music) to problems, as if one can approach any cultural form or event with a checklist: Postmodern? yes/no. Many discussions of postmodernism in music proceed along these lines, with the author wondering if that work or composer is postmodern or not because of its use of pastiche, or its intertextuality, or because it has crossed the great divide.

Timothy D. Taylor, "Music and Musical Practices in Postmodernity," in *Postmodern Music/Postmodern Thought,* ed. Judy Lochhead and Joseph Auner (New York: Routledge, 2002), 94.

7. In one of the few instances where Zorn considers the term in relation to his own music and/or practices, he has described postmodernism as "ambiguous." See Zorn's preface to *Arcana: Musicians on Music* (New York: Granary Books/Hips Road, 2000), v.

8. Gagne, *Soundpieces 2,* 530.

9. Ibid. I am not certain what Zorn intends here by "multiphonic." In this excerpted passage, Zorn is also referring to his working methods for a string quartet (possibly *Memento Mori*) in addition to *Elegy.* Zorn makes similar comments regarding *Aporias,* a work I examine in detail in chapter 4. Elsewhere, Zorn considers the audibility/inaudibility of these and other unifying devices. "Maybe nobody will know [these relations are there]! Maybe nobody will care even if they *do* know! But it makes me feel stronger about the piece." Quoted in Ann McCutchan, *The Muse That Sings: Composers Speak About the Creative Process* (Oxford: Oxford University Press, 1999), 169.

10. Extending the Schoenbergian line of thought, Zorn's preferred method of composing with "block structures" exerts a strong influence on the type of unity that is operative for a particular piece. One could say, then, that the "block structures" function as a way of presenting smaller musical ideas that—when taken together—produce the coherent whole. This is strikingly similar to the presentational form Arnold Schoenberg associated with popular music: juxtaposition or "stringing together." "Structurally," Schoenberg explains, "there never remains in popular tunes an unsolved problem, the consequences of which will show up only later. The segments do not need much of a connective; they can be added by juxtaposition, because of the absence of variation in them. There is nothing that asks for expansion. The small form holds the content firmly, constituting thus a small expansion but independent structure." Arnold Schoenberg, *The Musical Idea and the Logic, Technique, and Art of Its Presentation,* trans. Patricia Carpenter and Severine Neff (New York: Columbia University Press, 1995), 380.

11. McCutchan, *The Muse That Sings,* 170.

12. Peter Bürger, *Theory of the Avant-Garde,* trans. Michael Shaw, foreword Jochen Schulte-Sasse (Minneapolis: University of Minnesota Press, 1984), 72.

13. Ibid., 80.

14. Quoted in Gagne, *Soundpieces 2,* 528.

15. E-mail communication with the composer, January 11, 2004.

16. Edward Strickland, *American Composers: Dialogues on Contemporary Music* (Bloomington: Indiana University Press, 1991), 128.

17. Sergei Eisenstein, "A Dialectic Approach to Film Form," in *Film Form,* trans. Jay Leyda (San Diego: Harcourt Brace, 1977), 49–50.

18. Sergei Eisenstein, "The Montage of Attractions," in *The Film Sense,* trans. Jay Leyda (New York: Harcourt Brace Jovanovich, 1975), 232. Emphasis in original. This 1923 essay was written from the perspective of the theater.

19. I borrow the phrase "strategies of coherence" from Teresa de Lauretis and her investigations of similar issues in cinema, specifically the negotiations between narrative and anti-narrative strategies in some feminist filmmaking. See de Lauretis's chapter "Strategies of Coherence: Narrative Cinema, Feminist Poetics, and Yvonne Rainer" in *Technologies of Gender* (Bloomington: Indiana University Press, 1987), 107–26.

20. Kramer, "Beyond Unity," 22, 24.

21. Hal Foster, ed., *The Anti-Aesthetic: Essays on Postmodern Culture* (New York: New Press, 1998), xiii.

22. Hal Foster, *Recodings: Art, Spectacle, Cultural Politics* (New York: New Press, 1999), 123; Susan McClary, *Conventional Wisdom,* chapter 5. McClary problematizes the view of Zorn as the quintessential postmodern composer. In *Spillane,* for instance, McClary perceives the presence of a well-worn narrative representing a form of "self-actualization" by which an integrated and complete sense of self (in this case, Mickey Spillane's/Mike Hammer's self) is realized/represented. As McClary points out, this belief in the possibility of a whole self flies in the face of certain strains of postmodernist thought (particularly some poststructuralist varieties). I consider Zorn's complex position(s) relating to subjectivity in chapter 1.

23. William Duckworth, *Talking Music* (New York: Schirmer Books, 1995), 470.

24. Gagne, *Soundpieces 2,* 526.

25. See Andreas Huyssen, *After the Great Divide: Modernism, Mass Culture, Postmodernism* (Bloomington: Indiana University Press, 1986), 216–17, 160–77. I will have more to say on the avant-garde in the epilogue.

26. Gagne, *Soundpieces 2,* 530. Zorn's characterization of artists as "outsiders" is, of course, a very Romantic notion. Any attempt to unpack the many assumptions associated with such a characterization would take many pages or even another book! For some insight into how Zorn understands this position, he has mentioned to me (e-mail communication with the composer, October 19, 2005) how much he admires Colin Wilson's book *The Outsider* (Boston: Houghton Mifflin, 1956).

27. Michel Foucault, "A Preface to Transgression," in *Language, Counter-Memory, Practice,* ed. Donald F. Bouchard (Ithaca, N.Y.: Cornell University Press, 1977), 33–34.

28. In many ways, the in-between spaces where Zorn's musical poetics is enacted can be applied to his "Jewish" music. For example, Zorn's *Kristallnacht,* the jazz tunes composed for Masada, and the music that appears on Tzadik's Radical Jewish Culture series problematizes the very notion of what Jewish music and Jewish identity might mean. It is definitely not klezmer; at the same time, it does not serve as a memorial to Holocaust victims, nor does it lament Jewish *galut.* Although I do not pursue this line of thought in the present book, I hope to return to this topic in future work. The difficulties

presented by Zorn's "Jewish" music is examined by Michael Scott Cuthbert, "Free Improvisation: John Zorn and the Construction of Jewish Identity through Music," in *Studies in Jewish Musical Traditions: Insights from the Harvard Collection of Judaica Sound Recordings,* ed. Kay Kaufman Shelemay (Cambridge: Harvard College Library, 2001), 1–31. See also Adam Shatz, "Crossing Music's Borders in Search of Identity; Downtown, a Reach for Ethnicity," *New York Times,* October 3, 1999, AR1. Responses to Shatz's article by Larry Blumenfeld, Dave Douglas, and Bill Milkowski appeared in the *New York Times,* October 17, 1999, AR4.

29. Henri Lefebvre, *The Production of Space,* trans. Donald Nicholson-Smith (Oxford: Blackwell, 1991), 19–20. Maurice Blanchot expresses a similar sentiment regarding Marguerite Duras: "A rarefied space rendered infinite by the effect of rarity, up to the limit which nonetheless does not limit it." Zorn includes this quote on the back of his *Taboo and Exile* (Tzadik compact disc TZ 7325, 1999).

30. On the "Radical Jewish Culture" scene (a scene that includes Zorn and many other composers/musicians), see Tamar Barzel, "If Not Klezmer, Then What? Jewish Music and Modalities on New York City's Downtown Music Scene," *Michigan Quarterly Review* 42, no. 1 (Winter 2002): 79–94. See also Barzel, "'Radical Jewish Culture': Composer/Improvisers on New York City's 1990s Downtown Scene," PhD diss., University of Michigan, 2004.

31. On the "Cinema of Transgression," see Jack Sargeant, *Deathtripping* (London: Creation Books, 1995).

32. In this respect, I agree with Kevin Korsyn and his plea for new modes of writing in musical research, arguing that "it is not enough to change content, pouring new wine into old bottles; since the form of a genre carries its own content and its own messages, one must change the genres as well, by fostering dialogic relations among genres." Kevin Korsyn, *Decentering Music* (Oxford: Oxford University Press, 2003), 185. I have tried to adopt such an approach within individual essays, between essays, and at the level of the book as a whole. Craig Dworkin's *Reading the Illegible* (Evanston, Ill.: Northwestern University Press, 2003) has also been an important model for the present work.

33. Igor Stravinsky, *Poetics of Music in the Form of Six Lessons,* trans. Arthur Knodel and Ingolf Dahl, preface Darius Milhaud (New York: Vintage Books, 1959), 5. Emphasis in original.

34. Carl Dahlhaus, "Schoenberg's Poetics of Music," in *Schoenberg and the New Music,* trans. Derrick Puffett and Alfred Clayton (Cambridge: Cambridge University Press, 1997), 73–80. Emphasis added.

1. From the Fantastic to the Dangerously Real

1. Jonathan D. Kramer, "Beyond Unity: Toward an Understanding of Musical Postmodernism," in *Concert Music, Rock, and Jazz since 1945,* ed. Elizabeth West Marvin and Richard Hermann (Rochester, N.Y.: University of Rochester Press, 1995), 11–34; Tom Service, "Playing a New Game of Analysis: John Zorn's *Carny,* Autonomy and Postmodernism," *BPM Online* 5 (June 2002): www.bpmonline.org.uk/bpm5-playing.html; Susan McClary, *Conventional Wisdom* (Berkeley: University of California Press, 2000), 145–52. See also Kevin McNeilly, "Ugly Beauty: John Zorn and the Politics of Postmod-

ern Music," *Postmodern Culture* 5, no. 2 (1994–1995): http://muse.jhu.edu/journals/postmodern_culture/v005/5.2mcneilly.html.

2. Indeed, Ajay Heble remarks how "it's become something of a commonplace to say that listening to Zorn's music is a little like channel surfing with a remote control." See Heble, *Landing on the Wrong Note: Jazz, Dissonance, and Critical Practice* (New York: Routledge, 2000), 183.

3. Naked City released and recorded five studio albums and one extended play (EP) recording between 1989 and 1993. The band consisted of Zorn on alto saxophone, Fred Frith on bass, Bill Frisell on guitar, Wayne Horvitz on keyboards, and Joey Baron on drums. Yamatsuka Eye contributes vocals on some tracks. Although the band quit performing and recording in 1993, they did reunite for two live shows in 2003.

Painkiller's original lineup consisted of Zorn on saxophone, Bill Laswell on bass, and Mick Harris on drums. This band (active from 1991 until around 1994) released two EPs, one full-length album, and a number of live recordings. The group—with different drummers and sometimes with a vocalist—still performs.

4. Figures 1.1 and 1.2 were included on Naked City's album *Torture Garden.* Figure 1.3 appears on the band's *Leng Tch'e* EP. *Torture Garden* was originally released in 1989 on Toy's Factory/Earache/Shimmy Disc and is a collection of the "hardcore pieces" that would later be included on *Naked City* (Elektra/Nonesuch compact disc 979238-2, 1990) and Naked City's *Grand Guignol* (Avant compact disc Avan 002, 1992). *Leng Tch'e* was originally released as Toy's Factory compact disc TFCK 88604, 1992. All of these recordings are included on Naked City, *Black Box* (Tzadik compact disc TZ 7812-2, 1996) and, more recently, Naked City's *Complete Studio Recordings* (Tzadik compact disc TZ 7344-5, 2005).

5. Zorn has often emphasized the close relations between the music and artwork on all of his recordings. "For me, my record covers are *very* important. The cover has got to follow through with what the music is about. I don't just make music. I make *records.* I just don't give a tape to a record company + let them package it any way they want so it sells a lot. It has to *mean* something. The record package is *art.*" Tai Toshiharu and John Zorn, "About the Record Jacket of *Guts of a Virgin,*" *Eureka: Poems and Criticism* 29, no. 1 (1997): 138. Emphasis in original.

6. Elisa Lee, "Zorn's Album Art of Asian Women Sparks Controversy," *AsianWeek,* March 4, 1994, 1. See also Denise Hamilton, "Zorn's 'Garden' Sprouts Discontent Jazz," *Los Angeles Times,* August 15, 1994, 9; Alex Beels, "Musician John Zorn's Brutal Images of Asians Draw Fire," *Asian New Yorker,* May 1994, 5–6.

7. Ellie M. Hisama, "Postcolonialism on the Make: The Music of John Mellencamp, David Bowie, and John Zorn," in *Reading Pop: Approaches to Textual Analysis in Popular Music,* ed. Richard Middleton (Oxford: Oxford University Press, 2000), 329–46.

8. Ellie Hisama, "John Zorn and the Postmodern Condition," in *Locating East Asia in Western Art Music,* ed. Yayoi Uno Everett and Frederick Lau (Middletown, Conn.: Wesleyan University Press, 2004), 72–84.

9. See Gary Y. Okihiro, *Margins and Mainstreams* (Seattle: University of Washington Press, 1994), especially chapter 5, "Perils of the Body and Mind."

10. On the Chin incident, see Ronald Takaki, "Who Killed Vincent Chin?" in *A Look beyond the Model Minority Image: Critical Issues in Asian America,* ed. Grace Yun (New York: Minority Rights Group, 1989), 23–29. For an overview of the many books

written during this time that represented Japan as a "new threat," see Robert B. Reich's review of books in "Is Japan Really Out to Get Us?" *New York Times Book Review,* February 9, 1992. See also Okihiro, *Margins and Mainstreams,* 138 ff. On the *Miss Saigon* controversy, see Helen Zia, *Asian American Dreams: The Emergence of an American Other* (New York: Farrar, Straus and Giroux, 2000), 109–35. Finally, on the violence following the Rodney King verdict, see Robert Gooding-Williams, ed., *Reading Rodney King, Reading Urban Uprising* (New York: Routledge, 1993), especially the essays by Sumi Cho ("Korean Americans vs. African Americans: Conflict and Construction," 196–211) and Elaine Kim ("Home Is Where the *Han* Is," 219–35).

11. Hisama, "John Zorn and the Postmodern Condition," 78.

12. In this respect, the present chapter is modeled after the reading/interpretive strategies described in Ellen Koskoff's "Miriam Sings Her Song: The Self and the Other in Anthropological Discourse," in *Musicology and Difference,* ed. Ruth A. Solie (Berkeley: University of California Press, 1993), 149–63. A slightly different model can be found in Susan Rubin Suleiman, "Transgression and the Avant-Garde: Bataille's *Histoire de l'oeil,*" in *Subversive Intent: Gender, Politics, and the Avant-Garde* (Cambridge: Harvard University Press, 1990), 72–87.

13. Michel Foucault, *The History of Sexuality, Volume 1: An Introduction,* trans. Robert Hurley (New York: Vintage Books, 1990), 34.

14. Judith Butler, "The Force of Fantasy: Feminism, Mapplethorpe, and Discursive Excess," in *The Judith Butler Reader,* ed. Sara Salih with Judith Butler (Oxford: Blackwell, 2004), 186. Later, Butler remarks how "to say something is phantasmatic is not to say that it is 'unreal' or artificial or dismissible as a consequence. Wielded within political discourse, the real is syntactically regulated phantasm that has enormous power and efficacy" (187–88).

15. Hisama, "John Zorn and the Postmodern Condition," 84.

16. Oyama and Hwang quoted in Lee, "Zorn's Album Art of Asian Women Sparks Controversy," 1; Hisama, "John Zorn and the Postmodern Condition," 80.

17. Catharine MacKinnon, *Only Words* (Cambridge: Harvard University Press, 1993), 25.

18. Ibid., 21.

19. Hisama, "John Zorn and the Postmodern Condition," 80.

20. This equation is compounded by the fact that *Torture Garden* is the name of a book by Octave Mirbeau that most likely served as the inspiration for Zorn's album title. In this book, a young western woman with a morbid and lurid fascination for torture frequents a prison "yard"/"garden" where she routinely takes pleasure in seeing the Asian prisoners tortured. It is possible, therefore, to read the S/M photos as recontextualized forms of torture on Zorn's *Torture Garden* record.

21. These images are reproduced and described in Georges Bataille, *The Tears of Eros,* trans. Peter Connor (San Francisco: City Lights Books, 1989), 204–6. Bataille writes that, in Fu Chou Li's case, Leng Tch'e was chosen because the original sentence handed down—being burned alive—was deemed "too cruel" (204).

22. On the goals and practices of torture, see Elaine Scarry, *The Body in Pain* (New York: Oxford University Press, 1985), 27–59. Numerous writings address the complex politics and meanings of S/M practices. See, e.g., Gilles Deleuze, *Masochism: Coldness and Cruelty,* trans. Jean McNeil (New York: Zone Books, 1991); Karmen MacKendrick,

Counterpleasures (Albany: State University of New York Press, 1999); Kaja Silverman, *Male Subjectivity at the Margins* (New York: Routledge, 1992), especially chapters 5 and 6; Gini Graham Scott, *Erotic Power: An Exploration of Dominance and Submission* (Secaucus, N.J.: Citadel, 1983); and Linda Williams, *Hard Core: Power, Pleasure, and the "Frenzy of the Visible"* (Berkeley: University of California Press, 1989), 184–228.

23. Images of male participants in S/M scenes are included on Painkiller, *Rituals: Live in Japan* (Toys Factory compact disc TFCK 88627, 1993) and Painkiller, *Talisman: Live in Nagoya* (Tzadik compact disc TZ 7342, 2002). In all of the images on these records, the male is assuming the submissive position.

24. Andrea Dworkin, *Pornography: Men Possessing Women* (New York: Perigee Books, 1981), 150.

25. See the essays in Robin Ruth Linden, Darlene R. Pagano, Diana E. H. Russell, and Susan Leigh Star, eds., *Against Sadomasochism: A Radical Feminist Analysis* (East Palo Alto, Calif.: Frog in the Well, 1982).

26. MacKinnon, *Only Words,* 29. For a critique of MacKinnon's position, see Judith Butler, *Excitable Speech: A Politics of the Performative* (New York: Routledge, 1997), 65 ff.

27. MacKinnon, *Only Words,* 22.

28. Regarding my fictitious example, Aki Kawamoto has explained to me that if a person reading *Rapeman* is encountered on a train or bus, other Japanese passengers *would* probably sit next to him (or her) if that reader made no attempt to hide the *manga*. If, on the other hand, the passenger appeared to be hiding or concealing the name of the *manga*, other passengers would *not* be as willing to sit next to the reader. In an e-mail, Kawamoto explains:

> In Japanese society, such a passenger is considered quite "normal," "honest," "open," "natural," and even "safe," whereas someone who reads such a manga secretly is considered "dishonest," "introverted," and even "potentially dangerous." . . . If we sit next to such an "open" guy, we . . . feel we are "safe," so we never pick up our belongings. If we sit next to a guy who reads an ero manga but tries to hide it from others, then we might want to get away from him because he might be really into that manga (and he might even start masturbating right there).

A similar observation was expressed to me by Tomomi Nakashima.

29. Setsu Shigematsu, "Dimensions of Desire: Sex, Fantasy, and Fetish in Japanese Comics," in *Themes and Issues in Asian Cartooning: Cute, Cheap, Mad, and Sexy,* ed. John A. Lent (Bowling Green, Ohio: Bowling Green State University Popular Press, 1999), 140. See also Deborah Shamoon, "Office Sluts and Rebel Flowers: The Pleasures of Japanese Pornographic Comics for Women," in *Porn Studies,* ed. Linda Williams (Durham, N.C.: Duke University Press, 2004), 77–103. For a negative reading of *ero manga,* see Sandra Buckley, "Penguin in Bondage: A Graphic Tale of Japanese Comic Books," in *Technoculture,* ed. Constance Penley and Andrew Ross (Minneapolis: University of Minnesota Press, 1991), 163–93.

30. Shigematsu, "Dimensions of Desire," 140.

31. See Donald Richie's discussion of *eroductions* ("erotic productions") in *Some Aspects of Japanese Popular Culture* (Tokyo: Shubun International, 1981), 29–42.

32. I should clarify that the "poor production techniques" often encountered in

these films are not intended to evoke some sort of cinematic realism along the lines of cinema verité, where rough or shaky camera shots (perhaps from a hand-held camera or video camera) aim to create a sense of immediacy and intimacy between the viewer and the viewed. Instead, I am referring to the numerous slips in continuity (a half-empty glass in one shot is full in the next or a man's tie curiously disappears/appears in consecutive shots) and other technical mishaps. For instance, in a number of films I have viewed, it is sometimes possible to see the boom microphone at the top of the screen move back and forth between the speaking characters. I believe that these and other cinematic blunders were caused by the speed with which the film studios made and released these movies.

33. Anne Allison, *Permitted and Prohibited Desires: Mothers, Comics, and Censorship in Japan* (Boulder: Westview Press, 1996), 171. Allison also investigates the role of fantasy in Japanese business practices in her *Nightwork: Sexuality, Pleasure, and Corporate Masculinity in a Tokyo Hostess Club* (Chicago: University of Chicago Press, 1994). The role of fantasy in Japanese culture is also emphasized in Ian Buruma, *Behind the Mask: On Sexual Demons, Sacred Mothers, Transvestites, Gangsters, and Other Japanese Cultural Heroes* (New York: Meridian, 1985).

Of course, not all commentators agree with such a relatively harmless interpretation of Japanese pornography. See, e.g., Kuniko Funabashi, "Pornographic Culture and Sexual Violence," in *Japanese Women: New Feminist Perspectives on the Past, Present, and Future,* ed. Kumiko Fujimura-Fanselow and Atsuko Kameda (New York: Feminist Press at the City University of New York, 1995), 255–63.

34. Reprinted in Lawrence Ward Beer, *Freedom of Expression in Japan: A Study in Comparative Law, Politics, and Society* (Tokyo: Kodansha International, 1984), 336.

35. Ibid., 355–56, footnote 10.

36. Ibid., 337.

37. Allison, *Permitted and Prohibited Desires,* 163.

38. Quoted in R. P. Dore, *City Life in Japan: A Study in a Tokyo Ward* (London: Routledge & Kegan Paul, 1958), 160.

39. Allison, *Permitted and Prohibited Desires,* 147–50. In 1991, regulations against showing pubic hair began to relax, partly because of Kishin Shinoyama's *Santa Fe,* a collection of photographs of the then-popular singer/actress Rie Miyazawa.

40. Ibid., 151.

41. Beer, *Freedom of Expression in Japan,* 348. Emphasis added. The acquittal was later overturned by the Tokyo high court, which ruled that Condition 1 had been met. The Supreme Court later turned down an appeal in a "lengthy and complex" decision. On this ruling, see Beer, 349–53.

42. John Clammer, *Contemporary Urban Japan: A Sociology of Consumption* (Oxford: Blackwell, 1997), 59.

43. Allison, *Permitted and Prohibited Desires,* 78.

44. Mary Grigsby, "The Social Production of Gender as Reflected in Two Japanese Culture Industry Products: *Sailormoon* and *Crayon Shin-chan,*" in *Themes and Issues in Asian Cartooning,* ed. Lent, 207. Many of Grigsby's claims are tendentious; for a more balanced view, see Antonia Levi, *Samurai from Outer Space: Understanding Japanese Animation* (Chicago: Open Court, 1996), especially chapter 7 ("Outrageous Women").

45. Kanako Shiokawa, "Cute but Deadly: Women and Violence in Japanese Comics," in *Themes and Issues in Asian Cartooning*, ed. Lent, 120–21.

46. Shigematsu, "Dimensions of Desire," 133.

47. Ibid., 144–46.

48. Cited in Hisama, "John Zorn and the Postmodern Condition," 83. A version of this statement also appears in the "On the Artwork" notes appearing in *Black Box*. Here, the wording is slightly altered, and there is no mention of the images' "transgressive" qualities.

49. Zorn's familiarity with Bataille is also evident in the fact that his string quartet *The Dead Man* is inspired by a short story of the same name written by Bataille. One of the movements—or "specimens," as Zorn calls them—takes its name from another work by Bataille, "Blue of Noon."

Zorn's continued interest in the thought of Bataille can also be seen on a more recent recording, *Moonchild: Songs without Words* (Tzadik compact disc TZ 7357, 2006). On this record, one of the tracks, "Le Part Maudit," is a reference to Bataille's influential thoughts of a general economy predicated on waste and useless expenditure: the "Accursed Share."

50. References to Bataille's *Story of the Eye* appear in works that Zorn may have encountered while in Japan. In particular, Suehiro Maruo's *manga* "Shit Soup" and Nagisa Oshima's legendary film *In the Realm of the Senses* both include scenes that are clearly inspired by Bataille's work of fiction. The *manga* reproduced in Figure 1.1 may also be a reference to Bataille's work of fiction, specifically the emphasis placed on eyes.

51. Liner notes, *Black Box*, n.p.; Bataille, *The Tears of Eros*, 206–7. Italics in original. The pictures of Fu Chou Li exerted a strong hold over Bataille and are referred to repeatedly in his writings. See, e.g., Georges Bataille, *Inner Experience*, trans. Leslie Anne Boldt (Albany: State University of New York Press, 1988), 120 ff.; Bataille, *Guilty*, trans. Bruce Boone (Venice, Calif.: Lapis Press, 1988), 38. See also Peter Tracey Connor, *Georges Bataille and the Mysticism of Sin* (Baltimore: Johns Hopkins University Press, 2000), 1–7.

52. Bataille, *The Tears of Eros*, 206.

53. Georges Bataille, "The Psychological Structure of Fascism," in *Visions of Excess: Selected Writings, 1927–1939*, trans. Allan Stoekl with Carl R. Lovitt and Donald M. Leslie Jr. (Minneapolis: University of Minnesota Press, 1985), 137–38. See also Bataille, "The Use Value of D.A.F. de Sade (An Open Letter to My Current Comrades)," in *Visions of Excess*, 91–102. For a critical examination of these concepts, see Rodolphe Gasché, "The Heterological Almanac," in *On Bataille: Critical Essays*, trans. Leslie Anne Boldt-Irons (Albany: State University of New York Press, 1995), 157–208.

54. Bataille, "The Psychological Structure of Fascism," in *Visions of Excess*, 142–43. Bataille's equation of the heterogeneous with waste and unproductive expenditure forms the basis of his "general economy" as described in his "The Notion of Expenditure," in *Visions of Excess*, 116–29. This subject is treated more thoroughly in Georges Bataille, *The Accursed Share, Volume 1: Consumption*, trans. Robert Hurley (New York: Zone Books, 1991).

55. Georges Bataille, "Method of Meditation," in *The Unfinished System of Non-knowledge*, ed. Stuart Kendall, trans. Michelle Kendall and Stuart Kendall (Minneapolis: University of Minnesota Press, 2001), 78, 85.

56. Ibid., 84. Emphasis in original.

57. Bataille, "The Use Value of D.A.F. de Sade (An Open Letter to My Current Comrades)," in *Visions of Excess,* 97.

58. For a useful overview of Bataille's thought, see Michèle H. Richman, *Reading Georges Bataille: Beyond the Gift* (Baltimore: Johns Hopkins University Press, 1982).

59. In the notes to *Grand Guignol,* Zorn expresses similar ideas: "Our fascination with Fear, Terror, and Evil, like Death itself, knows no racial, cultural, or religious barriers. It resides in our collective unconscious, binding us together with ropes we try, but are ultimately unable to sever. Only through violent trauma, or the convulsive viscera of artistic vision does it rise to the surface, reminding us that it has, in truth, been there all along." (Liner notes to Naked City, *Grand Guignol,* n.p.)

60. Bataille, *The Unfinished System of Nonknowledge,* 95; "The Use Value of D.A.F. de Sade (An Open Letter to My Current Comrades)," in *Visions of Excess,* 97.

61. Example 1.1 is a slightly modified form of Zorn's handwritten chart of "Speedfreaks," which is reproduced in the booklet *Eight Million Stories: Naked City Ephemera* accompanying Naked City, *The Complete Studio Recordings* (n.p.).

62. Hisama, "John Zorn and the Postmodern Condition, 79–80.

63. It is also possible to read Hisama's remarks as a not-so-veiled dismissal of thrash/hardcore music in general.

64. E-mail communication with the composer, January 11, 2004.

65. Bataille, "Nonknowledge, Laughter, Tears," in *The Unfinished System of Nonknowledge,* 135.

66. Bataille, *Guilty,* 101. Emphasis in original.

67. While these images are, in terms of their depictions of violence and sexuality, just as graphic as those accompanying *Torture Garden* and *Leng Tch'e* (i.e., Man Ray's photographs of a bound woman wearing a leather (or rubber) suit and mask, medical photos of decapitated heads and heaps of severed body parts, etc.), they have not been subjected to the same type of scrutiny. Perhaps this is due to the fact that the men and women shown in these images are Caucasian and not Asian and/or the sources of these images (Man Ray, Hans Bellmer, etc.) have, in various ways, been "legitimized" by the academy (through their relations with surrealism). In other words, even if the images have the capacity to cause offense, their "real meaning" is much "deeper" and abstract, a luxury that is not afforded to the images discussed in the body of the chapter.

68. Suleiman, *Subversive Intent,* 74.

69. Ibid., 76.

70. Here I am thinking of certain Japanese films released as part of the Guinea Pig (*ginpiggu*) series. In at least two of the films released in this series (*The Devil's Experiment* and *Flowers of Flesh and Blood*), the filmmakers attempt to re-create the contents of snuff films. In support of the "image as speech act" model described in the body of this chapter, it is worth pointing out that copies of these and other films were found in the possession of Miyazaki Tsutomu, a serial killer who tortured and killed at least four Japanese girls in 1988 and 1989.

71. Liner notes to John Zorn, *Spillane* (Elektra/Nonesuch compact disc 9 79172-2, 1987). Elsewhere, Zorn talks about his time in Japan as a personal experience of "alienation and rejection." Ann McCutchan, *The Muse That Sings: Composers Speak about the Creative Process* (Oxford: Oxford University Press, 1999), 167.

72. Hisama, "Postcolonialism on the Make."

73. Coco Fusco, *English Is Broken Here* (New York: New Press, 1995), 46, 68, 27. See Gayatri Chakravorty Spivak, "Subaltern Studies: Deconstructing Historiography," in *In Other Worlds: Essays in Cultural Politics* (New York: Routledge, 1998), 270–304.

74. Fusco, *English Is Broken Here,* 32.

75. Susan Koshy, "The Fiction of Asian American Literature," *Yale Journal of Criticism* 9, no. 2 (1996): 321. The embedded quotation is from Lisa Lowe, "Heterogeneity, Hybridity, Multiplicity: Marking Asian American Differences," *Diaspora* 1, no. 1 (1991): 30.

76. On the perceived "inauthenticity" of Asian American identity, see Vincent J. Cheng, *Inauthentic: The Anxiety over Culture and Identity* (New Brunswick, N.J.: Rutgers University Press, 2004), 125–70. Quote on 142.

77. Viet Thanh Nguyen, *Race and Resistance: Literature and Politics in Asian America* (Oxford: Oxford University Press, 2002), 12.

78. Lisa Lowe, *Immigrant Acts: On Asian American Cultural Politics* (Durham, N.C.: Duke University Press, 2004), 9, 96. On the sometimes uneasy relations that exist between postmodern theories and/or practices in the context of Asian American studies in particular, see Keith Hiroshi Osajima, "Postmodernism and Asian American Studies: A Critical Appropriation," in *Privileging Positions: The Sites of Asian American Studies,* ed. Gary Y. Okihiro, Marilyn Alquizola, Dorothy Fujita Rony, and K. Scott Wong, (Pullman: Washington State University Press, 1995), 21–35. In the same volume, see also Dana Y. Takagi, "Postmodernism on the Edge," 37–45, and Colleen Lye, "Toward an (Asian) American Cultural Studies: Postmodernism and the 'Peril of Yellow Capital and Labor,'" 47–56. Takagi considers the uneasy relations that exist between many forms of postmodernist/poststructuralist theory and theorizing and a set of parallel concerns connecting Asian American studies and certain feminist theories.

79. John Kuo Wei Tchen, "Rethinking Who *We* Are: A Basic Discussion of Basic Terms," in *Voices from the Battlefront: Achieving Cultural Equity,* ed. Marta Moreno Vega and Cheryll Y. Greene (Trenton, N.J.: Africa World Press, 1993), 3; quoted in Hisama, "John Zorn and the Postmodern Condition," 83.

80. Stuart Hall, "Cultural Identity and Diaspora," in *Contemporary Postcolonial Theory: A Reader,* ed. Padmini Mongia (London: Hodder Arnold, 2003), 112–13.

81. Lowe, *Immigrant Acts,* 65, 82.

82. Ibid., 28–29. Emphasis added.

83. Ibid., 114. Emphasis added. Ileto's essay, "Outlines of a Nonlinear Emplotment of Philippine History," is reprinted in *The Politics of Culture in the Shadow of Capitalism,* ed. David Lloyd and Lisa Lowe (Durham, N.C.: Duke University Press, 1997), 98–131.

84. Here I am thinking of the arguments put forth in Michael Taussig's remarkable book *Defacement: Public Secrecy and the Labor of the Negative* (Stanford: Stanford University Press, 1999).

85. In the liner notes to *Grand Guignol,* Zorn identifies (among many others), the Marquis de Sade, Edgar Allan Poe, Salvador Dalí, Alfred Hitchcock, Hermann Nitsch, and Bataille. Liner notes to Naked City, *Grand Guignol,* n.p.

86. Here I am reminded of the limitations of such a position as described in Hal Foster, "Against Pluralism," in *Recodings: Art, Spectacle, Cultural Politics* (Port Townsend, Wash.: Bay Press, 1985), 13–20.

2. Magick and Mysticism in Zorn's Recent Works

1. Throughout this chapter, I adopt Aleister Crowley's preferred spelling of Magick with a *k*. "Magick" refers to the ability to communicate with enlightened individuals, demons, or angels; "mysticism" describes the ability of an individual to attain such an enlightened state.

According to Crowley, this particular spelling was adopted "in order to distinguish the Science of the Magi from all its counterfeits." Aleister Crowley, with Mary Desti and Leila Waddell, *Magick: Liber ABA, Book IV, Parts I–IV,* 2d rev. ed., ed. Hymenaeus Beta (York Beach, Maine: S. Weiser, 1997), 47. Crowley believed that Magickal practice does not exist apart from science and more traditional conceptions of rational thought but is, instead, an integral part of science and knowledge in general. In his introduction to *Magick,* Hymenaeus Beta notes that Crowley's intent "was not only to restore to Magick the respect and honor it commanded in earlier times; it was also to lay the cornerstone of a magico-religious system that would bridge the chasm between scientific skepticism and spiritual revelation" (xxiv). This interdependency between rational and speculative/occult forms of knowledge is discussed in the next section.

2. Even earlier, the voice of Aleister Crowley can be heard on "A Lot of Fun for the Evil One" included on John Zorn, *Filmworks IV* (Tzadik compact disc TZ 7310, 1997), a soundtrack for the 1994 S/M film of the same name directed by M. M. Serra and Maria Beatty.

3. Georges Bataille, "The Notion of Expenditure," in *Visions of Excess: Selected Writings, 1927–1939,* trans. Allan Stoekl with Carl R. Lovitt and Donald M. Leslie Jr. (Minneapolis: University of Minnesota Press, 1985), 118.

4. Georges Bataille, "Base Materialism and Gnosticism," in *Visions of Excess,* 51.

5. Bataille, "Materialism," in *Visions of Excess,* 15.

6. Ibid., 16. Emphasis in original.

7. Bataille, "The Big Toe," in *Visions of Excess,* 20–21. Emphasis in original.

8. This inadequacy of inverting values lies at the heart of the disagreement between the interpretation of the Marquis de Sade put forth by the surrealists and Bataille (and also touches upon the reality/fantasy distinctions described in the previous chapter). For Breton and many other surrealists, the "unreality" of Sade's writings qualify him as a visionary of the imaginative, thereby raising Sade and his writings to a higher level—the "sur-real"—where more nuanced and developed notions of truth and liberty reside. According to this view, Sade represents a proto-surrealist with Breton exclaiming "Sade is Surrealist in Sadism." André Breton, *Manifestos of Surrealism,* trans. Richard Seaver and Helen R. Lane (Ann Arbor: University of Michigan Press, 1972), 26. Bataille, by contrast, was never interested in "raising" Sade to a higher, loftier level. Referring to Breton and others, Bataille writes how the "behavior of Sade's admirers resembles that of primitive subjects in relation to their king, whom they adore and loathe, and whom they cover with honors and narrowly confine." Bataille, "The Use Value of D.A.F. de Sade (An Open Letter to My Current Comrades)," in *Visions of Excess,* 92. For Bataille, there is nothing imaginary about Sade's thoughts and ideas; instead, Sade's writings represent

a "heterological reality" that fundamentally resists the elevated readings advanced by Breton and others.

9. Within more "rational" or "idealized" philosophical modes of discourse, Benjamin Noys has described how "philosophical systems claim to be universal and enforce [claims according to] hierarchical oppositions, and in doing so they form the most complete attempt to dominate and eliminate base matter." However, Noys continues, the intrusive and transgressive nature of base matter "can disrupt the universalism of philosophy" as well as point to the "limits of discourse itself." Benjamin Noys, "Georges Bataille's Base Materialism," *Cultural Values* 2, no. 4 (1998): 510.

Of course, it is not only philosophical systems that "enforce hierarchical oppositions." Aesthetic systems are also quite capable of erecting similar distinctions. The associated aims of both art and artists working on either side of the "high" or "low" cultural divide immediately come to mind. It should come as no surprise, perhaps, that, given his Bataillean poetics—a poetics that recognizes and plays with the inherent instabilities of such artificial oppositions—Zorn considers the distinction between "high" and "low" music (and art in general) as "fucking bullshit." See Edward Strickland, *American Composers: Dialogues on Contemporary Music* (Bloomington: Indiana University Press, 1991), 128.

10. Bataille, "Base Materialism and Gnosticism," 51.

11. Ibid., 46. For a more extended and detailed examination of Gnosticism from the perspective of "otherness" and difference, see Karen L. King, *What Is Gnosticism?* (Cambridge: Belknap Press, 2005). See also Michael A. Williams, *Rethinking "Gnosticism": An Argument for Dismantling a Dubious Category* (Princeton, N.J.: Princeton University Press, 1996).

12. Bataille, "Base Materialism and Gnosticism," 47.

13. Ibid., 48.

14. For a more detailed treatment of Bataille's dualism, see Denis Hollier, "The Dualist Materialism of Georges Bataille," trans. Hillari Allred, *Yale French Studies* 78 (1990): 124–39.

15. Antonin Artaud, *The Theater and Its Double,* trans. Mary Caroline Richards (New York: Grove Press, 1958), 72. Zorn has acknowledged the importance of the thought and writings of Antonin Artaud (along with Crowley and Edgard Varèse) in the dedications to his *Moonchild, Astronome,* and *Six Litanies for Heliogabalus* recordings.

16. *Necronomicon* is included on John Zorn, *Magick* (Tzadik compact disc TZ 8006, 2004). The timings included in all of the examples/figures relating to *Necronomicon* are based on this recording.

17. On Lovecraft's evolving conception of the Necronomicon, see Daniel Harms and John Wisdom Gonce III, *The Necronomicon Files* (Boston: Weiser Books, 2003), 8 ff. This volume includes Lovecraft's "History of the *Necronomicon,*" 303–5.

18. See Zorn's comments describing *Magick* at www.tzadik.com.

19. A. E. Waite notes that the fifth *sefirah* of the demonic realm is *Golab* and that this *sefirah* is the "averse correspondence of GEBURAH" and the "Arch-demon of late Kabbalism . . . ASMODEUS." Arthur Edward Waite, *The Holy Kabbalah: A Mystical Interpretation of the Scriptures,* with an introduction by Kenneth Rexroth (New York: Carol, 1995), 257.

20. Asmodeus appears as the 32d demon listed in the *Lesser Key of Solomon* (*Goetia*) where he is described as a creature with three heads (a Bull, a Man, and a Ram) who belches flames of fire. He teaches arithmetic, geometry, and astronomy and can make men invisible. See Joseph H. Peterson, ed., *The Lesser Key of Solomon* (York Beach, Maine: Weiser Books, 2001), 21–22. It is possible that Zorn first encountered the figure of Asmodeus while working on the solo violin piece *Goetia* in 2002. I return to the figure of Asmodeus in my discussion of "Sacred Rites of the Left Hand Path."

21. And where (Movement) 3—when multiplied—by (Movement) 5 equals 15.

22. Concerning the symbolic significance of these strategically placed measures of 6, notice also that the final measure of 6 occurs in measure 61. So 61 and 6 may be an obscure reference to 616, an alternate reading of 666 found in some historical sources relating to the Beast that appears in Revelation 13:18. It is possible that this discrepancy arises from alternative spellings of the Roman emperor Nero (versus Neron), who may have been the original numerical//symbolic reference. Zorn is aware of this alternative reading as evidenced by the track "616" on *Moonchild* (Tzadik compact disc TZ 7357, 2006). Notice also that the three numbers of 616 sum to 13.

23. John Zorn, *IAO: Music in Sacred Light* (Tzadik compact disc TZ 7338, 2002). See www.tzadik.com. The timings included in all of the following examples/figures relating to *IAO* are based on this recording.

24. Crowley had to make a number of changes and alterations to IAO so that it would correspond to his own highly complex number symbolisms. See Aleister Crowley, *Magick: Liber ABA,* 533 ff. See also www.thelemapedia.org/index.php/IAO.

The resonances between Crowley's view of IAO and alchemy are clear if we recognize *I* as corresponding to natural matter, *A* as the destruction of that matter (placed in a crucible and burned), and *O* as the result, the philosopher's stone. The alchemical associations with IAO go back much further, as the name itself was often associated with Hermes Trismegistus. Adding to the complexity, IAO is also related to the Tetragrammaton and refers to the name of a sun god in Gnostic thought. Perhaps not coincidentally, an image reproduced in Bataille's "Base Materialism and Gnosticism" depicts the sun god IAO. (See Bataille, "Base Materialism and Gnosticism," 49, figure 6.)

25. Aleister Crowley, *Magick: Liber ABA,* 158, 160.

26. See especially Eisenstein's essays "A Dialectic Approach to Film Form" and "Methods of Montage," reprinted in Sergei Eisenstein, *Film Form,* trans. Jay Leyda (San Diego: Harcourt Brace, 1977). Eisenstein clarifies his understanding of "montage" by contrasting earlier usages—where the term is employed to describe editing techniques whereby images or frames are juxtaposed one after the other (in time)—with his own view of the term. "In my opinion," he writes:

> montage is an idea that arises from the collision of independent shots—shots even opposite to one another: the "dramatic" principle.
>
> [In montage] each sequential element is perceived not *next* to the other, but on *top* of the other. . . . This is, by the way, the reason for the phenomenon of spatial depth, in the optical superimposition of two planes of stereoscopy. From the superimposition of two elements of the same dimension always arises a new, higher dimension. In the case of stereoscopy the superimposition of two nonidentical two-dimensionalities results in stereoscopic three-dimensionality. (Eisenstein, "A Dialectic Approach to Film Form," in *Film Form,* 49–50)

27. Tony Rayns, "Aleister Crowley and Merlin Magick" (interview with Kenneth Anger), *Friends,* no. 14 (September 1970), and Jonas Mekas, "Movie Journal," *Village Voice,* May 17, 1973, both quoted in Alice L. Hutchison, *Kenneth Anger* (London: Black Dog, 2004), 179; Anna Powell, "The Occult: A Torch for Lucifer," in *Moonchild: The Films of Kenneth Anger,* ed. Jack Hunter (New York: Creation Books, 2001), 54–59.

28. Bruce Martin and Joe Medjuck, "Kenneth Anger," *Take One* 1, no. 6 (1967): 13, quoted in P. Adams Sitney, *Visionary Film* (Oxford: Oxford University Press, 2002), 100. Sitney discusses the film in detail on pages 95–102. See also Hutchison, *Kenneth Anger,* 89–103; Hunter, *Moonchild,* 65–73. *Inauguration of the Pleasure Dome* is included on *The Films of Kenneth Anger: Volume 1,* DVD (California: Fantoma Films FAN7048DVD, 2007).

29. Quoted in Sitney, *Visionary Film,* 95. See Crowley, *Magick: Liber ABA,* 267–74.

30. Sitney, *Visionary Film,* 97.

31. The instantly recognizable sigil of Baphomet depicts a goat's head included within an inverted pentagram that is circumscribed by two circles. Within the circles, the word "Leviathan" is written in Hebrew. While the sigil of Baphomet has a long history, it has certainly become more recognizable (even infamous) since the publication of Anton Szandor Lavey's *Satanic Bible* (New York: Avon Books, 1976), where this symbol is prominently reproduced on the book's cover.

32. This image is reproduced in Alexander Roob, *The Hermetic Museum: Alchemy and Mysticism* (Köln: Taschen, 1996), 186.

33. Crowley, *Magick: Liber ABA,* 271.

34. For a description of these and other instruments and their ritualistic meaning(s), see Crowley, *Magick: Liber ABA,* 58 ff.

35. Liner notes to *IAO.* Zorn's remarks here are only a slightly modified version of Crowley's comments regarding the act(s) and purpose(s) of writing in *Magick: Liber ABA,* 126.

It is also interesting to compare Zorn's comments with Antonin Artaud's vision of the director where:

> the director has become a kind of manager of magic, a master of sacred ceremonies. And the material on which he works, the themes he brings to throbbing life are derived not from him but from the gods. They come, it seems, from elemental interconnections of Nature which a double Spirit has fostered.
>
> What he sets in motion is the MANIFESTED.
>
> This is a sort of primary Physics, from which Spirit has never disengaged itself. (Artaud, *The Theater and Its Double,* 60)

I realize that many people might find Zorn's suggestion that the creation, recording, and distribution of his CD is an act of "Magick" a bit hard to swallow. However, in my conversations with the composer, I have never gotten the impression that the compositional strategies used in these and similar recordings—not to mention the intention(s) that lie behind their creation—are not meant seriously. I will return to this topic in the conclusion to this chapter.

36. A translation (that includes the figures and symbols) can be found at www .fraleralastor.com/verum.htm.

37. A brief description of the *Grimoirium Verum* appears in Arthur Edward Waite, *The Book of Ceremonial Magic* (Maple Shade, N.J.: Lethe Press, 2002), 96–99.

38. S. Liddell MacGregor Mathers, trans., *The Key of Solomon the King (Clavicula Salomonis)*, foreword by R. A. Gilbert (York Beach, Maine: Red Wheel/Weiser, LLC, 2004). In his preface, MacGregor Mathers says that *The Key of Solomon* is concerned primarily with matters relating to practical—or "white"—magic. He recognizes the affinities between *The Key of Solomon* and the *Grimoirium Verum* (and *The Lesser Key of Solomon* or *The Goetia*) but considers these last two to be wholly different because of their emphasis on "black" magic.

39. Ibid., 63.

40. Ibid., 68. This Pentacle appears on Plate III, following page 68.

41. Ibid., 73.

42. Ibid., 74. This text also appears in Psalm 113:13. Although it is difficult to read, MacGregor Mathers suggests that the text appearing on the three sides of the triangle is the first line of Genesis.

43. Crowley, *Magick: Liber ABA,* 276.

44. Gershom Scholem, *Kabbalah* (New York: Meridian, 1978), 102. See pages 87 ff. for a detailed description of these ideas.

45. See Rabbi Isaac ben Jacob ha-Kohen, "Treatise on the Left Emanation," in *The Early Kabbalah,* ed. Joseph Dan, trans. Ronald C. Kiener (New York: Paulist Press, 1986), 165–82; Scholem, *Kabbalah,* 122 ff.; Gershom Scholem, *Major Trends in Jewish Mysticism* (New York: Schocken Books, 1995), 235–39; Joseph Dan, "Samael, Lilith, and the Concept of Evil in Early Kabbalah," *AJS Review* 5 (1980): 17–40; Elliot Wolfson, "Left Contained in the Right," *AJS Review* 11, no. 1 (Spring 1986): 27–52.

46. Wolfson, "Left Contained in the Right," 28, 32.

47. For an idiosyncratic compendium of Hebrew words and their numerical values, see Aleister Crowley, *Sepher Sephiroth* in *777 and Other Qabalistic Writings of Aleister Crowley,* ed. Israel Regardie (Boston: Weiser Books, 1986).

48. Crowley, *Gematria,* in ibid., 27, 43. The equality between 13 and 1 derives from considering the shape and formation of individual letters, a practice Crowley refers to as Siphra Dzenioutha.

49. Crowley, *Gematria,* in *777 and Other Qabalistic Writings,* 30.

50. Asmodeus is sometimes understood as the ruling spirit of *Gevurah.* In his *Sepher Sephiroth,* Crowley identifies 15 with the "number of Abra-Melin Servitors of Asmodee [Asmodeus] and Magot, and of Paimon," all sub-princes under the control of "The Four Spirits and Superior Spirits" of Lucifer, Leviathan, Satan, and Belial (Crowley, *Sepher Sephiroth,* in *777 and Other Qabalistic Writings,* 2). See also Abraham the Jew, *The Book of the Sacred Magic of Abra-Melin the Mage,* trans. S. Liddell MacGregor Mathers (New York: Causeway Books, 1974), 104–22.

51. Aryeh Kaplan, trans., *Sefer Yetzirah: The Book of Creation,* rev. ed. (Boston: Weiser Books, 1997), 246.

52. Crowley, *777,* in *777 and Other Qabalistic Writings,* 49–50.

53. Regarding their names, many readers have probably recognized the association between Zorn and Anger, where *Zorn* is German for "anger." The relation can also be expressed in an obscure form of Gematria known as Albath, a form of Temura, or permutation. See Crowley, *Gematria,* in *777 and Other Qabalistic Writings,* 3. According to Albath, ZORN is equivalent to K. ANGeR, where both equal 29.

54. Zorn has mentioned to me that he has included "purifying numbers" in many of his mystical compositions, numbers such as 7, 3, and 11. E-mail communication with the composer, October 18, 2005. Unfortunately, I have been unable to find a reference to "purifying numbers" in the occult literature. Presumably, such numbers are designed to "neutralize" or balance the more overt "demonic" numbers at work in this movement. From a Crowleyian perspective, such a balance is unnecessary; given the dualist foundation for much of Crowley's thought, balance and equality are already present in every number, not to mention every phenomenon. This is exemplified by his famous equation 0=2 "devised to explain the Universe, and to harmonise the antinomies which it presents us at every turn." Crowley, "A Brief Essay upon the Nature and Significance of the Magical Alphabet," in *777 and Other Qabalistic Writings*, xix. I have yet to find the source of Zorn's notion of "purifying numbers," but it is quite clearly not derived from Crowley.

55. I would like to thank Meladee Kirton for suggesting the possible significance of 39 in "Leviathan" and "Mysteries." Of these two tracks, I am less convinced of the significance of 39 in "Mysteries" given Zorn's own remarks on this particular track. In the liner notes to *Protocols of Zion* (Tzadik compact disk TZ 7345, 2005), Zorn writes how, when he performs on a keyboard (as he does on "Mysteries"), he "pretty much has to hypnotize [himself]. I never know in the front of my brain exactly where I'm going to go, or what the next note will be (another example of a recording in this style is *Mysteries* [where Zorn plays organ]). One can literally hear me thinking out loud, making decisions on the spot, moment by moment."

56. These timings should be consistent on most commercial CD players. Six seconds of silence separate the movements of *Necronomicon* on *Magick*. On this same CD, thirteen seconds of silence separate *Necronomicon* from the next work, *Sortilège* for two bass clarinets.

57. Crowley, *Magick: Liber ABA*, 180.

58. Liner notes to *Magick*, n.p. Emphasis in original. Zorn expresses similar ideas in relation to his work *Shibboleth* in the notes to *From Silence to Sorcery* (Tzadik compact disc TZ 8035, 2007).

59. Mystic Fugu Orchestra, *Zohar* (Tzadik compact disc TZ 7106, 1995).

60. Scholem, *Major Trends in Jewish Mysticism*, 20–21

61. Many of the following points relating to this particular recording are discussed in Michael Scott Cuthbert, "Free Improvisation: John Zorn and the Construction of Jewish Identity through Music," *Studies in Jewish Musical Traditions: Insights from the Harvard Collection of Judaica Sound Recordings*, ed. Kay Kaufman Shelemay (Cambridge: Harvard College Library, 2001), 1–31. See especially 13–15.

62. From the description of *Zohar* at www.tzadik.com.

63. Excerpted and translated in Cuthbert, "Free Improvisation," 14.

3. Tradition, Gifts, and Zorn's Musical Homages

1. Hips Road at www.hipsroadedition.com. These and other names can also be found in the many published interviews or conversations with Zorn. See, e.g., Edward Strickland, *American Composers: Dialogues on Contemporary Music* (Bloomington: Indiana University Press, 1991), 124–40; Cole Gagne, *Soundpieces 2: Interviews with American Composers* (Metuchen, N.J.: Scarecrow Press, 1993), 509–42; William Duck-

worth, *Talking Music* (New York: Schirmer Books, 1995), 444–75; Ann McCutchan, *The Muse That Sings: Composers Speak about the Creative Process* (Oxford: Oxford University Press, 1999), 161–71.

2. Originally aired on July 8, 2000, on BBC Radio 3. The entire four-part interview is readily available in many bootlegging/trading circles.

3. E-mail communication with the composer, February 25, 2005.

4. Marcel Mauss, *The Gift: The Form and Reason for Exchange in Archaic Societies,* trans. W. D. Halls, foreword Mary Douglas (New York: W. W. Norton, 1990).

5. Useful overviews on Maussian and post-Maussian views on the gift and gift giving can be found in Mark Osteen, ed., *The Question of the Gift: Essays across Disciplines* (London: Routledge, 2002), 1–41. See also Alan D. Schrift, ed., *The Logic of the Gift: Toward an Ethic of Generosity* (London: Routledge, 1997), 1–22.

6. Mauss, *The Gift,* 3.

7. Ibid., 13 ff., 29, 33, 39 ff.

8. Ibid., ix, x.

9. Ibid., 10 ff.

10. Mauss's appeal to the Maori notion of *hau* has been criticized by many writers, most notably Claude Lévi-Strauss in his "Introduction à l'oeuvre de Marcel Mauss," in Marcel Mauss, *Sociologie et anthropologie* (Paris: Presses Universitaires de France, 1950). The relevant sections from Lévi-Strauss are reprinted and translated in *The Logic of the Gift,* ed. Schrift, 55 ff.

11. Mauss, *The Gift,* 11–12.

12. The metaphor of the circle and the limitations it imposes upon Mauss's understanding of a system of gift exchange is subjected to a deconstructive reading by Rodolphe Gasché, "Heliocentric Exchange," translated in *The Logic of the Gift,* ed. Schrift, 100–117.

13. Annette Weiner attempts to circumvent this limitation by appealing to "alienable" objects that are "lost" when given away and "inalienable" objects that allow an individual or group to "keep-while-giving." See Annette Weiner, *Inalienable Possessions: The Paradox of Keeping-While-Giving* (Berkeley: University of California Press, 1992). See also Chris A. Gregory, *Gifts and Commodities* (London: Academic Press, 1982). On the importance of "time" in gift giving, see the slightly similar (yet differently presented) views in Jacques Derrida, *Given Time I: Counterfeit Money,* trans. Peggy Kamuf (Chicago: University of Chicago Press, 1992), and Pierre Bourdieu, *The Logic of Practice,* trans. Richard Nice (Stanford, Calif.: Stanford University Press, 1990), esp. 98–111. Relevant sections from Bourdieu's work also appear in *The Logic of the Gift,* ed. Schrift, 190–230.

14. Jacques T. Godbout in collaboration with Alain Caillé, *The World of the Gift,* trans. Donald Winkler (Montreal: McGill-Queen's University Press, 1998), 19–20.

15. Ibid., 33, 45, 81.

16. Ibid., 214. The authors' language here is reminiscent of Ralph Waldo Emerson, who states: "The only gift is a portion of thyself. Thou must bleed for me." Emerson, "Gifts," in *The Logic of the Gift,* ed. Shrift, 26. Mauss also refers to Emerson's "rather curious" essay in *The Gift,* 65.

17. Godbout and Caillé, *The World of the Gift,* 129–30. The features associated with the gift as described here echo those developed by Georges Bataille and his notion of a

"general economy"—an economy predicated on waste, abundance, and nonutility (which itself is derived from Mauss and his description of the "potlatch" as it is presented in *The Gift*). See Georges Bataille, "The Notion of Expenditure," in *Visions of Excess*, trans. Allan Stoekl with Carl R. Lovitt and Donald M. Leslie Jr. (Minneapolis: University of Minnesota Press, 1985), 116–29; Georges Bataille, *The Accursed Share, Vol. 1: Consumption*, trans. Robert Hurley (New York: Zone Books, 1991).

18. Godbout and Caillé, *The World of the Gift*, 205.

19. Ibid., 17.

20. Ibid., 82–85.

21. Duckworth, *Talking Music*, 470. Given Zorn's comments here, it is tempting to situate Zorn within the so-called maverick tradition as described by Michael Broyles. See Broyles, *Mavericks and Other Traditions in American Music* (New Haven: Yale University Press, 2004).

22. A number of authors have considered the ways in which gift exchange can be applied to the idea of influence in the arts. See, e.g., Lewis Hyde, *The Gift: Imagination and the Erotic Property of Life* (New York: Random House, 1979); Nicoletta Pireddu, "Gabriele D'Annunzio: The Art of Squandering and the Economy of Sacrifice," in *The Question of the Gift*, ed. Osteen, 172–90; Stephen Collis, "Formed by Homages: H.D., Robert Duncan, and the Poetics of the Gift," in *The Question of the Gift*, ed. Osteen, 209–26; Adelaide Morris, "A Relay of Power and Peace: H.D. and the Spirit of the Gift," in *Signets: Reading H.D.*, ed. Susan Stanford Friedman and Rachel Blau Du Plessis (Madison: University of Wisconsin Press, 1990), 52–82.

23. Bloom's ideas are presented in his *The Anxiety of Influence* (New York: Oxford University Press, 1973) and *A Map of Misreading* (New York: Oxford University Press, 1975). Given some of the themes developed in the preceding chapter, an alternative to the gift model of influence employed here might consider connections between influence, tradition, and Kabbalah as described elsewhere by Bloom. See, in particular, his *Kabbalah and Mysticism* (New York: Seabury Press, 1975). To me, there seems to be a qualitative difference between the works examined in this chapter and how they figure into Zorn's musical poetics versus the more overt "occult" works examined in the previous chapter. Such qualitative differences can be substantiated, perhaps, by comparing the very different compositional strategies and techniques employed by Zorn in a work such as *Necronomicon* with *In the Very Eye of Night* or *Untitled*, examined below.

24. A somewhat related view of Zorn's homages is presented in Marcel Cobussen's online "interactive dissertation," located at www.cobussen.com/navbar/index.html. In the section entitled "Restitutions, Shibboleths, or Aporias," Cobussen considers Zorn's tributes not from the perspective of the gift but from the relationship that exists between a host body and a parasite. In the subsection "Saprophyte," Cobussen notes:

> Zorn is famous for his homages. And there are many. . . . But each project, each tribute, evolves differently and with a different musical language as a result, because the host demands these different approaches. Even if the host transforms into a hostage, even if Zorn's tributes have a violent side, it is the host who sets the rules. However, the host cannot sovereignly absorb this specific parasite; it is kicked off balance by it because the parasite has reprogrammed all the genetic material.

I find Cobussen's notion of the "reprogramming" of a host by a parasite highly suggestive, although I believe Cobussen is guilty of a sleight of hand here by equating a parasite with a virus. One thing I do not consider in the present chapter is how Zorn's tributes might force a different set of reading/interpretive strategies upon the work and thought of an individual dedicatee. However, it seems to me that Cobussen's metaphor of the parasite ultimately ends up being the type of restricted economy that the metaphor of the gift is able to overcome.

25. All of these quotes appear in Lauren Rabinovitz, *Points of Resistance: Women, Power & Politics in the New York Avant-Garde Cinema, 1943–71* (Urbana: University of Illinois Press, 1991), 67.

26. Jonas Mekas, "A Few Notes on Maya Deren," in *Inverted Odysseys: Claude Cahun, Maya Deren, Cindy Sherman*, ed. Shelley Rice (Cambridge: MIT Press, 1999), 131. Annette Michelson recognizes some contradictions between Deren's own work and thought and Deren's rather narrow understanding of surrealism's aims and methods. See Annette Michelson, "Poetic and Savage Thought: About *Anagram*," in *Maya Deren and the American Avant-Garde*, ed. Bill Nichols (Berkeley: University of California Press, 2001), 29–30.

27. Rabinovitz, *Points of Resistance*, 51–52. See also Maria Pramaggiore, "Performance and Persona in the U.S. Avant-Garde: The Case of Maya Deren," *Cinema Journal* 36, no. 2 (Winter 1997): 17–40. While Deren's films can and have been read against certain representations of—not to mention opportunities for—women in mainstream Hollywood practices, her films can also be read as a critique of the contemporary male-dominated world of American avant-garde cinema.

28. For an extended examination of this aspect of Deren's film poetics (with a close reading of *Meshes of the Afternoon*), see Theresa L. Geller, "The Personal Cinema of Maya Deren: *Meshes of the Afternoon* and Its Critical Reception in the History of the Avant-Garde," *Biography* 29, no. 1 (Winter 2006): 140–58.

29. In particular, see Renata Jackson, "The Modernist Poetics of Maya Deren," in *Maya Deren and the American Avant-Garde*, ed. Nichols, 47–76, quote on 47.

30. Maya Deren, *An Anagram of Ideas on Art, Form, and Film* (Yonkers, N.Y.: Alicat Book Shop Press, 1946), 26. Reprinted in its entirety in *Maya Deren and the American Avant-Garde*, ed. Nichols, 267–322, and in *The Legend of Maya Deren: A Documentary Bibliography and Collected Works. Volume I, Part Two: Chambers (1942–1947)*, ed. Vèvè A. Clark, Millicent Hodson, and Catrina Neiman (New York: Anthology Film Archives/Film Culture, 1988), 550–602. Both of these sources reproduce Deren's essay including the original pagination. Elsewhere in her essay (17), Deren describes art in general as "the dynamic result of the relationship of three elements: the reality to which a man has access—directly and through the researches of other men; the crucible of his own imagination and intellect; and the art instrument by which he realizes, through skillful exercize [sic] and control, his imaginative manipulations."

31. Deren, *Anagram*, 30.

32. Ibid., 39–40. Deren advances the same argument in her "Cinematography: The Creative Use of Reality," *Daedalus*, Winter 1960, 150–67; reprinted in *The Avant-Garde Film: A Reader of Theory and Criticism*, Anthology Film Archives Series 3, ed. P. Adams Sitney (New York: New York University Press, 1978), 60–73.

33. Zorn's jump-cut compositional technique—borrowed from film and put to great

use in much of his music from the late 1980s—could be understood in the context of an artificial or synthetic reality. For example, some of the more extreme tunes of Zorn's Naked City project seem to wear their synthetic quality like a badge, as disparate styles or genres are "strung together" in a seemingly random (linear and sequential) fashion (refer to the discussions of "Speedfreaks" and "Osaka Bondage" in chapter 1). This might give the impression that the recording studio is the unique medium here with its ability to create quick, clean edits and then reassemble these "moments" or "elements" into an artificial, constructed unity. However, the quick, stop-on-a-dime changes were performed and recorded in real-time and are not the result of any sort of studio "trickery." The result is the illusion of an illusion, that is, the appearance of artifice by the manipulation of a specific medium.

34. Deren, *Anagram,* 51.

35. Thus her opinion (again, evidence of Deren's essentialism) is that "the motion picture . . . should not be thought of as a faster painting or a more real play." Deren, "Cinematography: The Creative Use of Reality," 72. For Deren, poetry contains the potential for modifying or manipulating our sense of space and time, features I will address below.

36. Deren, *Anagram,* 48.

37. Ibid., 50–51.

38. Ibid., 17. Emphasis in original.

39. Jackson, "The Modernist Poetics of Maya Deren," 59.

40. Deren, *Anagram,* 25.

41. Ibid., 24. Emphasis in original.

42. Ibid., 20.

43. This piece appears on Zorn's *Songs from the Hermetic Theater* (Tzadik compact disc TZ 7066, 2001). In the liner notes, Zorn is listed as the producer/performer with recording and mixing credits attributed to Jamie Saft.

44. Concerning *The Very Eye of Night,* Lauren Rabinovitz refers to the film as a "dry exercise in filming dance" (*Points of Resistance,* 77), while P. Adams Sitney remarks how Deren's "art diminished" (*Visionary Film,* 40) later in her life.

45. From a description included on the DVD "Notes and Quotes" menu accompanying *The Very Eye of Night* (1952–59) on *Maya Deren: Experimental Films* (New York: Mystic Fire Video 76493, 2002).

46. One of the images of Zorn in the liner notes to *Songs from the Hermetic Theater* is a negative. This image appears next to a famous still of Deren looking out a window from *Meshes of the Afternoon.*

47. While conceived as a musical adaptation of Deren's poetics of film, Zorn's work also seems to resonate with a number of other musical works and styles. For example, works such as Cage's *Cartridge Music* and *Williams Mix* explore what Michael Nyman calls "amplified small sounds." Michael Nyman, *Experimental Music: Cage and Beyond,* 2d ed. (Cambridge: Cambridge University Press, 1999), 90. At the same time, Zorn's *In the Very Eye of Night* sits comfortably within a "microsound" style of composition as described by Curtis Roads in his *Microsound* (Cambridge: MIT Press, 2001).

48. In the discussion that follows, I will refer to particular moments from *In the Very Eye of Night* in minutes and seconds. All of these times are taken from the recording as it appears on *Songs from the Hermetic Theater.*

49. It should also be noted that Zorn composed the soundtrack to Martina Kud-láceks documentary *In the Mirror of Maya Deren,* released on *Filmworks X* (Tzadik compact disc TZ 7333, 2001). Zorns score for this film does not appear to exhibit the same types of recording/mixing intricacies as described in *In the Very Eye of Night.* Most likely, this is due to the fact that Zorn was composing music for a film *about* Deren and the narrative structure of this particular film and not—as with *In the Very Eye of Night*—creating a document directly influenced by Deren and her personal poetics of film.

50. Dickran Tashjian, *Joseph Cornell: Gifts of Desire* (Miami Beach: Grassfield Press, 1992), 15.

51. For an extended discussion on the role of childhood in Cornell's films, see Marjorie Keller, *The Untutored Eyes: Childhood in the Films of Cocteau, Cornell, and Brakhage* (Cranbury, N.J.: Associated University Press, 1986). For a useful biography on Cornell, see Deborah Solomon, *Utopia Parkway: The Life and Works of Joseph Cornell* (Boston: MFA, 2004).

52. E-mail communication with the composer, February 25, 2005.

53. On Cornell's relationship with surrealism, see Dawn Ades, "The Transcendental Surrealism of Joseph Cornell," in *Joseph Cornell,* ed. Kynaston McShine (New York: Museum of Modern Art, 1980), 15–41.

54. In a letter to Alfred Barr, Cornell explains that although "fervently admiring much of their work I have never been an official Surrealist, and I believe that Surrealism has far healthier possibilities than have been developed." Quoted in Ades, "Transcendental Surrealism," 19. Elsewhere, Carter Ratcliff has described how Cornell's "determination to see innocence everywhere flies gently in the face of the Surrealist desire to cultivate sexual extremes, both in imagery and practice, as a means of their apocalyptic dream." Carter Ratcliff, "Joseph Cornell, Mechanic of the Ineffable," in *Joseph Cornell,* ed. McShine, 54. If a label had to be attached to Cornell, he preferred "American Constructivist."

55. Lynda Roscoe Hartigan, "Joseph Cornell's Dance with Duality," in *Joseph Cornell: Shadowplay . . . Eterniday,* essays by Lynda Roscoe Hartigan and others, commentary Walter Hopps (New York: Thames & Hudson, 2003), 25.

56. Richard Vine, "Eterniday: Cornell's Christian Science 'Metaphysique,'" in *Joseph Cornell: Shadowplay . . . Eterniday,* 46.

57. Diane Waldman, *Joseph Cornell* (New York: George Braziller, 1977), 27.

58. Lindsay Blair, *Joseph Cornell's Vision of Spiritual Order* (London: Reaktion Books, 1998), 51–53.

59. Sandra Leonard Starr, *Joseph Cornell: Art and Metaphysics* (New York: Castelli, Feigen, Corcoran Gallery, 1982), 4. The phrase "The substance of things hoped for" is from Mary Baker Eddy's *Health and Science* (Boston: Christian Science Board of Directors, 1994), 468. Baker's wording is, of course, a paraphrase of Hebrews 11:1.

60. Vine, "Eterniday," 39–40.

61. Waldman, *Joseph Cornell,* 93.

62. Starr, *Joseph Cornell: Art and Metaphysics,* 4.

63. The phrase "association through synchronicity" is used by Blair to describe Cornell's working/thought processes. See Blair, *Joseph Cornell's Vision,* 120.

64. Concerned about how to portray his work to the public, Cornell finally hit upon a useful concept for characterizing his art in a diary entry: "What about 'constellations'

for experiments in going over past experiences and picking out certain points for a presentation." Quoted in Ades, "Transcendental Surrealism," 33.

65. Julien Levy, *Memoir of an Art Gallery* (New York: G. P. Putnam's Sons, 1977), 78.

66. Blair, *Joseph Cornell's Vision*, 97.

67. P. Adams Sitney, "The Cinematic Gaze of Joseph Cornell," in *Joseph Cornell*, ed. McShine, 69.

68. Ibid., 82. Sitney relates this view to numerous passages from Mary Baker Eddy's *Health and Science*.

69. From Walter Hopps's commentary accompanying a reproduction of this construction in *Joseph Cornell: Shadowplay . . . Eterniday*, 218.

70. Referring to Cornell's *Dovecotes* in general, Brian O'Doherty relates how "years ago I made charts of Cornell's boxes, searching for sets and systems; each time the evidence broke down, and I was struck by the ingenuity with which he *avoided* closure." Brian O'Doherty, *Dovecotes, Hotels, and Other White Spaces*, catalog from Joseph Cornell Exhibition at the Pace Gallery, New York, October 20–November 25, 1989, 9. Emphasis in original.

The intimate relationship between the boxes and the viewer's emotional response to his constructions was important to Cornell and was one reason he was hesitant to give his works titles. Lindsay Blair writes how "aspects of Cornell's method that further confirm his uncertainty regarding one particular viewpoint include his reluctance to title works, his habit of occasionally dating works over a period of years, and his way of allowing imagery and connections to flow over and out of the actual box space onto the sides and verso of his constructions." Blair, *Joseph Cornell's Vision*, 30.

71. Described at www.hipsroadedition.com. *Untitled*, performed by Erik Friedlander, appears on Zorn's *Madness, Love, and Mysticism* (Tzadik compact disc TZ 7065, 2001). Zorn's *Untitled* explicitly relates to Cornell's own works, many of which are "titled" *Untitled*.

72. One could say that form and content are collapsed in this piece, a trait that is common to a great deal of Zorn's concert music (see, e.g., *Le Mômo* and *Memento Mori*). On *Memento Mori*, for example, Zorn has written how "[at] the highest level life and art are the same, just as there is no true dividing line between form and content." Liner notes accompanying John Zorn, *The String Quartets* (Tzadik compact disc TZ 7047, 1999).

73. Because there are no measure numbers in Zorn's score, all of my musical examples/figures pertaining to *Untitled* will refer to the page number, system, and general location on these systems. In addition, I also identify the onset and location of these musical ideas as heard on the recording of *Untitled* on *Madness, Love, and Mysticism* (in minutes and seconds).

74. Hartigan, "Joseph Cornell's Dance with Duality," in *Joseph Cornell: Shadowplay . . . Eterniday*, 32. Continuing the alchemical associations often perceived in Cornell's work, Dore Ashton remarks how repetition is "central to Cornell's *oeuvre*. . . . [Cornell's] repetition is not the intellectualized notion of serialization, but more like the ritual repetition of an alchemist." Dore Ashton, *A Joseph Cornell Album* (New York: Viking Press, 1974), 111.

75. In the discussion that follows, I will identify many sonorities/melodic configurations using analytical strategies associated with set theory. My decision to utilize set-

class nomenclature should be understood as an expeditious tool; I do not claim that Zorn thought in "set-classes" (whatever this may mean) when composing this or any other work. While many of the pitch collections I focus on can be related to traditional tertian or extended sonorities familiar from tonal practices, just as many cannot. In my mind, set theory provides a ready-made analytical technique that allows me to trace and describe many of the recurring collections (both exact and modified) heard in *Untitled* without having to reinvent the analytical wheel or making the discussion any more unwieldy than it might be already. For those readers unfamiliar with set theory, see Joseph N. Straus's excellent *Introduction to Post-Tonal Theory,* 3rd ed. (Upper Saddle River, N.J.: Prentice Hall, 2005).

76. Zorn's performance indications throughout *Untitled* are in French, probably as a nod to Cornell, who was an unabashed Francophile.

77. The (0157) tetrachord is a relatively new sonority but one that will reappear in the coda.

78. Hopps in *Joseph Cornell: Shadowplay . . . Eterniday,* 208.

79. To my ears, this musical idea has strong connotations with the ascent of the soul at the end of Schoenberg's *Die Jakobsleiter.* Elsewhere, a similarly sounding moment occurs at the end of the Tenth Movement of Zorn's *Chimeras* (Tzadik compact disc TZ 7085, 2003).

4. Continuing the Spiral

1. William Duckworth, *Talking Music* (New York: Schirmer Books, 1995), 473.

2. Tom Service, "Playing a New Game of Analysis: John Zorn's *Carny,* Autonomy, and Postmodernism," *BPM Online* 5 (June 2002): www.bpmonline.org. uk/bpm5-playing .html.

3. Ann McCutchan, *The Muse That Sings: Composers Speak About the Creative Process* (Oxford: Oxford University Press, 1999), 169. On the same page, Zorn describes similar transformational or manipulative practices in other concert works. For example, in his *Rituals* for voice and chamber orchestra (1998), Zorn derives all of his pitch material from Karlheinz Stockhausen's *Kontrapunkt* by "taking thirty pitches and repeating them, over and over, in that order, throughout."

> If there's something I want, like a B-flat major chord, I can find it somewhere in my row. I'll say, "OK, if I skip three pitches and then skip four pitches, I'll get my B-flat major chord." So I'll do that for a while. Skip three, skip four, skip three, skip four. I do what I want with this information.

4. Ibid.

5. I will refer to these materials as "reference materials" and not by the more traditional term "sketch materials," because Zorn does not appear to have "sketched" out, reworked, or toiled over many of the musical ideas on these sheets. Instead, the information on these sheets (five 8½ × 11 pages—3 of which have writing on the front and back—and two sheets of 8½ × 14 pages—where one contains writing on the front and back) include notes, jottings, formal outlines, shapes, gestures, rhythmic ideas, and nu-

merous strings of pitches. Examining these sheets and the finished score, it appears that Zorn would outline larger musical forms, permutations for deriving pitch materials, and/ or rhythmic ideas and would then work directly to the score. These sheets, therefore, appear to contain the ideas to which Zorn would refer as he worked on his score (in addition to working out many of the precompositional details). Often, a single page or side of these reference materials is devoted to a single movement of *Aporias*. Material relating to the prelude, the interlude, and the postlude are spread out across multiple sheets.

I would like to thank the composer for providing me with these materials.

6. I will return to the subject of the work's title as well as the possible significance of the Latin text that appears near the bottom of the page at the end of this chapter.

7. The arabic numerals that appear to the right of Zorn's movements in figure 4.1 appear to be indications of length (in minutes).

8. Arnold Newman and Robert Craft, *Bravo Stravinsky* (Cleveland: World, 1967), 48. Elsewhere, Robert Craft has related how, in April 1968, Stravinsky began composing an "extra instrumental prelude to the *Requiem Canticles*, for a performance of the work in memory of Dr. Martin Luther King." Robert Craft, *Stravinsky: Chronicle of a Friendship* (New York: Alfred A. Knopf, 1972), 346, n. 1. Stravinsky was unable to complete this "extra prelude" in time for the May performance.

9. Quoted in Craft, *Stravinsky: Chronicle of a Friendship*, 376–77. Indeed, the *Requiem Canticles* was performed at Stravinsky's burial on April 15, 1971.

Louis Andriessen and Elmer Schönberger have also described the work as a "Requiem for the Requiem": "After [*Requiem Canticles*], every composer who writes a liturgical requiem for large choir and orchestra, preferably in his old age, will seem like a taxidermist." Louis Andriessen and Elmer Schönberger, *The Apollonian Clockwork*, trans. Jeff Hamburg (Oxford: Oxford University Press, 1989), 7.

10. In an interview with Cole Gagne from 1992, Zorn—referring specifically to *Elegy*—admits how he had discovered "really great ways to structure compositions in the past year." Cole Gagne, *Soundpieces 2: Interviews with American Composers* (Metuchen, N.J.: Scarecrow Press, 1993), 529.

11. In this respect, Zorn's aims are similar to those of Stravinsky and the latter's attempts at incorporating and translating a variety of structural and presentational features advanced by visual artists. On Stravinsky's fascination with the latent musical potentialities of cubism, for instance, see Glenn Watkins, *Pyramids at the Louvre* (Cambridge: Belknap Press of Harvard University Press, 1994), 229–74.

12. On the recording of this work, this movement is identified as "Con Mistero." John Zorn, *Aporias* (Tzadik compact disc TZ 7037, 1998). In the discussion that follows, I will refer to this movement as "Misterioso," the marking given in the score. Also, all of the timing indications included with my examples are drawn from this recording.

13. For an informative biographical account of Bacon's life, see Michael Peppiatt, *Francis Bacon: Anatomy of an Enigma* (Boulder: Westview Press, 1998).

14. Similar formal outlines exist for the "Dietrich," "Camarón," and "Messiaen" movements.

15. By referring to the discrete sections as "blocks," I am trying to be consistent with Zorn's understanding of the formal designs of many of his compositions. On numerous occasions he has referred to his method of composition as "composing with blocks." "The way I work is linear. I work in blocks. . . . That's something I learned from

Stravinsky and from cartoon music. Cartoon music and Stravinsky's early music—really *all* of his music—exist in block form. One thing happens, then it stops, and something else happens, then *it* stops, and something *else* happens." From an interview that originally appeared in *Ear* magazine, excerpted in *Future Jazz,* ed. Howard Mandel (Oxford: Oxford University Press, 1999), 170. Emphasis in original.

16. All of the examples from *Aporias* are my own transcriptions from the published score (in Zorn's hand). The score is extremely dense, so in an effort to make my examples as legible and user-friendly as possible, I have not included information such as dynamic markings, articulations, performance indications, or unpitched percussion parts. Also, I have added some time signatures where I felt they might benefit the reader. I have tried to maintain the spatial aspect of Zorn's score, a feature that is clearly designed to resemble the marvelous layout common to many of Stravinsky's later works.

17. In an e-mail communication to the author (July 22, 2006), Zorn does mention that he modified passages in Stravinsky's score by altering the clefs, notably with the so-called chords of death that sound in the Postlude (where the bells are read in alto clef and the vibraphone in bass clef).

18. Zorn appears to have momentarily forgotten (altered?) the clef he was working in, as the treble clef D♯ of the first solo viola would correspond to a bass clef F♯ in Stravinsky's score. This misreading (willful or simply a miscopying) is also present in Zorn's reference materials.

19. It is possible that this "spiraling" effect between the first and second solo viola lines is an oblique reference to a related compositional technique employed in the vocal part of the "Lacrimosa" movement of *Requiem Canticles*. See Claudio Spies, "Some Notes on Stravinsky's Requiem Settings," *Perspectives of New Music* 5, no. 2 (Spring/Summer 1967): 121; Joseph N. Straus, *Stravinsky's Late Music* (Cambridge: Cambridge University Press, 2001), 107, 110–11.

20. Zorn appears to have been particularly fond of this harmony and its voicing, as the same idea appears on a page with materials relating to both the "Messiaen" and "Cassavetes" movements.

21. Because he draws the pitch class content of this harmony from block 5, the F♯ in measure 112 of "Tuba Mirum" is replaced by the interpolated D that is the result of Zorn's copying "mistake," as described in note 18.

22. Notice the various numbers that appear to the left of this harmony in figure 4.2. It is quite possible that Zorn subjected block 5 to some sort of numeric permutation to derive these pitches and their particular groupings. Permutations such as those I am suggesting are evident in Zorn's reference materials, especially in the "Messiaen," "Cassavetes," and "Cage" movements where melodic figures and/or harmonies are the result of skipping every other pitch or extracting pitches according to other numeric means (i.e., "3-2-5-4-5-1-4" involves the reordering of a string of pitches beginning with the third pitch, then, the second, then the fifth, and so on). I have been unable to determine if such a permutation has been applied in this movement.

23. Zorn's reference materials do not appear to contain any indications relating to the last page of this movement. As the following account should make clear, it appears that Zorn shuffles, superimposes, and recombines the material associated with blocks heard earlier in the movement as well as composing new music.

24. In the first box of table 4.3, Zorn's D is the same pitch class that I have described

before and is, I believe, a misreading of Stravinsky's clef. Also, the final E♭ in Zorn's piano part would correspond to Stravinsky's E♮. There is a mark on Zorn's score that appears to be a flat sign; however, given that the score to *Aporias* is a photocopy in the composer's hand, it is possible that this mark is a hastily written natural sign.

25. For a detailed examination of Bacon's poetics of painting, see Martin Harrison, *In Camera: Francis Bacon, Photography, Film, and the Practice of Painting* (New York: Thames and Hudson, 2005).

26. See Sergei Eisenstein, "A Dialectic Approach to Film Form," in *Film Form,* trans. Jay Leyda (San Diego: Harcourt Brace, 1977), 45–63. Refer to chapter 2 for a discussion of Eisenstein's "theory of montage" as it relates to the work of Kenneth Anger.

27. Edward Strickland, *American Composers: Dialogues on Contemporary Music* (Bloomington: Indiana University Press, 1991), 128.

28. Referring to a performance of the work in Oakland, California, in 1968, Robert Craft describes the effect of the "Libera Me" as resembling the "cheering section at a football game." Craft, *Stravinsky: Chronicle of a Friendship,* 345.

29. Claudio Spies has described "the four-part simultaneities in the 'Libera Me' [as being] as difficult (or impossible) to relate to the serial chart as the eight, seven, five, and four-factor whole-note chords in the Postlude." Spies, "Some Notes on Stravinsky's Requiem Settings," 120. A short time later, Spies was happy to report that such difficulties had been resolved (at least in regard to the "Libera Me" movement). See his "Correction and Addendum: Some Notes on Stravinsky's Requiem Settings," *Perspectives of New Music* 6, no. 1 (Autumn/Winter 1967): 160).

30. Throughout this section, I adopt the hexachordal labeling system employed by Claudio Spies whereby P stands for "prime," R for "retrograde," I for "inversion," and IR for "inversion of the retrograde." Subscript arabic numerals refer to rotations (1=first rotation, 2=second rotation, and so on) while lowercase letters refer to hexachords (a for first hexachord, b for second hexachord). Compare my labels with Spies's example 11 in "Some Notes on Stravinsky's Requiem Settings," 110.

31. Similar observations on the hexachordal structure of this movement can be found in Karen Lesley Grylls, "The Aggregate Re-Ordered: A Paradigm for Stravinsky's 'Requiem Canticles,'" PhD diss., University of Washington, 1993, 185–87.

32. Stephen Walsh, *The Music of Stravinsky* (Oxford: Oxford University Press, 1993), 275.

33. Milton Babbitt briefly alludes to the "ear vs. mind" debate in his "Stravinsky's Verticals and Schoenberg's Diagonals: A Twist of Fate," in *Stravinsky Retrospectives,* ed. Ethan Haimo and Paul Johnson (Lincoln: University of Nebraska Press, 1987), 15–35.

34. E-mail communication with composer July 22, 2006.

35. A similar harmony is identified elsewhere on this page and does not include the B♭.

36. Although I have not seen any reference to this, it is possible that Zorn's *Hermeticum Sacrum* is based on Stravinsky's *Canticum Sacrum.*

37. Jacques Derrida, *Aporias,* trans. Thomas Dutoit (Stanford, Calif.: Stanford University Press, 1993). Zorn refers to Derrida's short book in McCutchan, *The Muse That Sings,* 169.

38. Gagne, *Soundpieces 2,* 529. A recording of *Elegy* was originally released in 1992 on the Japanese label EVVA (EVVA compact disc 3304) and was released in the United

States in 1995 as Tzadik compact disc TZ 7302. A remastered version from 1999 contains a photo of Genet, excerpts from his *A Thief's Journal* (in French and English), film stills from *Un Chant d'amour,* and a short note by Zorn.

Elegy was later incorporated into a music/film multimedia work/installation entitled *Elegy: For Jean Genet.* This work, a collaboration between Zorn and the filmmakers Ela Troyano and Tessa Hughes-Freeland, was premiered in 1993 as part of Zorn's fortieth birthday celebration and would later tour select venues in Europe. See Jack Sargeant, *Deathtripping* (London: Creation Books, 1995), 248–49.

39. Nicholas Rescher, entry on "Aporia," in *The Oxford Companion to Philosophy,* ed. Ted Honderich (Oxford: Oxford University Press, 1995), 41.

40. Derrida, *Aporias,* 8.

41. Ibid., 11. Italics in original.

42. Ibid., 8, 21. A similar idea is presented in the liner notes to Zorn's recording of *Aporias: "Is it possible to say **our** lives, or **my** death? Can death be a plural . . . is death even possible?"* [Italics and emphasis in original.] The source of this quotation is unclear; it does not appear, as we might expect, in Derrida's text.

43. Derrida, *Aporias,* 40.

Epilogue

1. Peter Bürger, *Theory of the Avant-Garde,* trans. Michael Straw, foreword by Jochen Schulte-Sasse (Minneapolis: University of Minnesota Press, 1984), 83

2. Ibid., 80. Bürger's understanding of the role of "shock" draws heavily on ideas set forth by Walter Benjamin. See especially Benjamin's "On Some Motifs in Baudelaire," in *Illuminations,* ed. Hannah Arendt, trans. Harry Zohn (New York: Schocken Books, 1969), 155–200.

3. Bürger, *Theory of the Avant-Garde,* 54. For a more detailed consideration of many of the limitations and paradoxes inherent within avant-garde movements from the first decades of the twentieth-century, see Hans Magnus Enzensberger, "The Aporias of the Avant Garde" in *The Consciousness Industry,* ed. Michael Roloff (New York: Seabury Press, 1974), 16–41.

4. Bürger, *Theory of the Avant-Garde,* 58. An extended examination of post-avant-garde movements and artists (and one that relies heavily on Bürger and is just as pessimistic) can be found in Stuart D. Hobbs, *The End of the American Avant Garde* (New York: New York University Press, 1997).

5. And there are many reasons not to. For an excellent critique of Bürger's essay, see Benjamin Buchloh, "Theorizing the Avant-Garde," *Art in America,* November 1984, 19–21.

6. In his "The Eighteenth Brumaire of Louis Bonaparte," Marx writes "Hegel somewhere remarks that all facts and personages of great importance in world history occur, as it were, twice. He forgot to add: the first time as tragedy, the second as farce." In Karl Marx and Friedrich Engels, *The Communist Manifesto and Other Writings* (New York: Barnes and Noble Classics, 2005), 63. Later Marx compares these subversive repetitions to the burrowing of a mole, recalling a line from *Hamlet* when describing the actions of Louis Bonaparte: "Well grubbed, old mole!" (156).

Bataille uses this same analogy when describing the aims and ideals of surrealism. See his "The 'Old Mole' and the Prefix *Sur* in the Words *Surhomme* and *Surrealist,*" in *Visions of Excess*, trans. Allan Stoekl with Carl R. Lovitt and Donald M. Leslie Jr. (Minneapolis: University of Minnesota Press, 1985), 32–44.

7. Hal Foster, *The Return of the Real* (Cambridge: MIT Press, 1996), 11.

8. Bürger, *Theory of the Avant-Garde*, 61.

9. Buchloh, "Theorizing the Avant-Garde," 21.

10. Foster, *The Return of the Real*, 13, 29.

11. Bürger, *Theory of the Avant-Garde*, 62–63.

12. Andreas Huyssen, *After the Great Divide* (Bloomington: Indiana University Press, 1986), 169.

13. Ibid., 174. My formulation of the avant-garde as an "incomplete project" is meant to be understood as a playful, subversive reference to Jürgen Habermas's "Modernity—An Incomplete Project" in *The Anti-Aesthetic: Essays on Postmodern Culture,* ed. Hal Foster (New York: New Press, 1998), 1–15.

14. Hugo Ball, *Flight out of Time: A Dada Diary,* ed. John Elderfield, trans. Ann Raimes (New York: Viking Press, 1974), 49.

15. Tom Bojko, "Music of the Saints: John Zorn on Beauty, Mystery, and the Importance of Giving," *Japan Times,* January 8, 2003.

16. John Zorn, *The Gift* (Tzadik compact disc TZ 7332, 2001).

17. The notes accompanying the release of *The Gift* are included on www.tzadik.com/index.php?catalog=7332.

18. It is worth pointing out that the chord progression in "Makahaa" and in "Makahaa (Reprise)" is also heard on many of Zorn's soundtracks for cartoons by Kiriko Kubo on *Filmworks VII: Cynical Hysterie Hour* (Tzadik compact disc TZ 7315, 1997). Compare those tracks on *The Gift* with tracks such as "Abacus Waltz," "Home Sweet Home," and "Making Ramen at Midnight" on *Cynical Hysterie Hour*. Zorn's invitation to "forget about the worries of the world" will resonate strongly for the attentive listener who makes the connection between Zorn's tracks on *The Gift* with the carefree and fun-loving music of *Cynical Hysterie Hour*. Furthermore, this oblique reference to his cartoon soundtracks adds new layers of meaning(s) when read in the context of the artwork included on *The Gift* as discussed in the next section.

19. This image is strikingly reminiscent of Joseph Cornell's well-known construction *Untitled (Bebe Marie)*.

20. Jean Baudrillard, *Seduction,* trans. Brian Singer (New York: St. Martin's Press, 1990), 69–70.

21. Another narrative is also discernible in the layout of the artwork on *The Gift*. Notice that images with a dark background all appear on one side of the notes while those with a lit background appear on the other. The interdependence of light and dark in Zorn's thought is examined more closely in chapter 2.

22. In an online review of *The Gift*, the reviewer picks up on the duplicitous nature of Zorn's record:

[*The Gift*] is similar in many ways to John Zorn's past output, though it does not appear to be at a first listen. Normally, Zorn focuses on dynamic jazz, offbeat movie music, and chaotic fusions that are so unique as to be almost indescribable. However, on [*The Gift*], this eccentric composer and saxophonist presents us with a sound that draws heavily on '50s pop instrumentals mixed with the lightheartedness of reggae rhythms. It doesn't take long before the joke reveals itself, though. Zorn uses [*The Gift*] to parody the false innocence of fifties tunes, in effect, making you feel guilty for enjoying the catchiness of some of the album's tracks. In the end, you are left with the feeling that you have opened [*The Gift*] only to find a much less-than-desirable present inside. So, like all of the composer's past work, the album mixes humor and good intent with evil and an underlying darkness, making for classic Zorn material.

This review originally appeared on www.interneted.com/Reviewpages/zorngift.htm and has since been removed. The quote can be found on the sidebar across from *The Gift* at www.omnology.com/zorn01.html.

23. Marcel Mauss, *The Gift: The Form and Reason for Exchange in Archaic Societies,* foreword by Mary Douglas, trans. W. D. Halls (New York: W. W. Norton, 1990), 62–63.

24. Jacques T. Godbout in collaboration with Alain Caillé, *The World of the Gift,* trans. Donald Winkler (Montreal: McGill-Queen's University Press, 1998), 10.

25. Bataille, "The Big Toe," in *Visions of Excess,* 20–21. Emphasis in original.

26. Leo Bersani, *The Culture of Redemption* (Cambridge: Harvard University Press, 1990), 2.

Bibliography

Abraham the Jew. *The Book of the Sacred Magic of Abra-Melin the Mage*. Trans. S. Liddell MacGregor Mathers. New York: Causeway Books, 1974.

Ades, Dawn. "The Transcendental Surrealism of Joseph Cornell." In *Joseph Cornell*, ed. McShine, 15–41.

Allison, Anne. *Nightwork: Sexuality, Pleasure, and Corporate Masculinity in a Tokyo Hostess Club*. Chicago: University of Chicago Press, 1994.

———. *Permitted and Prohibited Desires: Mothers, Comics, and Censorship in Japan*. Boulder.: Westview Press, 1996.

Andriessen, Louis, and Elmer Schönberger. *The Apollonian Clockwork*. Trans. Jeff Hamburg. Oxford: Oxford University Press, 1989.

Artaud, Antonin. *The Theater and Its Double*. Trans. Mary Caroline Richards. New York: Grove Press, 1958.

Ashton, Dore. *A Joseph Cornell Album*. New York: Viking Press, 1974.

Babbitt, Milton. "Stravinsky's Verticals and Schoenberg's Diagonals: A Twist of Fate." In Haimo and Johnson, eds., *Stravinsky Retrospectives*, 15–35.

Ball, Hugo. *Flight out of Time: A Dada Diary*. Ed. John Elderfield. Trans. Ann Raimes. New York: Viking Press, 1974.

Barzel, Tamar. "If Not Klezmer, Then What? Jewish Music and Modalities on New York City's Downtown Music Scene." Jewish in America (Part Two). *Michigan Quarterly Review* 42, no. 1 (Winter 2002): 79–94.

———. "'Radical Jewish Culture': Composer/Improvisers on New York City's 1990s Downtown Scene." PhD diss., University of Michigan, 2004.

Bataille, Georges. *Visions of Excess: Selected Writings, 1927–1939*. Trans. Allan Stoekl with Carl R. Lovitt and Donald M. Leslie Jr. Minneapolis: University of Minnesota Press, 1985.

———. *Guilty*. Trans. Bruce Boone. Venice, Calif.: Lapis Press, 1988.

———. *Inner Experience.* Trans. Leslie Anne Boldt. Albany: State University of New York Press, 1988.

———. *The Tears of Eros.* Trans. Peter Connor. San Francisco: City Lights Books, 1989.

———. *The Accursed Share, Volume 1: Consumption.* Trans. Robert Hurley. New York: Zone Books, 1991.

———. *The Unfinished System of Nonknowledge.* Ed. Stuart Kendall. Trans. Michelle Kendall and Stuart Kendall. Minneapolis: University of Minnesota Press, 2001.

Baudrillard, Jean. *Seduction.* Trans. Brian Singer. New York: St. Martin's Press, 1990.

Beels, Alex. "Musician John Zorn's Brutal Images of Asians Draw Fire." *Asian New Yorker,* May 1994, 5–6.

Beer, Lawrence Ward. *Freedom of Expression in Japan: A Study in Comparative Law, Politics, and Society.* Tokyo: Kodansha International, 1984.

Benjamin, Walter. *Illuminations.* Ed. Hannah Arendt. Trans. Harry Zohn. New York: Schocken Books, 1969.

Bersani, Leo. *The Culture of Redemption.* Cambridge, Mass.: Harvard University Press, 1990.

Blair, Lindsay. *Joseph Cornell's Vision of Spiritual Order.* London: Reaktion Books, 1998.

Bloom, Harold. *The Anxiety of Influence.* New York: Oxford University Press, 1973.

———. *Kabbalah and Mysticism.* New York: Seabury Press, 1975.

———. *A Map of Misreading.* New York: Oxford University Press, 1975.

Bojko, Tom. "Music of the Saints: John Zorn on Beauty, Mystery, and the Importance of Giving." *Japan Times,* January 8, 2003: http://search.japantimes.co.jp/member/member.html?fm20030108a1.htm.

Boldt-Irons, Leslie Anne, ed. *On Bataille: Critical Essays.* Trans. Leslie Anne Boldt-Irons. Albany: State University of New York Press, 1995.

Bourdieu, Pierre. *The Logic of Practice.* Trans. Richard Nice. Stanford, Calif.: Stanford University Press, 1990.

Breton, André. *Manifestos of Surrealism.* Trans. Richard Seaver and Helen R. Lane. Ann Arbor: University of Michigan Press, 1972.

Broyles, Michael. *Mavericks and Other Traditions in American Music.* New Haven: Yale University Press, 2004.

Buchloh, Benjamin. "Theorizing the Avant-Garde." *Art in America,* November 1984, 19–21.

Buckley, Sandra. "Penguin in Bondage: A Graphic Tale of Japanese Comic Books." In *Technoculture,* ed. Constance Penley and Andrew Ross, 163–93. Minneapolis: University of Minnesota Press, 1991.

Bürger, Peter. *Theory of the Avant-Garde.* Trans. Michael Shaw. Foreword by Jochen Schulte-Sasse. Minneapolis: University of Minnesota Press, 1984.

Buruma, Ian. *Behind the Mask: On Sexual Demons, Sacred Mothers, Transvestites, Gangsters, and Other Japanese Cultural Heroes.* New York: Meridian, 1985.

Butler, Judith. *Excitable Speech: A Politics of the Performative.* New York: Routledge, 1997.

———. "The Force of Fantasy: Feminism, Mapplethorpe, and Discursive Excess." In *The Judith Butler Reader,* ed. Sara Salih with Judith Butler, 183–203. Oxford: Blackwell, 2004.

Cheng, Vincent J. *Inauthentic: The Anxiety over Culture and Identity*. New Brunswick, N.J.: Rutgers University Press, 2004.

Cho, Sumi. "Korean Americans vs. African Americans: Conflict and Construction." In Gooding-Williams, ed., *Reading Rodney King, Reading Urban Uprising*, 196–211.

Clammer, John. *Contemporary Urban Japan: A Sociology of Consumption*. Oxford: Blackwell, 1997.

Clark, Vèvè A., Millicent Hodson, and Catrina Neiman, eds. *The Legend of Maya Deren: A Documentary Bibliography and Collected Works. Volume I, Part Two: Chambers (1942–1947)*. New York: Anthology Film Archives/Film Culture, 1988.

Cobussen, Marcel. "Deconstruction in Music." Interactive dissertation. Online at www .cobussen.com/navbar/index.html.

Collis, Stephen. "Formed by Homages: H.D., Robert Duncan, and the Poetics of the Gift." In *The Question of the Gift*, ed. Osteen, 209–26.

Connor, Peter Tracey. *Georges Bataille and the Mysticism of Sin*. Baltimore: Johns Hopkins University Press, 2000.

Coulombe, Renée T. "Postmodern Polyamory or Postcolonial Challenge? Cornershop's Dialogue from West, to East, to West. . . ." In *Postmodern Music/Postmodern Thought*, ed. Judy Lochhead and Joseph Auner, 177–93. New York: Routledge, 2002.

Craft, Robert. *Stravinsky: Chronicle of a Friendship*. New York: Alfred A. Knopf, 1972.

Crowley, Aleister. *777 and Other Qabalistic Writings of Aleister Crowley*. Ed. Israel Regardie. Boston: Weiser Books, 1986.

Crowley, Aleister, with Mary Desti and Leila Waddell, *Magick: Liber ABA, Book IV, Parts I–IV*. 2d rev. ed. Ed. Hymenaeus Beta. York Beach, Maine: S. Weiser, 1997.

Cuthbert, Michael Scott. "Free Improvisation: John Zorn and the Construction of Jewish Identity through Music." In *Studies in Jewish Musical Traditions: Insights from the Harvard Collection of Judaica Sound Recordings*, ed. Kay Kaufman Shelemay, 1–31. Cambridge, Mass.: Harvard College Library, 2001.

Dahlhaus, Carl. *Schoenberg and the New Music*. Trans. Derrick Puffett and Alfred Clayton. Cambridge: Cambridge University Press, 1997.

Dan, Joseph. "Samael, Lilith, and the Concept of Evil in Early Kabbalah." *AJS Review* 5 (1980): 17–40.

———, ed. *The Early Kabbalah*. Trans. Ronald C. Kiener. New York: Paulist Press, 1986.

de Lauretis, Teresa. *Technologies of Gender: Essays on Theory, Film, and Fiction*. Bloomington: Indiana University Press, 1987.

Deleuze, Gilles. *Masochism: Coldness and Cruelty*. Trans. Jean McNeil. New York: Zone Books, 1991.

Deren, Maya. *An Anagram of Ideas on Art, Form, and Film*. Yonkers, N.Y.: Alicat Book Shop Press, 1946.

———. Cinematography: The Creative Use of Reality." In *The Avant-Garde Film: A Reader of Theory and Criticism*, ed. Sitney, 60–73.

Derrida, Jacques. *Given Time I: Counterfeit Money*. Trans. Peggy Kamuf. Chicago: University of Chicago Press, 1992.

———. *Aporias*. Trans. Thomas Dutoit. Stanford, Calif.: Stanford University Press, 1993.

Dore, R. P. *City Life in Japan: A Study in a Tokyo Ward*. London: Routledge & Kegan Paul, 1958.

Duckworth, William. *Talking Music.* New York: Schirmer Books, 1995.

Dworkin, Andrea. *Pornography: Men Possessing Women.* New York: Perigee Books, 1981.

Dworkin, Craig. *Reading the Illegible.* Evanston, Ill.: Northwestern University Press, 2003.

Eco, Umberto. *Foucault's Pendulum.* Trans. William Weaver. New York: Ballantine Books, 1997.

Eddy, Mary Baker. *Health and Science.* Boston: Christian Science Board of Directors, 1994.

Eisenstein, Sergei. *The Film Sense.* Trans. Jay Leyda. New York: Harcourt Brace Jovanovich, 1975.

———. *Film Form.* Trans. Jay Leyda. San Diego: Harcourt Brace, 1977.

Emerson, Ralph Waldo. "Gifts." In Schrift, ed., *The Logic of the Gift: Toward an Ethic of Generosity,* 25–27.

Enzensberger, Hans Magnus. *The Consciousness Industry.* Ed. Michael Roloff. New York: Seabury Press, 1974.

Everett, Yayoi Uno, and Frederick Lau, eds. *Locating East Asia in Western Art Music.* Middletown, Conn.: Wesleyan University Press, 2004.

Foster, Hal. *The Return of the Real.* Cambridge, Mass.: MIT Press, 1996.

———. *Recodings: Art, Spectacle, Cultural Politics.* New York: New Press, 1999.

———, ed. *The Anti-Aesthetic: Essays on Postmodern Culture.* New York: New Press, 1998.

Foucault, Michel. *Language, Counter-Memory, Practice.* Ed. Donald F. Bouchard. Ithaca, N.Y.: Cornell University Press, 1977.

———. *The History of Sexuality, Volume 1: An Introduction.* Trans. Robert Hurley. New York: Vintage Books, 1990.

Fujimura-Fanselow, Kumiko, and Atsuko Kameda, eds. *Japanese Women: New Feminist Perspectives on the Past, Present, and Future.* New York: Feminist Press at the City University of New York, 1995.

Funabashi, Kuniko. "Pornographic Culture and Sexual Violence." In *Japanese Women,* ed. Fujimura-Fanselow and Kameda, 255–63.

Fusco, Coco. *English Is Broken Here.* New York: New Press, 1995.

Gagne, Cole. *Soundpieces 2: Interviews with American Composers.* Metuchen, N.J.: Scarecrow Press, 1993.

Gasché, Rodolphe. "The Heterological Almanac." In *On Bataille: Critical Essays,* ed. Boldt-Irons, 157–208.

———. "Heliocentric Exchange." In *The Logic of the Gift: Toward an Ethic of Generosity,* ed. Schrift, 100–117.

Geller, Theresa L. "The Personal Cinema of Maya Deren: *Meshes of the Afternoon* and Its Critical Reception in the History of the Avant-Garde." *Biography* 29, no. 1 (Winter 2006): 140–58.

Godbout, Jacques T., in collaboration with Alain Caillé. *The World of the Gift.* Trans. Donald Winkler. Montreal: McGill-Queen's University Press, 1998.

Gooding-Williams, Robert, ed. *Reading Rodney King, Reading Urban Uprising.* New York: Routledge, 1993.

Gregory, Chris A. *Gifts and Commodities*. London: Academic Press, 1982.

Grigsby, Mary. "The Social Production of Gender as Reflected in Two Japanese Culture Industry Products: *Sailormoon* and *Crayon Shin-chan*." In Lent, ed., *Themes and Issues in Asian Cartooning: Cute, Cheap, Mad, and Sexy*, 183–210.

Grylls, Karen Lesley. "The Aggregate Re-Ordered: A Paradigm for Stravinsky's 'Requiem Canticles.'" PhD diss., University of Washington, 1993.

Habermas, Jürgen. "Modernity—An Incomplete Project." In *The Anti-Aesthetic*, ed. Foster, 1–15.

Haimo, Ethan, and Paul Johnson, eds. *Stravinsky Retrospectives*. Lincoln: University of Nebraska Press, 1987.

ha-Kohen, Rabbi Isaac ben Jacob. "Treatise on the Left Emanation." In Dan, ed., *The Early Kabbalah*, 165–82.

Hall, Stuart. "Cultural Identity and Diaspora." In *Contemporary Postcolonial Theory: A Reader*, ed. Padmini Mongia, 110–21. London: Hodder Arnold, 2003.

Hamilton, Denise. "Zorn's 'Garden' Sprouts Discontent Jazz." *Los Angeles Times*, August 15, 1994.

Harms, Daniel, and John Wisdom Gonce III. *The Necronomicon Files*. Boston: Weiser Books, 2003.

Harrison, Martin. *In Camera: Francis Bacon, Photography, Film, and the Practice of Painting*. New York: Thames & Hudson, 2005.

Hartigan, Lynda Roscoe, Walter Hopps, Richard Vine, and Robert Lehrman. *Joseph Cornell: Shadowplay . . . Eterniday*. New York: Thames & Hudson, 2003.

Heble, Ajay. *Landing on the Wrong Note: Jazz, Dissonance, and Critical Practice*. New York: Routledge, 2000.

Hisama, Ellie M. "Postcolonialism on the Make: The Music of John Mellencamp, David Bowie, and John Zorn." In *Reading Pop: Approaches to Textual Analysis in Popular Music*, ed. Richard Middleton, 329–46 (Oxford: Oxford University Press, 2000).

———. "John Zorn and the Postmodern Condition." In *Locating East Asia in Western Art Music*, ed. Everett and Lau, 72–84.

Hobbs, Stuart D. *The End of the American Avant Garde*. New York: New York University Press, 1997.

Hollier, Denis. "The Dualist Materialism of Georges Bataille." Trans. Hillari Allred. *Yale French Studies* 78 (1990): 124–39.

Hunter, Jack, ed. *Moonchild: The Films of Kenneth Anger*. New York: Creation Books, 2001.

Hutchison, Alice L. *Kenneth Anger*. London: Black Dog, 2004.

Huyssen, Andreas. *After the Great Divide: Modernism, Mass Culture, Postmodernism*. Bloomington: Indiana University Press, 1986.

Hyde, Lewis. *The Gift: Imagination and the Erotic Property of Life*. New York: Random House, 1979.

Ileto, Reynaldo. "Outlines of a Nonlinear Emplotment of Philippine History." In *The Politics of Culture in the Shadow of Capitalism*, ed. David Lloyd and Lisa Lowe, 98–131. Durham, N.C.: Duke University Press, 1997.

Jackson, Renata. "The Modernist Poetics of Maya Deren." In Nichols, ed., *Maya Deren and the American Avant-Garde*, 47–76.

Kaplan, Aryeh, trans. *Sefer Yetzirah: The Book of Creation.* Rev. ed. Boston: Weiser Books, 1997.

Keller, Marjorie. *The Untutored Eyes: Childhood in the Films of Cocteau, Cornell, and Brakhage.* Cranbury, N.J.: Associated University Press, 1986.

Kim, Elaine. "Home Is Where the *Han* Is." In Gooding-Williams, ed., *Reading Rodney King, Reading Urban Uprising,* 219–35.

King, Karen L. *What Is Gnosticism?* Cambridge, Mass.: Belknap Press of Harvard University Press, 2005.

Korsyn, Kevin. *Decentering Music.* Oxford: Oxford University Press, 2003.

Koshy, Susan. "The Fiction of Asian American Literature." *Yale Journal of Criticism* 9, no. 2 (1996): 315–46.

Koskoff, Ellen. "Miriam Sings Her Song: The Self and the Other in Anthropological Discourse." In *Musicology and Difference,* ed. Ruth Solie, 149–63. Berkeley: University of California Press, 1993.

Kramer, Jonathan. "Beyond Unity: Toward an Understanding of Musical Postmodernism." In *Concert Music, Rock, and Jazz since 1945,* ed. Elizabeth West Marvin and Richard Hermann, 11–34. Rochester, N.Y.: University of Rochester Press, 1995.

Lavey, Anton Szandor. *The Satanic Bible.* New York: Avon Books, 1976.

Lee, Elisa. "Zorn's Album Art of Asian Women Sparks Controversy." *AsianWeek,* March 4, 1994.

Lefebvre, Henri. *The Production of Space.* Trans. Donald Nicholson-Smith. Oxford: Blackwell, 1991.

Lent, John A., ed. *Themes and Issues in Asian Cartooning: Cute, Cheap, Mad, and Sexy.* Bowling Green, Ohio: Bowling Green State University Popular Press, 1999.

Levi, Antonia. *Samurai from Outer Space: Understanding Japanese Animation.* Chicago: Open Court, 1996.

Lévi-Strauss, Claude. "Introduction à l'oeuvre de Marcel Mauss." In Mauss, *Sociologie et anthropologie,* ix–lii. Paris: Presses Universitaires de France, 1950. Translated excerpts in *The Logic of the Gift,* ed. Schrift, 45–69.

Levy, Julien. *Memoir of an Art Gallery.* New York: G. P. Putnam's Sons, 1977.

Linden, Robin Ruth, Darlene R. Pagano, Diana E. H. Russell, and Susan Leigh Star, eds. *Against Sadomasochism: A Radical Feminist Analysis.* East Palo Alto, Calif.: Frog in the Well, 1982.

Lowe, Lisa. "Heterogeneity, Hybridity, Multiplicity: Marking Asian American Differences." *Diaspora* 1, no. 1 (1991): 24–44.

———. *Immigrant Acts: On Asian American Cultural Politics.* Durham, N.C.: Duke University Press, 2004.

Lye, Colleen. "Toward an (Asian) American Cultural Studies: Postmodernism and the 'Peril of Yellow Capital and Labor.'" In *Privileging Positions,* ed. Okihiro et al., 47–56.

MacGregor Mathers, S. Liddell, trans. *The Key of Solomon the King (Clavicula Salomonis).* Foreword by R. A. Gilbert. York Beach, Maine: Red Wheel/Weiser, LLC, 2004.

MacKendrick, Karmen. *Counterpleasures.* Albany: State University of New York Press, 1999.

MacKinnon, Catharine. *Only Words.* Cambridge, Mass.: Harvard University Press, 1993.

Mandel, Howard, ed. *Future Jazz*. Oxford: Oxford University Press, 1999.

Marx, Karl, and Friedrich Engels. *The Communist Manifesto and Other Writings*. New York: Barnes and Noble Classics, 2005.

Mauss, Marcel. *The Gift: The Form and Reason for Exchange in Archaic Societies*. Trans. W. D. Halls. Foreword by Mary Douglas. New York: W. W. Norton, 1990. Originally published as "Essai sur le don. Forme et raison de l'échange dans les sociétés archaïques." *Année sociologique* Paris, 2e série, I (1923–24): 30–186.

———. *Sociologie et anthropologie*. Paris: Presses Universitaires de France, 1950.

McClary, Susan. *Conventional Wisdom*. Berkeley: University of California Press, 2000.

McCutchan, Ann. *The Muse That Sings: Composers Speak about the Creative Process*. Oxford: Oxford University Press, 1999.

McNeilly, Kevin. "Ugly Beauty: John Zorn and the Politics of Postmodern Music." *Postmodern Culture* 5, no. 2 (1994–95): http://muse.jhu.edu/journals/postmodern_culture/v005/5.2mcneilly.html.

McShine, Kynaston, ed. *Joseph Cornell*. New York: Museum of Modern Art, 1980.

Mekas, Jonas. "Movie Journal." *Village Voice*, May 17, 1973.

———. "A Few Notes on Maya Deren." In *Inverted Odysseys: Claude Cahun, Maya Deren, Cindy Sherman*, ed. Shelley Rice, 127–50. Cambridge, Mass.: MIT Press, 1999.

Michelson, Annette. "Poetic and Savage Thought: About *Anagram*." In *Maya Deren and the American Avant-Garde*, ed. Nichols, 21–45.

Morris, Adelaide. "A Relay of Power and Peace: H.D. and the Spirit of the Gift." In *Signets: Reading H.D.*, ed. Susan Stanford Friedman and Rachel Blau Du Plessis, 52–82. Madison: University of Wisconsin Press, 1990.

Newman, Arnold, and Robert Craft. *Bravo Stravinsky*. Cleveland: World, 1967.

Nguyen, Viet Thanh. *Race and Resistance: Literature and Politics in Asian America*. Oxford: Oxford University Press, 2002.

Nichols, Bill, ed. *Maya Deren and the American Avant-Garde*. Berkeley: University of California Press, 2001.

Noys, Benjamin. "Georges Bataille's Base Materialism." *Cultural Values* 2, no. 4 (1998): 499–517.

Nyman, Michael. *Experimental Music: Cage and Beyond*. 2d ed. Cambridge: Cambridge University Press, 1999.

O'Doherty, Brian. *Dovecotes, Hotels, and Other White Spaces*. Catalog from Joseph Cornell Exhibition at the Pace Gallery, October 20–November 25, 1989. New York: Pace Gallery, 1989.

Okihiro, Gary Y. *Margins and Mainstreams*. Seattle: University of Washington Press, 1994.

Okihiro, Gary Y., Marilyn Alquizola, Dorothy Fujita Rony, and K. Scott Wong, eds. *Privileging Positions: The Sites of Asian American Studies*. Pullman: Washington State University Press, 1995.

Osajima, Keith Hiroshi. "Postmodernism and Asian American Studies: A Critical Appropriation." In *Privileging Positions*, ed. Okihiro et al., 21–35.

Osteen, Mark, ed. *The Question of the Gift: Essays across Disciplines*. London: Routledge, 2002.

Peppiatt, Michael. *Francis Bacon: Anatomy of an Enigma*. Boulder.: Westview Press, 1998.

Peterson, Joseph H., ed. *The Lesser Key of Solomon.* York Beach, Maine: Weiser Books, 2001.

Pireddu, Nicoletta. "Gabriele D'Annunzio: The Art of Squandering and the Economy of Sacrifice." In *The Question of the Gift,* ed. Osteen, 172–90.

Powell, Anna. "The Occult: A Torch for Lucifer." In *Moonchild: The Films of Kenneth Anger,* ed. Hunter, 54–59.

Pramaggiore, Maria. "Performance and Persona in the U.S. Avant-Garde: The Case of Maya Deren." *Cinema Journal* 36, no. 2 (Winter 1997): 17–40.

Rabinovitz, Lauren. *Points of Resistance: Women, Power & Politics in the New York Avant-Garde Cinema, 1943–71.* Urbana: University of Illinois Press, 1991.

Ratcliff, Carter. "Joseph Cornell, Mechanic of the Ineffable." In *Joseph Cornell,* ed. Mc-Shine, 43–67.

Rayns, Tony. "Aleister Crowley and Merlin Magick" (interview with Kenneth Anger), *Friends,* no. 14 (September 1970), quoted in Alice L. Hutchison, *Kenneth Anger,* 179 (London: Black Dog, 2004).

Reich, Robert B. "Is Japan Really Out to Get Us?" *New York Times Book Review.* February 9, 1992.

Rescher, Nicholas. "Aporia." In *The Oxford Companion to Philosophy,* ed. Ted Honderich, 41. Oxford: Oxford University Press, 1995.

Richie, Donald. *Some Aspects of Japanese Popular Culture.* Tokyo: Shubun International, 1981.

Richman, Michèle H. *Reading Georges Bataille: Beyond the Gift.* Baltimore: Johns Hopkins University Press, 1982.

Roads, Curtis. *Microsound.* Cambridge, Mass.: MIT Press, 2001.

Roob, Alexander. *The Hermetic Museum: Alchemy and Mysticism.* Köln: Taschen, 1996.

Sargeant, Jack. *Deathtripping.* London: Creation Books, 1995.

Scarry, Elaine. *The Body in Pain.* New York: Oxford University Press, 1985.

Schoenberg, Arnold. *The Musical Idea and the Logic, Technique, and Art of Its Presentation.* Trans. Patricia Carpenter and Severine Neff. New York: Columbia University Press, 1995.

Scholem, Gershom. *Kabbalah.* New York: Meridian, 1978.

———. *Major Trends in Jewish Mysticism.* New York: Schocken Books, 1995.

Schrift, Alan D., ed. *The Logic of the Gift: Toward an Ethic of Generosity.* London: Routledge, 1997.

Scott, Gini Graham. *Erotic Power: An Exploration of Dominance and Submission.* Secaucus, N.J.: Citadel, 1983.

Service, Tom. "Playing a New Game of Analysis: John Zorn's *Carny,* Autonomy, and Postmodernism." *BPM Online* 5 (June 2002): www.bpmonline.org.uk/bpm5-playing.html.

Shamoon, Deborah. "Office Sluts and Rebel Flowers: The Pleasures of Japanese Pornographic Comics for Women." In *Porn Studies,* ed. Linda Williams, 77–103. Durham, N.C.: Duke University Press, 2004.

Shatz, Adam. "Crossing Music's Borders in Search of Identity; Downtown, a Reach for Ethnicity." *New York Times,* October 3, 1999, AR1.

Shigematsu, Setsu. "Dimensions of Desire: Sex, Fantasy, and Fetish in Japanese Comics." In *Themes and Issues in Asian Cartooning,* ed. Lent, 127–63.

Shiokawa, Kanako. "Cute but Deadly: Women and Violence in Japanese Comics." In *Themes and Issues in Asian Cartooning,* ed. Lent, 93–125.

Silverman, Kaja. *Male Subjectivity at the Margins.* New York: Routledge, 1992.

Sitney, P. Adams. "The Cinematic Gaze of Joseph Cornell." In *Joseph Cornell,* ed. McShine, 69–89.

———. *Visionary Film.* Oxford: Oxford University Press, 2002.

———, ed. *The Avant-Garde Film: A Reader of Theory and Criticism.* Anthology Film Archives Series 3. New York: New York University Press, 1978.

Solomon, Deborah. *Utopia Parkway: The Life and Works of Joseph Cornell.* Boston: MFA, 2004.

Spies, Claudio. "Some Notes on Stravinsky's Requiem Settings." *Perspectives of New Music* 5, no. 2 (Spring/Summer 1967): 98–123.

———. "Correction and Addendum: Some Notes on Stravinsky's Requiem Settings." *Perspectives of New Music* 6, no. 1 (Autumn–Winter 1967): 160.

Spivak, Gayatri Chakravorty. *In Other Worlds: Essays in Cultural Politics.* New York: Routledge, 1998.

Starr, Sandra Leonard. *Joseph Cornell: Art and Metaphysics.* New York: Castelli, Feigen, Corcoran Gallery, 1982.

Straus, Joseph N. *Stravinsky's Late Music.* Cambridge: Cambridge University Press, 2001.

———. *Introduction to Post-Tonal Theory.* 3d ed. Upper Saddle River, N.J.: Prentice Hall, 2005.

Stravinsky, Igor. *Poetics of Music in the Form of Six Lessons.* Trans. Arthur Knodel and Ingolf Dahl. Preface by Darius Milhaud. New York: Vintage Books, 1959.

Strickland, Edward. *American Composers: Dialogues on Contemporary Music.* Bloomington: Indiana University Press, 1991.

Suleiman, Susan Rubin. *Subversive Intent: Gender, Politics, and the Avant-Garde.* Cambridge, Mass.: Harvard University Press, 1990.

Takagi, Dana Y. "Postmodernism on the Edge." In *Privileging Positions,* ed. Okihiro et al., 37–45.

Takaki, Ronald. "Who Killed Vincent Chin?" In *A Look beyond the Model Minority Image: Critical Issues in Asian America,* ed. Grace Yun, 23–29. New York: Minority Rights Group, 1989.

Tashjian, Dickran. *Joseph Cornell: Gifts of Desire.* Miami Beach, Fla.: Grassfield Press, 1992.

Taussig, Michael. *Defacement: Public Secrecy and the Labor of the Negative.* Stanford, Calif.: Stanford University Press, 1999.

Taylor, Timothy D. "Music and Musical Practices in Postmodernity." In *Postmodern Music/Postmodern Thought,* ed. Judy Lochhead and Joseph Auner, 93–118. New York: Routledge, 2002.

Tchen, John Kuo Wei. "Rethinking Who *We* Are: A Basic Discussion of Basic Terms." In *Voices from the Battlefront: Achieving Cultural Equity,* ed. Marta Moreno Vega and Cheryll Y. Greene, 3–9. Trenton, N.J.: Africa World Press, 1993.

Toshiharu, Tai, and John Zorn. "About the Record Jacket of *Guts of a Virgin.*" *Eureka: Poems and Criticism* 29, no. 1 (1997): 133–39.

Vine, Richard. "Eterniday: Cornell's Christian Science 'Metaphysique.'" In *Joseph Cornell: Shadowplay . . . Eterniday,* 36–49. New York: Thames & Hudson, 2003.

Waite, Arthur Edward. *The Holy Kabbalah: A Mystical Interpretation of the Scriptures.* With an introduction by Kenneth Rexroth. New York: Carol, 1995.

———. *The Book of Ceremonial Magic.* Maple Shade, N.J.: Lethe Press, 2002.

Waldman, Diane. *Joseph Cornell.* New York: George Braziller, 1977.

Walsh, Stephen. *The Music of Stravinsky.* Oxford: Oxford University Press, 1993.

Watkins, Glenn. *Pyramids at the Louvre.* Cambridge, Mass.: Belknap Press of Harvard University Press, 1994.

Weiner, Annette. *Inalienable Possessions: The Paradox of Keeping-While-Giving.* Berkeley: University of California Press, 1992.

Williams, Linda. *Hard Core: Power, Pleasure, and the "Frenzy of the Visible."* Berkeley: University of California Press, 1989.

Williams, Michael A. *Rethinking "Gnosticism": An Argument for Dismantling a Dubious Category.* Princeton, N.J.: Princeton University Press, 1996.

Wilson, Colin. *The Outsider.* Boston: Houghton-Mifflin, 1956.

Wolfson, Elliot. "Left Contained in the Right." *AJS Review* 11, no. 1 (Spring 1986): 27–52.

Zia, Helen. *Asian American Dreams: The Emergence of an American Other.* New York: Farrar, Straus and Giroux, 2000.

Zorn, John, ed. *Arcana: Musicians on Music.* New York: Granary Books/Hips Road, 2000.

Index

Page numbers in italics indicate illustrations.

John Brackett

is Assistant Professor of Music at the University of Utah.
His research interests include early approaches to twelve-tone
composition, the music of John Zorn and the New York "Downtown"
scene, the intersections between the philosophy of science and
postwar American music theory, and the analysis
of pop and rock music.